WITHDRAWN

Monnet and the Americans

Clifford P. Hackett, Editor

Monnet and the Americans

The father of a united Europe and his U.S. supporters

Jean Monnet Council
Washington D.C.

Library of Congress Cataloging-in-Publication Data
Monnet and the Americans : the father of a united Europe and his U.S.
   supporters / Clifford P. Hackett, editor.
       p.   cm.
   Includes bibliographical references (p.) and index.
   Contents: Jean Monnet : a biographical essay / Richard Mayne --
Jean Monnet and the Roosevelt administration / Clifford P. Hackett-
- Dean Acheson and Jean Monnet / Douglas Brinkley -- Eisenhower,
Dulles, Monnet, and the uniting of Europe / Pascaline Winand --
Catch the night plane for Paris : George Ball and Jean Monnet /
David DeLeo -- The transnational partnership : Jean Monnet and Jack
McCloy / Thomas Schwartz -- Monnet and the "insiders" : Nathan,
Tomlinson, Bowie, and Schaetzel / Sherrill Browne Wells -- Monnet
and the American press / Don Cook and the editor.
   ISBN 0-9642541-0-7. - ISBN 0-9642541-1-5 (pbk.)
   1. Monnet, Jean, 1888-1979.   2. Statesmen--Europe--Biography.
3. European Federation.   4. United States--Foreign relations-
-Europe. 5. Europe--Foreign relations--Europe.   I. Hackett,
Clifford P.
D413.M56M66 1995
940.5'092- -dc20
[B]   94-48830
                                      CIP

To Edward M. Strauss Jr., founder of the Jean Monnet Council, and to Henri Rieben, founder of the Fondation Jean Monnet Pour L'Europe

Table of Contents

The Contributors

Douglas Brinkley is associate professor of history and director of the Eisenhower Center at New Orleans University. He earned his doctorate from Georgetown University and has edited several books on key personalities in US-European relations in addition to writing *After the Creation: Dean Acheson and American Foreign Policy 1953-1971* (1991) and co-authoring *Driven Patriot: The Life and Times of James Forrestal* (1993)

Don Cook was a correspondent in Europe for a quarter century for the International Herald Tribune and the Los Angeles Times. He has written several books on Europe including *Floodtide in Europe* (1965) and *Ten Men in History.* (1981) He finished a book on Britain and the American Revolution shortly before his death in March 1995.

David DiLeo completed his doctorate at the University of California, Irvine and is a professor of history at Saddleback College in Mission Viejo, California. He is the author of *George Ball, Vietnam and the Rethinking of Containment* (1991).

Clifford Hackett. Following ten years in the foreign service in Europe, he spent more than 13 years working on Capitol Hill where he became interested in the European Community. His book on its history and institutions, *Cautious Revolution: The European Community Arrives* (1990), will appear in a new edition in 1995. He co-edited *Jean Monnet:The Path to European Unity* (1991).

Richard Mayne is an English writer who worked with Monnet in 1956-58 and again in 1963-66 in the Action Committee for a United States of Europe. He wrote *Postwar, The Dawn of Today's Europe* (1983) and several other well-received books on postwar Europe and translated Monnet's memoirs into English. He is also a BBC broadcaster and a book and film critic.

Thomas Schwartz is associate professor of history at Vanderbilt University, Nashville, TN. He wrote *America's Germany: John J. McCloy and the Federal Republic of Germany* (1991) and "Victories and Defeats in the Long Twilight Struggle: The United States and Western Europe in the 1960s" in Diane Kunz ed., *The Diplomacy of the Crucial Decade* (1994). His doctorate is from Harvard University; his earlier studies were at Oxford and Columbia.

Sherrill Brown Wells teaches contemporary European history in the Elliott School of International Affairs at George Washington University. She has taught at Rutgers and North Carolina State University and served as a senior historian at the Department of State where she edited Foreign Relations of the United States. She received her Ph.D. from the London School of Economics and authored French Industrial Policy: A History, 1945-81 (1991).

Pascaline Winand is a research associate at the Belgian National Fund for Scientific Research and maitre de conference at the Free University of Brussels. Her dissertation from that institution was published as *Eisenhower, Kennedy and the United States of Europe* (1993). She is collaborating with Monnet's longtime assistant, Max Kohnstamm, on his memoirs.

Abbreviations

Some common abbreviations in the text and endnotes include:

DDEL Dwight D Eisenhower Library, Abilene, KS
EC European Community
ECSC European Coal and Steel Community
EEC European Economic Community
EU European Union
Euratom European Atomic Energy Community
FDRL Franklin D Roosevelt Library, Hyde Park NY
FJM Fondation Jean Monnet Pour l'Europe, Lausanne, Switzerland
FRUS Foreign Relations of the United States (Serial)
HSTL Harry S Truman Library, Independence, MO
JFKL John F Kennedy Library, Cambridge, MA
JM:PEU *Jean Monnet: The Path to European Unity,* NY, NY, 1991
JMM Jean Monnet, *Memoirs,* Garden City, NY, 1978
LBJL Lyndon B Johnson Library, Austin, TX
NATO North Atlantic Treaty Organization
PL Princeton University Library, Princeton, NJ

Monnet and the Americans

1
Introduction

By the Editor

Jean Monnet, born in Cognac, France in 1888, died in his home outside Paris in 1979 a citizen of the united Europe he helped create. The transition from Frenchman to European citizen was the main story of his long life, yet that life had many sub-themes. Among the most important of these were his relations with the United States and with many Americans.

This book describes some of these American links to Monnet. Most of them involve Americans who were themselves actively committed to a united Europe but some began long before one Europe was anything but a distant vision. One involves principally Monnet's work in World War II when he lived for several years in Washington working with quiet and unassuming devotion to getting American war production behind the battle against Nazi Germany and its allies. Several of the American friendships start with Monnet's work in World War I and its aftermath in the Versailles Peace Conference.

What these Americans have in common and what tied them to Jean Monnet is at once a complicated and a simple truth: Monnet had a special relationship to both the United States and to its people and both he and the Americans he dealt with knew of this tie. In his *Memoirs*, written close to the end of his life, Monnet tried to describe his first impressions of North America, gained as an 18 year old in pre-WW I Canada:

> At Winnipeg...I saw trainloads of Scandinavian immigrants pulling in. They were not refugees: they were not starving. They had come to hard, rewarding work---the conquest of new lands....
> Here, I encountered a new way of looking at things: individual initiative could be accepted as a contribution to a general good. In contrast to the static balance of the old Europe, this was the dynamism of a world on the move. Each had its merits; each could be explained. But American expansion needed no explanation: it was spontaneous, like necessity itself. To my European eyes, this sponteneity looked like confusion; but I very soon ceased to think in those terms. I

became convinced that there could be no progress without a
certain disorder, or at least without disorder on the surface....
        I also went to the United States, from New York to
California. Everywhere I had the same impression: that where
physical space was unlimited, confidence was unlimited too.
Where change was accepted, expansion was assured. The
United States had retained the dynamism of the Western
pioneers. But to that they had added organization. To
organize change---that, I saw, was necessary, and it could be
done. (JMM p. 45-6)

Monnet probably did not have these concise and assimilated
thoughts at age eighteen. But the impressions he gained in those years
endured and grew with more experience with the New World and it
citizens. In fact, Monnet probably had more extensive knowledge of the
United States and Canada and more friends in North America than he
did in either France or Britain, at least until after World War II.

The reasons for this unusual aspect of a Frenchman is covered
partly in Richard Mayne's biographical essay but here it might be noted
that Monnet's business career, which occupied most of his life before
1939, was international and, largely, American in character. First, as a
representative of the family's cognac firm, Monnet dealt with an
international product, with most of its customers outside France and
many in England and the United States. Even his firm's largest
competitors in his hometown of Cognac were of Scotch-Irish origin. The
Charente region where Cognac is located is said to face across the
English Channel and the Atlantic Ocean, not toward Paris.

In his second business career, as an investment banker from 1925
to 1939, Monnet was an official of an American firm, Blair and Co,
stationed briefly in Paris and later in the United States. His English,
fluent from his two year apprenticeship in London and his work in
Canada before World War I, was now almost bilingual. He had an
apartment in New York City, lived briefly in San Francisco as a bank
holding company vice president, and knew his way around Washington
quite well. He also knew Moscow, Shanghai, Hong Kong and various
European cities even better for many years than he knew Paris.
Everywhere he went he felt comfortable with the local Americans
whether they were the bankers or the diplomats or, later, the journalists.

Of the essays in this volume, one describes Monnet's long and
close relations with John Foster Dulles which began at the Versailles
Peace Conference. Later, sealing the friendship, Dulles loaned Monnet
and a partner money in 1935 to go into investment banking themselves
instead of working for others. In Versailles Monnet also met Walter
Lippmann, later to become a close journalist friend, as journalist Don

Cook's essay notes.   Monnet had a special affinity for journalists, especially Americans. He grouped them with bankers, industrialists and lawyers as people he could rely on for advice and information in the United States whenever his frequent visits brought him there. These were people "who could not afford to make mistakes" he said in his memoirs.

The two world wars, in both of which Monnet played key roles in getting war supplies to the Allies, introduced him to many Americans who then or later played important public roles in both American and European affairs. Only some of these are covered in this volume--- people like Dean Acheson, George Ball, Dwight Eisenhower, Felix Frankfurter, Harry Hopkins, John McCloy and Henry Morgenthau; unfortunately there are others quite important to Monnet but omitted for reasons of time and space like Dwight Morrow and Lewis Strauss, to mention two, and those also important but mentioned only briefly, like Presidents Kennedy and Johnson and diplomats David Bruce and Robert Murphy.

But there were dozens, perhaps hundreds of Americans whom Monnet knew, worked with, influenced and was influenced by, whose names and careers were not widely recorded in the history of the great events of the twentieth century where Monnet was active. The final essay in this book is about four of these "insiders," people who played key roles in the Second World War and postwar periods. They represent the much larger group mentioned and must stand here for an important point in Monnet's American connections: he did not "collect" people for their fame or position, least of all for their worth in impressing others. Monnet was eminently practical when it came to people as he was with almost everything else. He wanted, in the words of his friend Dwight Morrow, to do something rather than to be someone.

He knew all American presidents from Hoover to Nixon but he influenced them as much by knowing their key subordinates as he did by dealing directly with the chief executives. (He only knew Hoover briefly during World War I, never in the White House; he knew Truman and Nixon only slightly.) They valued Monnet's advice and information which came, they knew, without national prejudice or personal motives. He also knew that the top people in government tend to become isolated; he supplied ideas and let others take the credit when they used them.

No man could deal with such a collection of Americans in business and government and public affairs without sometimes crossing them.   In business Monnet could play his affairs closely and, occasionally, with a brusque kind of detachment. Sometimes he treated even friends and staff that way. In the 1939-45 period in Washington he was almost always distrusted by some like Henry Morgenthau (who disliked all international bankers) and once he antagonized key people, probably including President Roosevelt, for playing an independent hand which supported General de Gaulle's ascendency in the French Committee of National Liberation. Finally, some people distrusted Monnet because he was such an anglicized Frenchman, a few others because he did not seem French enough when, for example, he argued in public with fellow-Frenchmen.

Why single out Americans among the many people Monnet dealt with in his long and productive life? Not out of national pride, which would be alien to the Monnet style and not because his whole story can be properly told only through his American friends. Rather, the Jean Monnet Council, established in 1985 to support studies of Monnet's life so that his achievements might be studied and applied to contemporary problems, decided that while Monnet and the Americans was part of a larger story it was one that needed to be told by itself. The Monnet memoirs similarly only tell part of his story since they concentrate on his work which culminated in the creation of the European Community---the work of getting men to cooperate for a common good.

The Council previously published another book of essays, *Jean Monnet: The Path to European Unity* (New York, St. Martin's Press, 1991) which contained both European and American assessments of those accomplishments. This volume adds therefore one more stone to the larger mosaic which is slowly being formed of the record of the life and work of one of the great men of the twentieth century.

Some Acknowledgements

A generous grant from the National Endowment for the Humanities made this book possible. The Franklin D. Roosevelt Library Association cosponsored a conference with the Jean Monnet Council in 1990 at the presidential library in Hyde Park, NY at which preliminary versions of these papers were presented.

Douglas Brinkley was involved at the start of the project with ideas and enthusiasm beyond his own essay; J. Robert Schaetzel, the

Council President, and the council members, supported the idea of the book from the beginning of the council's organized activities in 1987. Retired General Andrew J. Goodpaster suggested the title.

The authors of these papers themselves are indebted to many librarians, archivists, friends and family members for support throughout a long project which sometimes involved extensive and trying revisions of their first papers.

In 1985, Edward M. Strauss Jr, an American businessman and engineer, brought back from Switzerland a commitment to found an American organization ---ultimately the Jean Monnet Council--- devoted to the work of Monnet. Professor Henri Rieben, president of the Fondation Jean Monnet Pour l'Europe in Lausanne, was responsible for forming that commitment by leading Ed Strauss to a fuller understanding of Monnet's role in Europe and his relations with America. Jean Monnet benefitted throughout his life from people like these two inspired men who recognized the value of his work and carried it forth on their own. To the Riebens and the Strausses in Monnet's life this book is dedicated.

2
Jean Monnet: A Biographical Essay

Richard Mayne

Jean Monnet is best known as the "Father of Europe." He inspired the first European Community organization -- the European Coal and Steel Community -- in 1950. He formulated the plan for a European Defense Community in the same year. When that failed, he supplied the impetus for the European Economic Community and Euratom. He helped to steer their development and enlargement. Before he died in 1979 he had been made an Honorary Citizen of Europe. His ashes now rest in the Panthéon in Paris, transferred there by the President of France.

But Monnet was 62 when he proposed the Coal and Steel Community; and already by that age he had accomplished enough to deserve a place in history. In two world wars, he had helped to make a decisive contribution to the cause of the Allies; in the second, through his role in Lend-Lease and in Roosevelt's Victory Program, he had helped to save Britain, speed the liberation of Europe, and so spare many human lives. Between the wars, he had been a key figure in the early, hopeful days of the League of Nations, then an international banker and an adviser to governments. In the later days of World War II, he helped to reconcile General de Gaulle and General Giraud, preventing discord and likely bloodshed in France. After the war, he played a little-known role in the Marshall Plan which helped Europe to recover. He did the same for France by initiating and heading the national *Commissariat au Plan*.

Earlier, Monnet had helped to liquidate the Kreuger match empire, taken part in the reconstruction of China, made and lost a fortune on Wall Street, and contracted a runaway marriage. In the summer of 1940, he had persuaded Winston Churchill to make the abortive offer of Franco-British union. For several years during World War II, he had even been a senior British civil servant. Harold Macmillan aptly called him, indeed, "a devoted friend of Britain."

Monnet's achievements earned him many other verbal tributes, as well as medals, honorary doctorates, and other decorations. Willy Brandt called him "a wise counselor to those in government." Konrad

Adenauer described him a "a true man of peace." Dean Acheson saw him as "one of the greatest of Frenchmen." "No man in the twentieth century," wrote David Schoenbrun, "had ever influenced so many governments in Europe, America, and Asia." And the United States diplomat Robert Murphy, although critical of Monnet, thought he was "in many respects more remarkable than de Gaulle."

                    *   *   *

Jean Omer Marie Gabriel Monnet was born on Friday, November 9, 1888, in the quiet town of Cognac on the Charente river, about halfway between Angoulême and the Bay of Biscay. The walls of some of the buildings, especially near the river, still look blackish, owing to microscopic fungus encouraged by the fumes of alcohol. For Cognac is and was the home of French brandy, surrounded by the vineyards which produce more than a hundred different species of grape.

Monnet's paternal grandfather was a smallholder, and his maternal grandfather a barrel-maker who became a vintner; but his father, one of the first pupils at Cognac College, became a businessman and director of the "Society of Cognac Vine-growers" founded in 1838 to enable smallholders to compete against the purchasing monopoly of the big firms. As the society's director, he printed his own name, "J.G. Monnet'" on the brandy bottles, and traveled far afield to market his wares. Equally, the family house in Cognac was always filled with foreigners, from Britain, Germany, Scandinavia, and America. From his childhood there Monnet learned, he said, two things. One was patience -- "the only way to make good brandy." The other was practical acquaintance with broad horizons. "Our concerns took us a long way from Cognac, but never far from the cognac it produced."

Monnet disliked school, and left it after taking the first part of his school-leaving examination. "At the age of sixteen I bought a bowler hat and assumed my responsibilities." These meant preparing to enter the family firm; and the first step was to spend two years with a wine merchant in London, learning English. The second, at eighteen, was to go to North America to visit clients and develop a retail network. "Don't take any books," said his father. "No one can do your thinking for you. Look out of the window; talk with people. Pay attention to your neighbor." When the West was still opening up, Monnet discovered a new spirit of personal initiative and confidence. One day in Calgary, Alberta, he asked a blacksmith how he could get up-country to visit some farmers. The blacksmith pointed to his own horse. "You can take this animal. When you come back, just hitch him up in the same place." When Monnet traveled south into the United States, he found that they "had retained the dynamism of the Western pioneers, like those I had seen in action at Winnipeg. But to that they had added organization."

Still selling brandy, Monnet traveled to Greece, Russia, Sweden, and again to England. He was on his way back from there to Cognac in 1914, when on the train in Poiters station he heard that France was mobilizing for war. His younger brother left to join the hussars; but Monnet was medically unfit, and he fretted to help the war effort. In London, he had discovered that France and Britain, although allies, were very far from coordinating their national efforts to secure the flow of vital was supplies. Determined, despite his father's doubts, to alert the authorities in Paris, the 26-year-old Monnet turned to a local lawyer, Maître Fernand Benon, who had worked with René Viviani, the French Prime Minister. Benon agreed to introduce him, and they were on the point of leaving for Paris when news came that the Government had withdrawn to nearby Bordeaux. In the second week of September, Viviani received Monnet in his office at the Faculty of Letters. That very morning, the Prime Minister had heard that his two sons had been killed in the Battle of the Marne. He listened gravely as Monnet argued for joint Allied bodies to estimate the combined total of French and British resources, allocate them on an agreed plan, and share out the cost. Then he sent Monnet to see Alexandre Millerand, the War Minister. Two months later, Monnet was in London in the French Civil Supplies Service -- based, to his quiet amusement, in Trafalgar House, Waterloo Place.

It was only then that he realized how anarchic supply arrangements were, not only between the Allies but also on each side separately. Patiently but urgently, he worked to improve matters. In November 1915, a first inter-Allied agreement was reached. It was followed by a Conference of Ministers of Commerce and by an Allied Wheat Executive --- the model, Monnet thought, for further joint organizations, eventually covering oils, grains, fats, sugar, meat, and nitrate. At last came the Allied Military Transport Committee with its own Executive, set up in March 1918.

Monnet's British opposite number in these efforts had been Arthur (later Lord) Salter, then a young official in the Department of Transport. After World War I they became colleagues again, this time in a still broader context: the secretariat of the newly founded League of Nations.

Monnet had no hand in drafting the League Covenant. Those who did, he noted, "were careful to avoid setting up a genuine authority independent of the member states, or even a first nucleus of autonomous international power." But he saw the need for urgent action to build a lasting peace, and he accepted when A.J. Balfour, the British Foreign Secretary, and Georges Clemenceau, the French Prime Minister, invited him to become Deputy to the League's British Secretary-General, Sir Eric Drummond. Here, he played an active part in the partition of Upper Silesia between Germany and Poland, in the unsatisfactory settlement of the Saar (which France insisted on keeping), and above all in the reconstruction of Austria. He also argued powerfully, but unsuccessfully, against Raymond Poincaré's insistence on German reparations on a large scale. As an international civil servant, indeed, Monnet was very much his own man. A reporter at the time described him as "short, quick, mysterious, with great charm and a sparkle in his eyes." Although his staff prepared dossiers for him, he piled them on his desk without reading them, preferring to be briefed in person. He never kept to office hours or administrative routine, and was "even more pragmatic than the British."

Later, looking back, Monnet realized the weakness of the league; but he would have continued his efforts there had it not been for a crisis in the family brandy firm. One day in the autumn of 1921, his sister Marie-Louise came to beg him to return to Cognac and take matters in hand. The postwar slump, the fall in prices, and the slackening of demand had affected J.G. Monnet's business far more than it had touched the giant firms. There was even talk of bankruptcy -- which Monnet promptly scotched. Part of the trouble was his father's desire to hang on to long-maturing vintage brandy, locking up capital and inhibiting sales. The market, Monnet saw, wanted good quality brandy of less venerable age and more moderate price. His dispute with his father pained them both; but the lucky accident of a price rise enabled Monnet to reorganize the firm. After that, he handed its day-to-day running to his cousins, keeping some shares in it but otherwise remaining free.

At this point he was approached by Blair and Co., a large American investment which during the war had negotiated French and other loans on the U.S. market. Blair was now extending its interests in Europe; and in August 1926 it established the French Blair and Co. Foreign Corporation, based in Paris, with Monnet as its vice president. He took as his assistant a young French economist named René Pleven, who long afterwards became Prime Minister of France.

While a banker, Monnet was involved in many varied projects, and met many very diverse people, including the American lawyer John Foster Dulles and the Swedish match magnate Ivar Kreuger -- "the formidable swindle of his fictitious wealth," as Monnet later realized, was "built on a scaffolding of falsehood." At Blair, Monnet helped to stabilize the Polish and Rumanian currencies; when Blair merged with Amadeo Giannini's Bancamerica in May 1929, he went to San Francisco as vice president of the new conglomerate. After the Wall Street crash, Giannini's holding company, Transamerica, was found to be seriously over-valued. Monnet and his Blair partner Elisha Walker persuaded Giannini to take a long holiday abroad while they reorganized the company; but on February 13, 1932, Giannini recovered control. Monnet had lost. He had also made and lost a great deal of money.

In August 1929, however, he won a far more valuable prize. It was in Paris; and, as Monnet described the event: "An Italian couple were among those having dinner with us. He was a businessman. That night, I saw his young wife for the first time. She was very beautiful. We forgot the other guests."

Monnet continued his discreet narrative: "I think I can trace back to that first meeting the beginning of a love that was mutual and indestructible. I was forty years old; she was little more than twenty. We soon decided that we must be together for life. Many obstacles stood in their way. Silvia was married under Italian law, which forbade divorce. I looked into a number of solutions: I found that divorce and remarriage were possible under Soviet law. We decided on that as a solution. We met in Moscow on November 13, 1934, and everything went as simply as could be. Many years later, Monseigneur Henri Donze, Bishop of Tarbes and Lourdes and a great friend of the family, married us in Lourdes itself."

Monnet's travels continued. In 1933 he had gone to China for the first time; now he and Silvia went for a year to Shanghai in a private capacity to launch a Chinese reconstruction plan. The secret of dealing with the Chinese he discovered was simple: "Act as you speak, so that there is never any contradiction between what you say and what you do." He met Chiang Kai-shek, whose wife told Monnet: "The General likes you. He says there is something Chinese in you." He learned among other things that he must ask three times before receiving a precise answer, because to answer too quickly would be impolite. He also learned that it was no use trying to invest foreign capital in China without Chinese participation. Having realized that, in June 1934 Monnet secured the agreement of a number of Chinese banks to the establishment of the China Finance Development Corporation, to inject long-term capital into private and public concerns. One of its first and most important achievements was to restore and develop China's rail communications network.

Early in 1936, Monnet returned to New York and to investment banking in partnership with George Murnane. Already, on a visit there in the previous September, he had been dining with Murnane when John Foster Dulles had arrived with news of Adolf Hitler's decrees against the Jews in Germany. Presciently, Monnet remarked: "A man who is capable of that will start a war." In March 1936, when Hitler occupied the left bank of the Rhine, the former German Chancellor Heinrich Brüning was in New York, and he told Monnet: "The Allies must enter Germany. Otherwise, sooner or later, there will be war."

Monnet watched with disquiet the creation and rapid growth of Hitler's and Goering's Luftwaffe. So did France's Defense Minister, Edouard Daladier, whom he met at the beginning of 1938. So too did William Bullitt, the US ambassador to Paris, with whom he drafted a "Note on the possible establishment of an aeronautical industry out of reach of enemy attack." The Munich crisis that September saw Daladier become Prime Minister as well as Defense Minister. After the Munich Conference, he invited Monnet to lunch with Bullitt and the French Air Minister Guy La Chambre. "If I had three or four thousand aircraft," said Daladier, "Munich would never have happened." And on October 3, 1938, he decided to send Monnet to the United States for urgent talks with President Roosevelt.

After an initial foray that month, Monnet returned to Paris on November 4 and reported that the United States could supply the aircraft France needed in 1939. If the first orders were placed before the end of 1938, the first deliveries could be made in April. On December 9, Daladier sent Monnet back with instructions to order a thousand aircraft for delivery by July 1939. In the event, he was able to place orders for 600, with a firm option on 1500 more by the beginning of 1940. Meanwhile, France also ordered thousands of aero-engines -- so many that in the summer of 1939 Pratt & Whitney had to double the size of their plant. In the words of Edward R. Stettinius, these orders "were almost revolutionary in their effect upon our aircraft industry, and they laid the groundwork for the great expansion that was to come in 1940 and the years that followed."

When war came, Monnet proposed to Daladier that the Allies should set up at once a joint supply organization similar to that which had taken years to establish in World War I, and draw up a balance-sheet of their resources and needs. By November 1939, the British and French Governments had formed an Anglo-French Coordinating Committee with Monnet as its Chairman -- "an Allied official", his letter of appointment stressed, pledged to adopt "an Allied rather than a national point of view." Needless to add, this language had been drafted by Monnet himself.

Hitler's invasion of Belgium and the Netherlands on May 10, 1940, outflanking the French defensive Maginot Line, lent power and urgency to Monnet's plea that the Allies act jointly to open up the American arsenal for arms and munitions as well as aircraft. But Hitler's blitzkrieg was more powerful and urgent still. Soon, the British Army had fallen back on Dunkirk, and the "little ships" evacuation had begun. Monnet persuaded Churchill, by now British Prime Minister, to prolong the operation for 36 hours so as to rescue 26,000 French troops; but he was less successful in arguing that the French and British air forces be used as one in the Battle for France. Instead, with his friend and colleague Arthur Salter, Monnet decided as he wrote later "to raise our sights and try to recover on the political level the control of events that was escaping us in the field."

In essence, this was to propose a solemn declaration of indissoluble union between Britain and France -- with one Parliament, one Cabinet, one army, one currency. With the help of Desmond Morton, Churchill's security adviser, Salter, Pleven (Monnet's assistant), and Sir Robert Vansittart, Permanent Under-Secretary at the Foreign Office, Monnet drafted a document to this effect; and with the help of Neville Chamberlain, now Lord President of the Council, Churchill was persuaded to discuss it in Cabinet.

With some modifications, the Cabinet approved it, and a French version was read over the telephone to Paul Reynaud, now French Prime Minister, in Bordeaux, to which the Government had withdrawn as in World War I. He was delighted, and proposed a meeting at Concarneau in Brittany on the following morning, Monday June 17. The British party was about to set out when news came that Reynaud had resigned, and that the French President Albert Lebrun has appointed Marshal Pétain in his stead.

Even so, Monnet made one last attempt to rally the French Government. While Lord Lloyd, the Colonial Secretary, flew with a British team to Bordeaux, Monnet took a Sunderland flying-boat, the *Claire*, with Pleven, Emmanuel Monick (financial atttaché at the French Embassy in London), and Robert Marjolin, his assistant. The idea was to have room on board to bring back some leading political opponents of capitulation. Alas -- none would accept the offer; and Monnet's group flew back with an assortment of ordinary refugees.

Monnet now faced a dilemma; whether to join forces with General de Gaulle, with whom he was in daily contact in London, or to continue his efforts to secure supplies. His aircraft orders were assigned to Britain for the symbolic sum of one dollar; and they helped to win the later bomber battle. But he doubted whether de Gaulle was wise "to form an organization which might seem in France as if it were set up under the protection of Britain." He proposed instead that resistance be organized in French North Africa, and in what he later called "a less personalized form." "My dear friend," replied the general, "at such a time as this it would be absurd for us to cross one another, because our fundamental aim is the same, and together perhaps we can do great things." But although they continued to meet and discuss matters, they did not work together for another three years.

On July 2, 1940, Monnet formally resigned from the Anglo-French Coordinating Committee, which in effect had ceased to exist. In a note to Churchill, he added: "I therefore place my services at the disposal of the British Government in such capacity as they can be most useful." Churchill asked him to go to Washington to work with the head of the British Purchasing Commission, his friend and colleague Arthur Purvis. When he landed en route in Bermuda, a British customs official looked suspiciously at his French passport and his instructions from Churchill. "It just doesn't make sense," he said, "for a Frenchman to hold a British job at this point."

In fact, it made a great deal of sense. Before leaving London, Monnet had written of the need to "establish a reserve of weapons beyond the range of the bombers." President Roosevelt was willing to help; but his hands were tied by American isolationism, fear of war, and unpreparedness. Monnet saw his role as exposing the problems and contradictions, and starting a wide-ranging debate among his many U.S. contacts, including Felix Frankfurter, Henry Stimson, Jack McCloy, Averell Harriman, and Dean Acheson. He also got to know Harry Hopkins, James Byrnes, Walter Lippmann, and James Reston -- all in their different ways key figures in preparing to make the United States what Monnet himself first called "the arsenal of democracy." On the evening when he used the phrase, Frankfurter begged him not to repeat it. "Why not?" asked Monnet. "Because I think I can soon find a very good use for it." He did. A few days later, the President used it in a famous radio "Fireside Chat."

As before, Monnet's procedure was to draw up a "balance-sheet" of what was needed, in what form, and how it was to be produced. But speed was the key. "I knew from experience that it took four months for supplies to come off the production line." In the summer of 1941, the U.S. economist Stacy May brought back from London a 60-page balance-sheet of Britain's needs. It caused a shock in Washington; but after the Japanese attack on Pearl Harbor in December, it became clear that existing efforts would have at least to be doubled. Monnet actually persuaded the President to increase the General Staff's munitions program by a further 50%. Aircraft production rose to 300,000; tank production to 100,000; ship production to 184,000; machine-gun production to 2.7 million; steel production to 430 million tons. That effort, Maynard Keynes estimated after the war, probably shortened the conflict by a whole year.

In November 1941, Jean and Silvia Monnet had a daughter. They named her, for France, Marianne. Within little more than a year, with the Victory Program well launched, Monnet once more turned towards specifically French problems following the "Torch" landings in North Africa on November 8: the establishment of Free French authority there, the subsequent assassination of Admiral Darlan in Algiers and the danger that his successor, General Henri Giraud, would in effect divide the French, whose pivotal leader had hitherto been General de Gaulle. Worried in addition by the anti-democratic, anti-Semitic, and generally reactionary character of the Algiers administration, Monnet asked Harry Hopkins whether he could be sent to Algeria on behalf of the Munitions Assignment Board. Officially, his role was to center on the rearmament of French forces. In reality, his task was to try to reconcile Giraud and de Gaulle.

Giraud, he soon found, was courageous, upright, stubborn, vain, conservative, and a child in politics. Eventually, under pressure from Monnet, from Roosevelt's representative Robert Murphy, and from Churchill's representative Harold Macmillan, Giraud abrogated some (and, by implication, all) of the Vichy laws which he had hitherto let stand in North Africa. He was also persuaded to repudiate the 1940 armistice and to recognize the French Resistance. De Gaulle, in London, welcomed these steps forward; and two months later, once he was assured that the Conseil National de la Résistance, painstakingly set up by Jean Moulin, had pledged him its allegiance, he at last consented to come to Algiers. He landed there on May 30, 1943. Two days later, a joint Executive Committee, with de Gaulle and Giraud as its co-Presidents, met in the Lycée Fromentin: its other members were André Philip and René Massigli from London, and General Joseph Georges Catroux -- putting Giraud in effect in a minority -- and adopted the title of Committee of National Liberation. Gradually, de Gaulle outmaneuvered Giraud; and when the Committee became the Provisional Government, there was no longer any question as to who was at its head. Monnet was its member in charge of supplies, both nominally and in practice; but he had played a key role in holding the frail coalition together, and also, through his U.S. contacts, ensuring its support by the American administration.

In early summer of 1944, in a interview with a journalist from Fortune magazine, John Davenport, Monnet discussed his thoughts about the future of France and Europe now that the liberation seemed to be at hand. "The countries of Europe; he said, "are too small to give their peoples the prosperity that is now attainable and therefore necessary... The States of Europe must form a federation or 'European entity' which will make them a single economic unit." He had long been discussing these ideas with his colleagues in Algeria: René Mayer, Hervé Alphand, Robert Marjolin, and Etienne Hirsch. It was characteristic, at this stage, that the emphasis was on "prosperity" and economics. When he returned to liberated Paris in September 1944, Monnet confessed: "My heart ached to see how impoverished and exhausted people were.... I realized that I had no choice: at all costs we must keep up the flow of supplies from overseas." But France itself must make a collective effort. "Everyone," Monnet told de Gaulle, "must be associated in an investment and modernization plan."

"That is what has to be done, and that is the name for it," answered the general. "Send me your proposals before the end of the year."

That conversation took place in Washington in August 1945. Monnet was at the time still involved in securing further Lend-Lease supplies, with the help, among others, of George Ball. But he lost no time in meeting de Gaulle's deadline; and in early December he sent him a five-page note. The method it proposed was "to bring together in each sector the administration department concerned, the best qualified experts, and the representatives of industry and the trade unions (working people, whitecollar workers, and employers)." This in itself was an innovation for France. So too was Monnet's proposal to set up a Commissariat-General of the Plan, attached not to an economic ministry with its attendant bureaucracy, but directly to the Prime Minister's office, and as immune as possible from the effects of any political crisis, cabinet reshuffle, or government change.

After much hectic and informal work in rented rooms at the Hotel Bristol, the tiny staff of the Plan, with Monnet at its head, was established in the small private house at 18 rue de Martignac that it still occupies today. The total strength was no more than a hundred or so; and Monnet's personal staff was only four or five, including in particular Etienne Hirsch and (slightly later) the mercurial Pierre Uri. Another innovation on which Monnet insisted was to have a small dining room on the premises, so that work could continue uninterrupted and formalities could be relaxed.

Around this minute nucleus, vast numbers of others revolved. Civil servants, chairmen of companies, Communist labor unionists -- people from all walks of life and every part of France met with the Commissariat in "Modernization Commissions" to discuss production targets and supply needs in the specialized priority sectors where they were expert; and each year Monnet and his staff produced an indicative Plan. Its distinctive style became its trademark: short sentences, numbered paragraphs marking the transition from one idea to the next without clumsy bridging passages, a limited number of concrete words, and few adjectives. Newcomers, anxious to shine, got their drafts back with the comment: "Too intelligent; rewrite." And although the annual plan had no coercive legislative force, it had immense influence, especially in the early years. As Monnet wrote later: "More important than the figures themselves was the method whereby they had been reached, and the experience this had given to those responsible for the French economy."

But that economy, as Monnet had stressed in talking with friends and colleagues in wartime, was inescapably linked with those of its neighbors. The Marshall Plan or European Recovery Program acknowledged this by insisting that American aid be allocated on lines agreed jointly by its recipients. And although the hope of establishing a European customs union as a counterpart to Marshall Aid were in the end disappointed, the establishment of OEEC, the Organization for European Economic Cooperation, like that of the Council of Europe, at least recognized interdependence of a sort.

Merely cooperative ventures, however, seemed to Monnet inadequate. "In my opinion," he wrote after one postwar visit to the United States, "Europe cannot long afford to remain almost exclusively dependent on American credit for her production and American strength for her security.... To match the American effort, the countries of Western Europe must turn their national efforts into a truly European effort."

His first move in this direction was to try to inaugurate joint economic planning by Britain and France. The opportunity came when Maurice Petsche, the French Finance Minister invited Monnet to dinner with Sir Stafford Cripps, at the beginning of March 1949. "You won't reach agreement," said Monnet, "unless you make it your ultimate aim to merge the British and French economies." To this end, Monnet proposed informal talks; and at the end of April Sir Edwin Plowden, the head of the British planning organization, whom Monnet had met at the beginning of the war and whom he liked and respected, came to France to discuss what might be done. He brought with him two British officials, Alan Hitchman and Robert Hall. Monnet was flanked by Uri and Hirsch. They spent four days together at Monnet's country retreat at Houjarray outside Paris. But although they exchanged useful information, it became clear that the British view of their purpose was limited to immediate material ends, such as "exchanging U.K. coal for French foodstuffs," and that the idea of merging French and British economic planning, let alone that of merging the respective economics, was out of the question in British eyes.

Among the subjects discussed at Houjarray had been the rising economic power of postwar Germany. German friction with France had centered on the Saar, which France sought to annex; but more fundamental was the problem of Western Germany's role in the new European system. The United States was anxious to include the new Federal Republic in the Western political, economic, and military effort; the Soviet Union was implacably opposed to it. France was uneasy at the prospect of German revival; and Britain was inclined to side with the United States. The issue was due to come to a head in May 1950, at a Western Foreign Ministers' meeting in London. It was now that Monnet saw the chance to make his key contribution to the development of postwar Europe. Essentially, it linked the immediate problem of Germany with the contemporary discussion of European unity; and it did so by focusing on a very specific and concrete idea.

Instead of tackling the central difficulty head-on, Monnet applied his habitual method of seeking to change its context -- a procedure involving what later became known as "lateral thinking."

What he proposed, in other words, was not a new, general European institution, not a specific settlement of the "German problem"; it was to take one key element in Franco-German relations and deal with that in such a way as to alter the entire perspective. Coal and steel, he saw, were at that time the essential elements of economic power and the raw materials for war. So he proposed to pool French and German output of those materials in an organization transcending both countries, with common and equal institutions open to other nations willing and able to join. Henceforth, there was to be no question of dominating Germany, but equally no danger of a resurgent Germany's dominating France. And the joint institutions which would oversee the countries' joint resources of coal and steel would themselves be the possible embryo of further European integration.

Monnet first put his ideas to Paul Reuter, a young law professor from Eastern France whom he had met at rue de Martignac. Then, with Reuter, Hirsch, Uri and his faithful secretary Madame Miguez, he worked at Houjarray on a draft text. He sent it to the French Prime Minister Georges Bidault -- who failed to take it up; but he also gave a copy to Bernard Clappier, head of the private office of Robert Schuman, the Foreign Minister, who was anxious to make some kind of proposal to the Foreign Ministers' conference he was due to hold with Dean Acheson and Ernest Bevin in London on May 10. Schuman read the proposal overnight, and accepted it. So it was that Monnet's coal and steel pool proposal became the Schuman Plan.

Before putting the Plan to the French Cabinet, Schuman sent a trusted emissary in secret to explain his political purpose to the Federal German Chancellor, Konrad Adenauer, in Bonn. With Adenauer's agreement telephoned to him in Paris, Schuman then raised his proposal at the end of the morning meeting of the French Cabinet on May 9. It was accepted. At six that same evening, the press was summoned to the Foreign Office to hear Schuman read the text and its striding preamble: "It is no longer a time for vain words, but for a bold, constructive act." That act was in effect the launching of what became the European Union.

Six nations joined at once in the process of putting flesh on the bones of Monnet's proposal: France and Germany, Italy, Belgium, the Netherlands, and Luxembourg. That Britain did not was no fault of Monnet's or Schuman's. Both went to London to explain the aim of their proposal; and Monnet engaged in a long exchange of official messages which at length revealed Britain's unwillingness to accept the idea of trying to establish institutions which in some respects would be superior to national governments. Wary at the way in which British opposition had weakened the structure of both OEEC and the Council of Europe, Monnet and the French Government insisted that the principle of so-called "supranationality" should not be excluded from negotiations on the Schuman Plan: but they tried at the same time to reassure the British that its practical implications were entirely subject to negotiation, and that any commitment to negotiate was not in itself a commitment to accept the result of the negotiations in advance. The Dutch, who expressed similar reservations, found the French reassurance perfectly adequate. The British did not; and they thereby excluded themselves and their influence from some 23 years of Community development. They did, however, establish the first of many diplomatic delegations to the new Community, and formed an association agreement with it, mainly as a result of Monnet's pressure and persuasion. It was also characteristic of Monnet's concern for Britain that he recruited to his personal staff -- long before Britain joined the Community in 1973 -- no fewer than four young Englishmen, in practice bilingual in English and French.

Monnet chaired the Schuman Plan negotiations, as head of the French delegation; and his methods surprised some colleagues from other countries, accustomed to establishing national positions in advance. His motto was to "put the problem on the other side of the table" and to seek common approaches to it. This often meant that members of his own delegation would argue with each other, in plenary session, just as vigorously as with their colleagues from other countries. It was creative, and it was free. Above all, it secured solidarity in problem-solving. Thus it was that the two institutions adumbrated in the original Schuman Declaration -- an independent High Authority and some form of arbitration by an independent Court -- were complemented, in response to suggestions from around the table, by a Common Assembly (embryo of the European Parliament) and by what was then called the "Special" Council of Ministers, representing national governments.

Monnet was appointed first President of the High Authority, which set itself up in Luxembourg after a failure to agree on even a "provisional" site for the new Community's institutions. As at the French Plan, his aim was to keep his staff small. In the early days, it was hand-picked. Lights burned at all hours in the High Authority's headquarters; and Sunday picnics might well be interrupted by an urgent summons to work. To one colleague whom complained at the lack of local entertainment, Monnet memorably answered: "Europe will not be made in night-clubs." He was an exacting, exasperating, inspiring and exhilarating chief. But his administrative methods daunted traditional bureaucrats. Essentially, he was intent on forcing the pace and promoting new ideas.

He had already done so while the Schuman Plan was under negotiation. Facing American pressure for German rearmament, France felt herself in an even more acute form of the same dilemma as that concerning German economic recovery. And Monnet saw a similar way out. Instead of trying to postpone the decision or to keep Germany subordinate, why not pool defense -- or a substantial part of it -- in much the same way and with the same institutions as the pooling of coal and steel? After much discussions and many drafts, Monnet put this plan to René Pleven, his erstwhile assistant, now Prime Minister of France. Pleven accepted it, and proposed it in the French National Assembly on October 24, 1950. The same six nations negotiated the Pleven Plan into a Treaty for a European Defense Community (EDC); but Monnet played little part in its further promotion, and after years of delay, although ratified by all of the Six except France and Italy, E.D.C. was defeated on a procedural motion in the French Assembly on August 30, 1954.

His first term of office as President of the High Authority was due to expire in February 1955: but the failure of EDC, together with a bout of ill-health, made Monnet restless. On November 9, 1954, he called his colleagues together and announced in advance his decision to resign on the following February 10, "in order to be able to take part with complete freedom of action and speech in the achievement of European unity." What he had in mind was what came to be called "the re-launching of Europe" after the defeat of EDC.

Initially, Monnet saw this in terms of extending the principles of the coal and steel community to the joint European development of nuclear energy for peaceful ends. Atomic power was new: there were as yet few vested national interests; and it was a field in which, as Monnet wrote, "the prospect of fresh national rivalry... alarmed me; but, equally, that of a vast common enterprise attracted me, provided that a careful distinction were maintained between civil and military ends." The French engineer Louis Armand nicknamed that enterprise "Euratom." But Monnet also foresaw the need at the same time to extend the scope of the E.C.S.C. institutions to cover not just a "common market" in coal, coke, steel, iron ore, and scrap, but the whole of the member countries' economy. He also hoped, once again, to associate Britain with this new Community venture.

After some discussion, Monnet secured the agreement of the Belgian statesman Paul-Henri Spaak, who did his best to convert his Benelux colleagues, Joseph Bech from Luxembourg, Johan Willem Beyen, the Foreign Minister of the Netherlands. But there were difficulties elsewhere. Antoine Pinay, now French Foreign Minister, was reluctant to reopen the European debate; and the Germans were less keen on the Euratom idea than Monnet had expected. In response, Monnet and Pierre Uri improved and expanded the proposal for a general "Common

Market"; and on the basis of these ideas Spaak drafted a four-page "Benelux Memorandum", a copy of which he sent to Monnet on May 6, 1955, with the simple covering note: "herewith your child."

By this time, Monnet had long been fretting to leave Luxembourg and the High Authority; but his lawyers had advised that he must remain until a successor was appointed. On June 1, 1955, the Foreign Ministers of the Six met in Messina to begin discussing this question as well as the far bigger issues raised by the Benelux Memorandum. By June 3, they had settled both. They appointed René Mayer President of the High Authority, and they set up a committee under Paul-Henri Spaak to propose, with help from the High Authority and with representatives from Britain, how to implement the Benelux Memorandum. With Europe thus "re-launched", Monnet even thought of asking to resume the presidency of the High Authority. But it would have been impossible; and in his memoirs he made no mention of the idea.

"So, in the early summer of 1955," he wrote, "I found myself a private citizen once more after sixteen years of uninterrupted public service." How best could he continue to promote the European cause? One of his close associates, François Duchêne, suggested that he might enter French politics: but Monnet demurred. He had already toyed with the thought on returning to France from America in 1945. He had concluded then that it was not his role. He was no orator, though he would have liked to be. He disliked jostling for power and dispersing his efforts over many disparate problems. The idea of "belonging to a party" repelled him, because it meant following a party line of which he might not be totally convinced. His task was to prepare the future -- "which by definition is outside the glare of present publicity." And "although it takes a long time to reach the men at the top, it takes very little to explain to them how to escape from the difficulties of the present.... When ideas are lacking, they accept yours with gratitude -- provided they can present them as their own. These men, after all, take the risks; they need the kudos."

Monnet now, therefore, set out to institutionalize the "gray eminence" activity he had pursued for so long as a single individual. The form it took was "the Action Committee for the United States of Europe" -- a body composed of the political parties and trade unions of all the six Community countries, with the exception of Communists, Gaullists, and neo-fascists. They, and not their representatives, were technically the Committee's members, giving it exceptional authority and weight. The policies adopted by the Action Committee, in other words, became *ipso facto* the policies of the parties (and governments) and the trade unions concerned.

Monnet had wondered whether to include in the Committee various militant "European" pressure groups; but he had concluded that they were not always effective or responsible, and that they also lacked power. He also omitted employers' organizations. But the trade unions, in his view, were essential; it was they, in Germany, who had helped to win over the social democrats to the European cause while Monnet was still in Luxembourg.

After much travel and countless telephone conversation, the Action Committee formally came into being on October 13, 1955. As always, Monnet kept its headquarters' staff small: Max Kohnstamm, the Dutch Secretary-General of the High Authority, who became the Committee's Vice President; Jacques Van Helmont, also from the High Authority; François Duchêne, who had recently left it; later, he was replaced by Richard Mayne. Together with three secretaries, they worked from the flat in Paris, at 83 avenue Foch, which Monnet shared with his brother-in-law. But when the Committee met in plenary session it brought together some of the best-known names in European politics.

The Action Committee's tasks were, first, to provide a favorable political environment for the negotiation, ratification, and application of the new Community Treaties for Euratom and the Common Market; secondly, to help provide technical suggestions for further developments in Europe; and, thirdly, to deal with major problems of "crisis management." Naturally, all three activities overlapped. Examples of the first were the securing of support for the new treaties in the national Parliaments; of the second, proposals for direct elections to the European Parliament, greater aid to developing countries, and backing for the abortive project of a "Multilateral Force": or M.L.F. This in itself was one aspect of "crisis management" after the veto imposed by General de Gaulle on Britain's belated bid to join the Community and the disarray in the Atlantic Alliance after President Kennedy was shot.

Monnet finally dissolved the Action Committee in May 1975. By then, many of its aims had been achieved. The "new" Communities were in being, and their institutions had been merged. The Economic Community, in particular, was flourishing, despite internal crises and the oil-priced inflation and depression. Britain and other countries had joined the Community, after two vetoes by the late General de Gaulle. A "European Council" had been established -- regular meetings of the Heads of State or Government, which Monnet had originally wanted to

call "the Provisional Government of Europe." New links had been forged
with countless developing countries. The European Parliament was soon
to be directly elected, and to propose new steps in European integration.
The Community had successfully negotiated major steps in freer trade on
a world basis, in more and more equal partnership with the United
States.

But Monnet had one further task to accomplish: to produce a
best-selling masterpiece. He had published one book in the 1950s, a
compilation from his speeches entitled *Les Etats-unis d'Europe ont
commencé.* Now, he planned to write his memoirs -- not to explain,
justify, or glorify his achievements, but to demonstrate for future
generations how further progress might be made. He had long since
been struck by a remark from the Swiss philosopher Henri-Frédéric
Amiel: "each man's experience starts again from the beginning. Only
institutions grow wiser: they accumulate collective experience." Monnet
saw his memoirs as a way of encapsulating the experience of his own
long lifetime -- his last political act.

"I can't write," he once remarked to a colleague, "but I know how
to correct." To draft the memoirs, he invoked the help of a fine French
stylist, now a distinguished novelist, his former close assistant François
Fontaine. He asked Richard Mayne to translate them into English. He
kept a close and watchful eye on the work, and pronounced himself very
satisfied at the end.

The last page of the *Memoirs* reproduced the decision of the
European Council in April 1976, declaring Jean Monnet "Honorary
Citizen of Europe." He was then 87. He lived for three more years. His
funeral service was attended by the president of France and the
chancellor of Germany -- among countless others famous or obscure. A
smaller group of friends attended his burial in a country graveyard near
Houjarray. Ten years later, on the centenary of his birth, on November 9,
1988, a vast crowd in Paris watched as his remains were transferred to
the Panthéon in a ceremony presided over by François Mitterand, the
French President.

France had honored one of her two greatest sons this century.
Europe was left to mourn the man who had given it shape.

3

Jean Monnet and the Roosevelt Administration

Clifford P. Hackett

It was a self-assured Jean Monnet who arrived in Washington in October 1938 by ship on his way to meet Franklin Roosevelt at his private home in Hyde Park on New York's Hudson River shore. The Frenchman was experienced both in international affairs and in working with Americans but nothing in his previous years prepared him for the intensive interaction with the leaders of the New Deal which would follow in the next seven years.

The year 1938 became a crucial one for Europe and for Monnet. This final prewar year began with sharp conflicts within France. French Defense Minister Daladier insisted, against fiscal and political obstructionists, that the country must rearm. Hitler had already intimidated the Austrian Chancellor, Kurt Von Schuschnigg to resign in favor of a pro-Nazi successor. The incorporation of Austria into the Third Reich followed in March. By September the Nazi ruler was at work pressuring Czechoslovakia in a similar way. Although Britain, France and the Soviet Union were bound by treaties, alliances and interests in stopping Hitler they were unprepared, in spirit or material resources for the effort.

Monnet would soon witness the transition from American isolationism which at times affected the entire administration, to the fullest commitment to winning the Second World War for which the country was to be the principal supplier and financier, an important source of military manpower, and, by the end, a leader in waging the war and planning the peace. It was enough to dazzle even an experienced America-watcher like Monnet who had first been to the New World soon after the turn of the century and who had lived and worked there on and off throughout his life.

From 1938 to 1945, Monnet went from being a buyer of aircraft for France, to chairman of the London-based Anglo-French Coordinating Committee, then a Washington member of the British Supply Council before going to Algiers as an informal representative of the Roosevelt administration. When he returned from North Africa he came as a representative of the Free French forces to work for two more years with that administration for France's lend lease supplies and a generous post-liberation policy from Washington. In each of these roles Monnet was armed with his insider-outsider style; he practised a kind of benevolent penetration of institutions, using them only for their own good, or more precisely, for the good of the enterprise which now was victory over Hitler.

Monnet first assessed the Nazi regime in September 1935 when having dinner in suburban New York with his partner, American investment banker George Murnane and Foster Dulles, a lawyer with whom both Monnet and Murnane worked closely. Dulles reported that Hitler's first decrees against the Jews had just been published. Monnet concluded that "a man who would do that would start a war."

The following spring Monnet talked with former German chancellor, Heinrich Bruening, soon after the Rhineland was reoccupied by Germany. If the Allies do not enter Germany now, Bruening said, Hitler and his army will think themselves invincible. But the British and the French could not agree to act. Hitler gained strength by their failure. Before the French recognized the need to rearm, more than another year passed.

By October, 1938 Monnet was preparing to meet Franklin Roosevelt on France's belated rearmament. By the end of the year, he was on another, extended visit to the United States where he spent Christmas and New Year's day seeking the latest American aircraft. He was not the first, or the only, French agent to seek desperately needed American arms but he was the most persistent.[1]

Monnet arrived back in New York on October 19, 1938 on his first aircraft mission for France. His way was smoothed by Ambassador William Bullitt who proceeded Monnet from Paris to Hyde Park and told the President about the Frenchman's key role. When Monnet arrived at the comfortable presidential home, 40 miles north of New York City, he was impressed by the warmth of his host and his friendly, informal manner.

The President, Bullitt and Monnet discussed France's needs, including the possibility France could buy American aircraft parts and assemble them in a factory across the border in Quebec. Roosevelt was so enchanted with the idea that he sketched a map from his knowledge of the border area indicating where a French factory could be located. Monnet asked for the sketch as a souvenir of his first meeting with Roosevelt. Monnet and Bullitt then went to Washington where they met with Secretary of the Treasury Henry Morgenthau whose department handled foreign military sales. Monnet then hurried home to consult with Daladier.

The origins of the plan to build French factories somewhere in Canada, perhaps across from Buffalo or Detroit, are not clear. Monnet, who had lived in Canada as a young man, certainly would have been open to a plan which called for cooperation between Canada and the United States, and may have originated it. Managers, workers and supplies from the United States would have to be involved, pleasing some Americans. Avoiding the American Neutrality Act by using a cross border location would also have appealed to both Bullitt and Monnet, as well as to the President. The French government would have felt comfortable in a country with historical ties to France.

Monnet celebrated his fiftieth birthday on November 9, 1938, when he was just back in Paris from this first mission in the United States. For Europe, it was the date when any innocence about Hitler was lost for it saw the start of direct Nazi violence against the continent's Jews. It must have been a birthday anniversary Monnet would recall to the end of his long life. It was the day the world remembers as Kristallnacht.

Two of Monnet's three closest acquaintances in these early prewar visits to Washington were Jewish-Americans --- Felix Frankfurter and Henry Morgenthau --- both of whom helped activate the Roosevelt adminstration's concern about Nazi Germany. They were dedicated, as was Monnet, to sounding an alarm about Hitler's goals.

The third, Harry Hopkins, was also a man who could remind one of Monnet; was the social worker who ended as the closest presidential adviser in foreign affairs any less versatile or committed than the cognac salesman who ended as the father of a united Europe?

Henry Morgenthau's father had been American ambassador to Turkey during the First World War and a strong Wilson supporter on the fringes of the Paris Peace Conference where he may have met Monnet. The younger Morgenthau went to Washington in 1934 when, as political friend and Hudson Valley neighbor of Roosevelt, he was soon named Secretary of the Treasury. Monnet was often in the capital at that time on international investment matters and their paths apparently crossed.

The Morgenthaus, father and son, were party loyalists, each with a close friendship to the first two Democratic presidents of the twentieth century. The Morgenthaus represented the liberal side of their party and of their patrons. As an early opponent of Hitler, Monnet should have fallen easily into the Morgenthau orbit but instead he was seen in the treasury department as suspect, with shadowy connections in the European and New York financial worlds.

Monnet worked closely with many Americans in these years just before and during the war, some of whom became much more important to him in later work. George Ball and Robert Nathan are the best examples of the people Monnet picked up during the war and used in rebuilding Europe. They represented the American lawyer-statesman he admired, as did Henry Stimson, Jack McCloy and Dean Acheson. William Bullitt, journalist and diplomat, represented another favored type for Monnet.

But the three key administration figures --- one in the treasury department, one in the White House, the third in the Supreme Court --- were different. They were vital to Monnet's wartime work yet they had almost nothing to do with him after the war. (Hopkins was dead in 1946 when Morgenthau was retired by the Truman administration; Frankfurter stayed on the court and kept up a friendly but long-distance relation with Monnet after the war).

Yet without Frankfurter, Hopkins and Morgenthau there would not have been a Monnet story to tell in these crucial war years which prepared the Frenchman for the postwar reconstruction of France and Europe. Further, without the detailed accounts of the activities of these three, it would be difficult to tell a coherent story of how the Roosevelt administration fought the war, especially in the early years.

Each of the three was personally close to the President of the United States who relied on them for inspiration, loyalty, argument and friendship. Their proximity to Roosevelt drew Monnet to each like iron filings to the magnetized object.

In 1938 Monnet was still engaged in investment banking with his partner, George Murnane, from which he only slowly extricated himself in the following months. Some of these business deals made

Monnet an object of suspicion for Henry Morgenthau. For example, Monnet and Murnane had been brought together in partnership in 1935 by Foster Dulles, a prominent Republican lawyer of the firm Sullivan and Cromwell. Morgenthau considered this law firm, which had represented the Spanish government of dictator Francisco Franco in a suit against the Treasury Department, an enemy of the New Deal. When Monnet used Sullivan and Cromwell in some work involving a possible French aircraft assembly firm to be built in Canada, Morgenthau sputtered to Ambassador Bullitt, "Monnet doesn't seem to realize we have a new administration here." [2]

Morgenthau regarded the New York financial community, of which Monnet was a member, as hostile to the New Deal. He carried a suspicion about Monnet throughout their years of working together, believing somehow that a man involved with international banking could not be fully committed to the fight against Hitler.

Monnet returned to Washington in December 1938 after his consultations in Paris with Daladier and Guy La Chambre, the Minister for Air. Morgenthau increasingly felt himself pressured by Monnet's demands for access to the still feeble American aircraft industry, especially with the Frenchman supported by President Roosevelt's own strong desire to aid the European democracies by every step short of war or outright illegality. On the other side, Morgenthau knew that parts of the U.S. government were hostile to any foreign aircraft sales which could undermine the American buildup of its miniscule airforce and its supporting industry. And the state department was cautious about this mysterious French mission by Monnet who was not a government official and whose links to the foreign ministry or the French Ambassador in Washington were unclear.

To ground some of this suspicion, Morgenthau insisted that Monnet make public his second mission in Washington. On his arrival in October, the French Embassy was apparently not even aware he was in the country. Monnet told the treasury secretary that the Daladier government --- the defense minister had become prime minister --- was reluctant to publicize the mission but probably did not tell him why: the French government was itself divided on the question of buying American planes both because of the dollar outflow and because French aircraft manufacturers wanted the business themselves.

In a meeting on the last day of 1938, Morgenthau told Monnet: "I want to talk very frankly to you. Our mutual good friend, Ambassador Bullitt, has put me in an almost impossible position.... The whole

United States Army is opposed to what I am doing and I am doing it secretly and I just can't continue, as Secretary of the Treasury, forcing the United States Army to show you planes which they say they want for themselves." [3]

But this was not the end of Morgenthau's concerns about the French. He was also worried about the Neutrality Act. Perhaps it would be better, Morgenthau and his staff suggested, to have the French government open its own office in Canada for arms procurement.

Monnet seems bewildered by this argument. This *was* a French government corporation which he was trying to start in Canada. He also told the treasury secretary that he was ready to invest $250,000 of his own money as would other members of the corporation's board of directors. Morgenthau could not believe what he was hearing. "Might I ask why you should do it [invest your own money]?"

Monnet replied, "I do a lot of things in this affairs that I should not be doing. I have been the instrument through which this thing is being worked out and I find no other solution." [4]

Early in the new year, a spectacular aircraft accident further undermined the Monnet mission and shook the Roosevelt administration. Two members of Monnet's team went to California, over the U.S. Army's objections, to test a new Douglas light bomber. The American test pilot, intent to demonstrate the plane's capabilities to a skeptical French observer, pushed the plane into a stall and crash onto an airport parking lot. The pilot was killed when his parachute delayed opening; the French observer was injured but conscious when rescuers arrived. The press overheard a conversation in French and the story was out: the French were test flying the latest, most secret American planes.

When Monnet returned to France in early 1939 after this second mission to America, he continued to balance his private business interests with a growing commitment to help France face and survive the German challenges. By April, Monnet was being pressed to return to Washington to help France find a way out of its debt problems which increasingly restricted its options for rearming with American help.

Before he could leave, family problems arose. His father had a stroke in early April in Cognac. Monnet went home to be with the man who had been an important guide from his childhood but also a stubborn obstacle when Jean Monnet had to reorganize the family cognac

firm in 1923. Years later a friend said that the death of his father was
an even more severe blow than his mother's passing which came sixteen
years later.[5]

Symbols of the tensions and conflicts in Monnet's Franco-
American life arose in the person and the family of Charles Lindbergh,
America's hero of the 1927 trans-Atlantic solo flight. Lindbergh's wife,
Anne Morrow, was the daughter of one of Monnet's close friends,
Dwight Morrow, who worked with Monnet in London in the First World
War. Lindbergh was also an acquaintance of Ambassador Bullitt who
brought the Monnets and the Lindberghs together several times in Paris
in early 1939.

Anne Morrow Lindbergh, who attended a family dinner with
Monnet just before his father's final illness, wrote of the Monnets,
father and son, that evening:

> A wonderful old man --- quick, gay, full of life and
> humor. Much joking between him and Jean. Jean is very proud
> of him. I like him for it. He is always mysterious though, in a
> quiet and completely orthodox way. Interrupted by telephone
> calls, having to leave for England or America on something
> frightfully important but no one having the slightest idea what
> he is doing. It was a nice evening. He was not the man of the
> world tonight but only a simple, devoted, charming, admiring
> son.[6]

The daughter of Dwight Morrow later described the two worlds
between which she was now caught: her father's --- urbane, international, democratic; and her husband's --- respectful of strength,
suspicious of democracy, inexperienced in diplomacy or negotiation.
Monnet represented her father's world and its values. He must have
sensed what Dwight Morrow's daughter was enduring when her
husband said publicly that the French airforce had no chance against
the Germans, whose factories and squadrons he had just visited.

Anne and Charles Lindbergh were at another dinner at
Monnet's apartment in Paris a few months later with Guy La Chambre,
the French Minister for Air. Later, the minister invited Lindbergh to
several meetings with advisers about the Canadian factory plan
Monnet had helped assemble. But the flyer-hero was out of sympathy
with rearming France which he thought should seek some kind of
accomodation with Germany. Increasingly, Lindbergh spoke out
against the French and American plans for building up the Allied air
strength against Hitler. Lindbergh and his wife returned to America

the next year where he became a vocal and increasing bitter opponent of Roosevelt's rearmament plans, and, implicitly, of Monnet as well.[7]

Ambassador Bullitt persisted to get Monnet to Washington once more, in May 1939, to work on France's financial problems. Monnet again saw Roosevelt who was ready to help France and Britain, subject to the stiff limits which isolationism still placed on him.[8]

On September 1, 1939, the French and British ultimatum to Hitler over his invasion of Poland was rejected. Their declaration of war followed immediately. The United States, watched now ever more closely by Monnet, began to plan more aid to the allied powers under relaxed neutrality legislation.[9] Monnet now made a total commitment to the war effort.

With the start of the European war, even with its six month hiatus known as "the phony war," personal plans changed rapidly for those anticipating a new American role. For some, like the Lindberghs who had hoped to continue living in Europe, perhaps even in Germany which Charles admired, the war meant a forced return home; others, like Monnet, saw the American role as decisive to the defeat of Hitler whose victory, they knew, would be catastrophic for Europe.

As American involvement deepened, so did the divide between these two men whom Anna Lindbergh and her family had brought together. Public opinion in America began to separate into two groups, corresponding to the basic positions of Charles Lindbergh and Monnet: those, like Lindbergh, who hoped America could stay out of the war and who saw neutrality in deed and thought as essential to that goal; and those like Monnet who abhorred any kind of neutrality between Hitler and his enemies and who were prepared to do whatever necessary to aid Britain and France. Monnet, of all America watchers, knew his side was still in the minority in the winter of 1939-40.

This shift from part to full-time work for Allied war supplies required adjustments in Monnet's personal life. He gave up his pleasant Fifth Avenue apartment across from Central Park. He asked his partner, George Murnane, to allow him to draw $1000 a month from the partnership; his wife, Silvia, who had been getting $1800 monthly while living in New York with Anna when Monnet was shuttling across the Atlantic in 1938-39 could soon join him in Paris. He and Murnane negotiated a new division of income from the partnership, reducing Monnet's share to 25%. Murnane would manage all operations in Monnet's extended absence.[10]

Monnet now took over the partnership's Paris apartment on Rue Fabert, overlooking the Invalides and the Seine River, giving him a place to stay after he had sold his older and larger city house near the university quarter, also on the Left Bank. Eventually Silvia joined Jean in Paris, leaving daughter Anna with the Donald Swatlands in their New Jersey home for the uncertain year from mid-1939 until late summer 1940.[11]

Monnet's vantage point for prodding America would now shift again. He manuevered with Daladier to be named head of a new allied coordinating committee which Monnet saw as crucial to the war effort. Ambassador Bullitt wrote Roosevelt that Daladier wanted Monnet either in London or, if the British objected to a single Allied purchasing office (or to Monnet), in Washington as France's ambassador. But, Bullitt added, Monnet was too valuable for merely running an embassy, a hint of the Ambassador's own impatience with his status.[12]

After some intra-allied manuevers, Monnet was named chairman of the Anglo-French Coordinating Committee (AFCC) in October 1939 with headquarters in London. Monnet approached this assignment with sharp memories of the strains and disappointments of a similar job in the First World War. He was determined to profit by those lessons. Others, lacking that experience or disputing its relevance, opposed Monnet's approach of coordinated purchases.

Monnet's peripatetic life settled, for ten months at least, into the London job. He and Silvia lived in an apartment on Mount Street. For exercise, he walked each morning through St. James Park on his way to the office on Richmond Terrace. He started drawing the French franc equivalent of about $1000 a month as his pay. He was proud to be an Allied official, as the press termed him.[13] In December, back in Paris briefly, Monnet was invited by Ambassador Bullitt to lunch with Premier Daladier, Air Minister La Chambre and René Pleven, Monnet's aide, who was on his way to New York to continue spurring the Americans to greater production, particularly of aircraft. Bullitt reported to Roosevelt on the meeting, asking him to see Pleven who was also spending time with Arthur Purvis, a Canadian businessman who had just opened an AFCC office in New York.

But with Monnet stationed in London, a gulf grew between him and Bullitt which was greater than the few hundred miles separating them. Monnet was captivated by the energy the new Conservative prime minister, Winston Churchill, brought to the rebuilding of His

Majesty's armed forces. Churchill had preached in a personal political wilderness for more than a decade about the need to rearm. Now, replacing a cautious and misguidedly optimistic Neville Chamberlain, Churchill was ready to act. In Monnet he had a willing junior partner representing Daladier, La Chambre and the few others in the French government who were prepared to pay what it cost for France to rearm as well.

Curiously, Bullitt grew pessimistic. He seemed to absorb the defeatism of much of the French political and military leadership and communicated it to Washington. Roosevelt once complained that the Ambassador would cable a buoyant message in the morning, followed by a pessimistic one on the same subject after lunch with a French official.

In London, as head of the fragile French-British coordinating effort, Monnet was in constant danger of being undercut by the traditional outlook of civil servants in both governments. A British diplomat in Paris at the time of France's fall said Monnet "seemed a mixture of gangster and conspirator" as he went about seeking suitable men for an alternative to the defeatism which finally produced the Petain government. The diplomat added that while he did not care for Monnet, "in England they think him the cat's pyjamas."

Not everyone in the British capital shared that view either, although Monnet's experience and skills with allied supply problems were well recognized in London. Sir Frederick Philipps, a high British treasury official, indicated drily to a colleague that some people, including some in the French Ministry of Finance and the U.S. treasury department, did not trust Monnet "and I am among them." As in the First World War, Jean Monnet found that he was making enemies by disregarding the hierarchies of government. Phillips' reference to U.S. treasury suspicions of Monnet indicated that Morgenthau had communicated his own doubts on Monnet to the allied powers for whom the treasury secretary was in a powerful position as manager of America's foreign military procurement.[14]

When the German blitzkrieg broke through weak French and Belgian defenses in May 1940, Monnet shifted urgently but briefly from arms procurement to bolstering Allied solidarity and to keeping France in the war. He tried, with Charles de Gaulle who was also in London, to persuade the British and French governments to unite in a desperate wartime political union which would include a single parliament and combined armed forces. Winston Churchill, who had just become prime minister, reluctantly supported the idea. But the French government under Paul Reynaud could not continue under the defeatism of the French armed forces and the withdrawal of British forces in the Dunkirk evacuation. Phillipe Petain, the great hero of the First World War, succeeded Reynaud, with a government committed to an armistice.

The plane orders which Monnet had so carefully nurtured were jeopardized by France's withdrawal from the conflict. Quick-footed work by Monnet and the Washington and New York members of the British Purchasing Commission, including a lawyer whom Foster Dulles had recommended as the BPC counsel, transferred the contracts from French to British hands for a nominal sum.[15]

Britain stood alone now against the Nazis and each man had to decide his place. Reynaud, Daladier and many other French leaders and parliament members stayed in France where many were imprisoned. Others collaborated or otherwise tolerated the occupation which left about half the country in French hands with the government at Vichy. But Monnet, de Gaulle and many others fled France.

Monnet and de Gaulle, back in London, discussed where to make this fight. They recognized their differences; the general stayed in London to place himself at the center of the French resistance forces outside France. Monnet arranged, with an exchange of letters with Churchill, to be assigned to the British Purchasing Office in Washington. He showed his indifference to government hierarchy once again by going to work for Arthur Purvis, head of the BPC, whom Monnet had until recently supervised as part of the Anglo-French Coordinating Committee from London.[16]

The fall of France was a momentous blow to the nation, to its citizens and for its allies. While Britain girded for a Nazi attack, the United States moved more vigorously to help. Roosevelt's nomination in 1940 of two activist Republicans --- Henry Stimson as Secretary of War and Frank Knox as Secretary of the Navy --- indicated both a political move to disarm the Republicans in the coming presidental election and a willingness to suspend conventional partisanship.

Monnet's arrival in Washington was part of Churchill's response to this new urgency yet also an unusual move. Monnet was a French official with a French diplomatic passport. He was a national of a defeated ally. It is a tribute to the British, especially Churchill who had to agree personally to the assignment, that they found in Monnet a unique combination of experience with both supply questions and with the United States.[17]

If 1940 marked a year of great change in Monnet's personal life with his move from London to Washington, the next year became a critical one for both him and the United States which moved in 12 months from a reluctant and hesitant supplier of military goods to an isolated Britain to a fully committed (if still militarily feeble) combatant ready to work with both Britain and the Soviet Union to defeat Germany and Japan.

Monnet was present for this transformation, having arrived in Washington in August 1940, not long after the destroyers-for-bases deal with Britain which marked the beginning of a more active U.S. aid program for that country. The destroyer deal proceeded under an ingenious interpretation of existing law published first as a letter to the editor in the New York Times of August 11, 1940 by four distinguished international lawyers including Dean Acheson, Charles C. Burlingham, George Rublee, and Thomas D. Thatcher. Two of them --- Acheson and Rublee --- were close Monnet friends whom he would soon see again in the United States.

Although many thought that the United States received the better part of the destroyer deal by gaining useful British bases for hemispheric defense for aged warships, both Churchill and Roosevelt knew that the transaction, together with an earlier relaxation of the Neutrality Act, moved the United States to an active war role.[18]

A major shift in American political life came about between Monnet's arrival in 1940 and his full engagement six months later in pushing defense production. In the summer of 1940, the country began a divisive political campaign over a third term for Franklin Roosevelt. Monnet witnessed most of this unique event where a Roosevelt campaign theme was that an experienced hand on the helm would keep America out of Europe's wars. Many believed that the country could avoid another involvement in Europe if it stayed clear of Britain's cause. The powerful "America First" movement was built on solid and widespread resentment that Europe had once again gotten itself into a mess and once more wanted American help in getting out. Anna and Charles Lindbergh, Monnet's acquaintances from Paris in 1938, were fully involved in America First and thus directly opposed to the work of both Monnet and Roosevelt in helping Britain survive.

Soon after arrival, Monnet was being escorted around key government offices by Felix Frankfurter, recently named to the Supreme Court by President Roosevelt. Justice Frankfurter spent considerable time with Monnet in 1940-41, initially introducing him to the key policy people he did not yet know. Then he pressed Monnet's ideas and memos on France, on North Africa and on Hitler's "New Order" on many people, starting with the President.

The Monnets and the Frankfurters soon became close acquaintances, dining in each other's home and sharing family experiences. Frankfurter was especially taken with the Monnet family style including the cook and butler couple who came with the Monnets from London and Paris and whom the Monnets occasionally lent to them for the Frankfurters frequent dinner parties. The borrowed French cook's bourgeois cuisine was a wartime highlight for the Frankfurters.[19]

Later, Monnet would come by Frankfurter's office in the Supreme Court almost daily to compare notes on their respective efforts to boost American involvement in supporting Britain, and eventually, the Soviet Union, in the war against Hitler. The day after Pearl Harbor, Frankfurter announced to his law clerk that he had been "called to war." The clerk was to take care of the court business, Frankfurter would check in regularly, but meanwhile he, Monnet and others had to press forward with helping the President win the conflict with Germany and Japan. Frankfurter's frenzied pace even included forwarding a letter from 10 year old Anna Monnet to the President with whom, Frankfurter's cover note said, Anna had "fallen in love" when witnessing the inauguration. The President dutifully replied.[20]

The mood in Washington, and in the country, in late 1940 was not hospitable to Monnet's efforts even after Roosevelt's historic electoral victory. The country was not yet united behind Roosevelt's international efforts, abetted by Morgenthau, Frankfurter and some others. One problem in the pre-Pearl Harbor period was convincing the military leaders to raise their requirements, an essential step to ratchet up the civilian production output. Caution and budget restrictions made military leaders reluctant to move; political considerations slowed the civilian leadership. The President had fought an election campaign on the theme of keeping America out of war; anticipating enlarged military needs seemed to contradict the commander-in-chief. Further, continuing legal restrictions on sales to belligerents slowed production until, in March 1941, the Lend Lease Act was signed.[21] Finally, even some British officials wanted to slow arms purchases for fear of bankrupting the national treasury.

The British wanted to believe, however, that their beleaguered role merited and received wide American recognition. But this was not the case. Part of Monnet's early work in the capital was conveying to London the sobering account of American detachment from the British war efforts.

The scale of Monnet's work at the British Supply Council can be gauged from the testimony by Morgenthau in early 1941 at the lend lease legislative hearings. From the start of the war in September 1939 to early 1941, Britain had paid for and taken delivery of $1.3 billion in supplies. It had on order another $1.4 billion. This total of nearly three billion dollars of British orders in 18 months compared with total U.S. government outlays of fourteen billion in fiscal year 1941. Monnet was greatly involved in this impressive volume, both in nine months in London as head of the AFCC and in his first year in Washington. With the passage in early 1941 of the legislation, even "counting the dollars" would be made easier for Britain.[22]

The importance of solidarity between Britain, the United States and the French resistance was a major theme in Monnet's work during his first few months in Washington. He also had a specific goal within the larger one: keeping France from joining Hitler's "New Order" and preventing North Africa from coming under German control. In this work, Monnet was again fortunate in having the right American friends.

The arrival of Monnet's old Republican friend, Henry Stimson as secretary of war --- a bipartisan stroke by Roosevelt which confounded his electoral opponents --- brought another business-era acquaintance to power. With Stimson came an old Monnet friend, John J. McCloy, now special assistant to the secretary of war. Monnet had known Stimson in the early 1930s when he was secretary of state under President Hoover. McCloy and Monnet worked together in Paris in the late 1920s when McCloy opened a Paris law office which serviced, among other clients, Blair and Company, an investment banking firm where Monnet worked. The Stimson-McCloy team at the War Department would become one of Monnet's closest ties to the Roosevelt administration.

Stimson was very impressed when Monnet briefed him at lunch in December 1940 on the French situation including the rivalries to lead the Free French forces. Stimson called Monnet's luncheon presentation "one of the most interesting I have ever had.... [Monnet] gave me a most clear and penetrating analysis of the situation in France and of the personalities involved and, what was more important, he had some constructive suggestions of what the United States could do." [23] His lunch with Stimson, at which Frankfurter may also have been present, concentrated on the dangers of the Nazi "New Order" which had already been endorsed by some French collaborationists.

Two weeks after the lunch, Monnet wrote a new version of the "New Order" memorandum he had given the War Secretary. In it, Monnet now stressed the need for the President to speak out clearly against the German strategy of enticing France into a "United Europe brought about by coercion, fear and terror." Monnet believed it crucial for the American leader to show solidarity not only with British war efforts but also against the insidious suggestion of the Germans that a European equivalent of the American union would come from Hitler's "New Order."

Roosevelt never spoke publicly as Monnet advised; at his next major statement the President instead addressed global issues (the "Four Freedoms") and national priorities (rearmament and economic warfare against the Axis powers). Monnet's plea for special prominence for France fell between these macro-themes.[24]

Earlier Monnet did have unanticipated success with a presidential speech when his phrase "arsenal of democracy" was incorporated into one of Roosevelt's "fireside chats" at the end of December. Monnet had used the words casually in a conversation with Frankfurter who immediately claimed it for presidential use. A few days later, the phrase which captured the American role at the time so perfectly was passed through to presidential speech writers to emerge in Roosevelt's confidence cadence as he defined the American role beside Britain.[25]

Monnet's relations with other top administration leaders were more complex. While he knew Stimson, McCloy and Morgenthau over many years, most other New Deal leaders involved in supply matters had to be met and conquered by Monnet's charming directness and honesty. But these skills sometimes failed. Secretary of State Cordell Hull, a Tennessee congressman for many years with few international ties, never trusted Monnet, partly because he saw him as de Gaulle's agent.

The state department, for two years after the fall of France, maintained a rigid support of the Vichy regime in the belief that some resistance to Hitler within France was better than the complete occupation of the country. Hull persisted in this view, which Monnet thought unspeakably naive, until the Germans, in late 1942, finally occupied the Vichy zone. But Hull never overcame his distrust of Monnet who is not even mentioned in the voluminous Hull memoirs. There was, in fact, no one of any stature in the state department close to Monnet or to his flexible views on de Gaulle in his wartime years in Washington. With the exception of Dean Acheson who returned to Roosevelt's government in February 1941, Monnet did not have a friend in the department.

In response to Hull's complaints about Monnet's role, Stimson reassured the secretary of state that Monnet was being treated by the war department "purely as an agent here to purchase supplies [and] that his authority and our authority was limited to that subject in all our talks." This was not literally true since Stimson's diary shows he was clearly attracted to Monnet's clear analyses of the French political situation and was being kept informed by Monnet of what was happening in North Africa. He also passed a Monnet memo on Europe to "Wild" Bill Donovan, who became head of the office of strategic services, the predecessor of the Central Intelligence Agency.[26]

Neither Monnet's duties nor his status in Washington were clear when he arrived in late summer 1940. He had been asked to bring to Arthur Purvis, head of the British Purchasing Commission, the papers used in London by the Anglo-French Coordinating Committee. But how he would work with the British, the Americans or with the various French groups in the country was not defined.

Even at the start of 1941, Monnet's status was not as clear as his memoirs indicate or as simple as Stimson and Frankfurter suggest. Monnet's account was reconstructed thirty years later when many of the petty tensions and frustrations of the war years had been forgotten. But in a long letter in early 1941 from his friend, Tommy Brand, there is a hint of these problems.

Brand, writing from London from the vantage of a position backstopping Monnet's supply efforts, wrote that "you may be hurt and certainly irritated by the way in which we have dealt with personal questions concerning yourself. First, P[urvis] and M[orris] W[ilson, his deputy] had to do more than just be glad of your services. It is now quite clear that they really want you to stay and help them and have a real confidence in your judgment." Apparently this desire by the Purvis team for Monnet's presence had not been made evident to him when he arrived in August 1940. Brand hinted that there had been opposition to the Monnet appointment from within the American government as well. "One or two [in the U.S. Administration] had to accept you as one of us and at first they were critical of your inclusion." Brand also notes that the British foreign office, and others in London, shared those doubts.

Monnet's outspokeness had also been a problem, Brand hinted. "Certain events caused you to express your feelings very strongly when you were here. This incident was... magnified by certain people but it has not been forgotten." [27]

By 1941, the Roosevelt administration was shifting slowly to a full commitment to England's survival and to the defeat of Hitler. The President had discovered a popular explanation for aiding the English without upsetting the popular American fears of involvment in a European war: we would not give or sell war supplies to England but only lend them until the war was over. It was like lending your neighbor a garden hose to put out a fire on his roof, Roosevelt explained.

The quaint interwar authority of the treasury department for foreign arms purchases ended even before the Lend Lease Administration opened for business in early March. One of Henry Stimson's first steps as War Secretary was to insist to the President that all military orders for foreign countries be handled by the war department. Henry Morgenthau was out of the military procurement business and removed from immediate proximity to Monnet.[28]

Even after his arrival, and eventual acceptance, in January 1941, as a member of the new supply council, it was not clear exactly what Monnet did as a council member. He was the only non-British official on the council where most members headed a supply organization dealing with a specific commodity. His office with the council was centrally located in Washington on one of the floors of the Willard Hotel which the British government rented for its expanding supply organization.

Robert Nathan recalls that Monnet always came to his office or he visited Monnet at home. Sometimes they walked together before breakfast; Monnet called Rock Creek Park "mon park," Nathan recalls, because it was directly accessible from his backyard, a feature of the fenceless American life which delighted Monnet.

Monnet invariably visited American officials in their offices, urging greater efforts and larger goals in the retooling of American industry for wartime production. Closer American friends, like Nathan, Philip Graham, one of Frankfurter's law clerks and later a lend-lease official, and a few others, he invited home for breakfast or for an early morning walk in the park.

According to a Monnet secretary, he seldom met with other council members and spent much of his time outside the office. Nathan was not even aware Monnet had an office in the Willard Hotel.[29]

Nathan and Stacy May were two of these key Americans with whom Monnet spent much time. Nathan, a key New Deal economist, recalls meeting Monnet sometime soon after his arrival in Washington, probably at about the time of Roosevelt's "arsenal of democracy" speech. But identifying the United States as Britain's arsenal was only the first of a series of needed steps. The immediate problem, Nathan recalled, was how to calculate exactly what Britain needed and how America could produce it. Monnet never assumed the United States would enter the war as a fighting ally. But he knew that the enormous productive capacity of the country had to be engaged.

Monnet was not an economist and certainly not a technician capable of close monitoring of industrial production. He relied on others for such expertise but he effectively pressed Nathan and others to raise quotas for the critical war materials even when told that unplanned increases would actually confuse and delay production. His singular effectiveness was as a persuasive advocate of whatever was needed to win the war. But this talent seemed to limit his understanding of other aspects of the problem of production.[30] Nathan makes clear that Monnet was involved in only one side of the bargaining involved in war production goals: demanding larger productive capacity. Monnet was not patient when Nathan expressed his grave concerns that highly excessive goals would almost certainly result in chaos in the armaments industries. We would end producing less than the optimum number of planes, ships, tanks, guns and ammunition. He listened but he preferred to take a risk of seeking higher arms production rather than settling for a lower, more secure numbering by being more cautious.

Nathan gradually refined the concept of "feasibility" which applied some established economic principles to wartime planning of production. The feasibility study has since become a popular concept but when Nathan explained it Monnet seemed to regard it like an excuse to delay full production.[31]

The Monnets had travelled much in their six years of marriage and they apparently adjusted rapidly to life in Washington. They arrived in Washington in late summer 1940, accompanied by Amélie and André Horré, a French couple who had worked as cook and butler for the Monnets in Paris and then in their London apartment for the ten months they had just spent there. Their daughter Anna soon joined them, ending her year-long stay with friends in New Jersey where she had been shielded from the Monnets hectic wartime life in Paris and London.

The Monnet's comfortable house at 2415 Foxhall Road was on an attractive, tree-lined street, then on the edge of the city, north of Georgetown. Silvia Monnet became pregnant in February 1941, a few months after the family's arrival. Jean and Silvia, and her 10 year old daughter, Anna, from her first marriage spent a quiet initial 15 months in Washington until after the birth of a second daughter, Marianne, in November 1941.

Besides the Horrés, they had a chauffeur to help with the frequent entertaining and to run errands in the family car; driving was a skill Monnet never acquired. A nurse was added to the household staff and Silvia, a painter, became more active thereafter in her own pursuits, including volunteer work with Ellen McCloy on behalf of Navy families. For awhile, aiding young navy wives became almost a fulltime task for the energetic Silvia Monnet.

Monnet apparently lived well beyond his 200 pound sterling monthly salary alloted by the British government through the Ministry of Supply and based on what he had earned in London as an allied official. Converted into dollars, his salary would have been about $11,000 a year--more than a member of Congress but less than a cabinet member. It is not even clear he ever accepted this salary. Morgenthau reported that Monnet told people he never accepted a British salary because he wanted to be able to tell fellow Frenchmen after the war that he --- unlike de Gaulle whose London office drew eight million pounds a year from the UK treasury --- was not supported by the British in wartime.

A U.S. treasury department investigation of Monnet reported that his 1940 gross income was $54,000, a sizeable amount of money. Most of this income must have been from partnership and investment sources. Yet three years later he had severe money problems and had to seek financial advice from a close British friend. Part of this problem was a claim of $45,000 by the U.S. Treasury for back taxes. His partnership with Murnane was also dissolved by 1944 with a loss of income which was only partially replaced by a salary from the Free French.

Under these circumstances, his willingness to spend money in such a period for a substantial home in an expensive neighborhood and for a household staff which was certainly large even for the truly wealthy by American wartime standards may seem surprising yet it is consistent with Monnet's lifelong attitude toward money. He wanted the quality things --- good clothes, ample housing, first class travel and a personal staff --- which only money could buy. He spent freely for these things. But, to close friends, he never seemed greatly concerned with making, or losing, large sums of money which happened occasionally in his business career.[32]

In a major radio address at the White House correspondents dinner on March 15 1941, Roosevelt explained the expanded aims of the United States to aid Britain war efforts. He noted that Congress had just passed the lend lease legislation. Soon after, Arthur Purvis wrote the President that the speech "brought to me [and] to tens of millions of others, a sense of leadership at its height." Five months later, Purvis was killed in an airplane crash on his way back to Washington from Britain.[33]

Monnet had written the President a personal note several months earlier, also to praise a presidential speech (which used the Monnet phrase "arsenal of democracy"). Like Purvis, Monnet took the occasion to remind Roosevelt of his work for British supplies. But Monnet's note may have been motivated by some anxiety about his own role in Washington including how he should fit into the Anglo-American structure to which he found himself attached. It was difficult and frustrating work because there was both political opposition to Roosevelt's desire to aid Britain and simple inertia within the American government.

He had other good reasons to feel uneasy in his first year in Washington. His pay status was uncertain, the pregnancy of his wife, Silvia, confined her to the rented family house with little opportunity for entertaining and the earlier suspicions of treasury secretary Morgenthau were resurfacing with Monnet's full time presence in Washington.

Not surprisingly, Monnet gives no hint in the memoirs of these problems since he was directing his thoughts to the future, not the past. But he conveyed them in 1941 to Brand and perhaps others in London and Washington. Further, he certainly had to prepare a defense of his role for those like Morgenthau, who threatened to undermine his work in Washington.

However concerned Monnet was with these personal matters, he never seemed to deviate from his self-directed task of prodding American officials to increase defense production. Frankfurter's words on Monnet --- "a teacher to our defense establishment" --- might have been put even stronger by some. Monnet was a prod and, occasionally, a scold to those who seemed less committed than he was.[34]

Robert Nathan, who worked as closely with Monnet as any American in this period, occasionally clashed with him on the means to their agreed goal of increased production. Nathan wrote:

> Monnet was an impatient man because he knew better than most the grave jeopardy of Great Britain. He would not waste precious time with small talk or socializing.... He had an unusual ability to spot effective operators and quickly discard those who were not in a position to help. He was persistent when he sensed an opportunity to recruit an effective operator. But he had no time or energy for ineffectual or phony persons.[35]

His singlemindedness was baffling to some, overwhelming to others. He would not be deterred, deflected or distracted. He could smile if it helped or, more often, be concise, even curt, especially with his own staff. But even those offended sometimes by his brusque style tended to forgive him because they became drawn into his personal network of intensive and selfless concentration on the common goal. He persuaded others to act for the common cause above all by his own example. Frankfurter also recalled this aspect of Monnet. "He had blinders on. For the things that he's interested in he doesn't dissipate his energies, or doesn't take time off, or doesn't listen to anything else. [In] Jean Monnet, the central quality that I call resolution, will, was manifested in an extreme intensity." [36]

Monnet was also learning the importance of repetition and simplification in presenting his ideas. He became attached to the "balance sheet" as a way presenting or remembering details. For Monnet in 1941, the balance sheet was a list of planes, ships and armaments needed by the Allies to overcome the Axis. Jotting notes and calculations became Monnet's way of handling problems without a large staff or a trusted secretary. These slips of paper also helped overcome an erratic memory, especially for figures.

Monnet was not a member of the small, inner circle of pro-
interventionists called, among themselves, the "goon squad." Nathan
was a member, as was Isaiah Berlin of the British Embassy joined by a
few other key officials. Nor did Monnet consider himself a member of
an influential "study group" which met informally and included, at
different times and places, Ben Cohen, of the White House staff,
Frankfurter, McCloy and Hopkins.[37]

Monnet's first encounter with Harry Hopkins, a key Roosevelt
aide, came at the start of 1941 when the former secretary of commerce
moved into the White House and became, in fact, the president's
special assistant to win the war. A trip to London to meet Churchill
was the first assignment for Hopkins. Roosevelt sent his trusted
assistant to London to establish exactly how the United States could
best help Britain's war efforts.[38]

Hopkins was easy to misjudge. The Iowa-born social worker
wore a rumpled and casual exterior which belied his inner intensity. To
some he appeared the unsophisticated midwesterner out of place in the
New Deal administration marked by eastern establishment figures.
Nothing could be farther from the mark. Hopkins was well read in
English literature, was very knowledgeable about the theater, had
traveled to England in the late 1920s and wrote poetry for relaxation for
many years. But above these interests, Hopkins was a man of action
and these actions, especially those on behalf of the New Deal, were
dramatic, insistent and, at times, ruthless. In this and other
characteristics, he made a proper match for Jean Monnet.

Monnet also underestimated Hopkins initially. He told Robert
Sherwood, Hopkin's biographer, that he first doubted Roosevelt's plan
to send his aide to meet Churchill. He mistakenly believed Hopkins
had never before traveled abroad and, perhaps, that Hopkins' tattered
informality might grate the Conservative government in London.

After their first meeting at the Frankfurter's, Monnet changed
his mind. The two men learned easily to work together, partly because
both were functional optimists. Each had to believe that his
respective tasks were both efficatious in the war effort and certain to be
successful. Both left the details (and the drudgery) to others. They
worked toward the larger concepts which they presented with striking
persuasiveness. Monnet and Hopkins were a team made for these
wartime tasks.

When Hopkins returned from London, he made a point of spending an evening at the Monnet home with the family. The presidential advisor had no purpose, Monnet said, except to get to know him and his family better. But the relaxed meeting was welcomed by both men; Hopkins now recognized the value of Monnet's advice and Monnet sensed that the presidential adviser was to become a central figure in arming England with the hints by Roosevelt that more explicit and more urgent aid was needed.

For Monnet, this shift had a personal benefit. Hopkins, now a friend, was assuming responsibility for Monnet's sector, replacing Henry Morgenthau, who remained suspicious of Monnet even after working with him for nearly three years. With Hopkins, a mutual optimism helped him and Monnet face the common and separate problems in the coming months.[39]

But they faced obstacles within their respective bureaucracies. Before 1941 was over, the United States entered the war against the Axis powers after suffering a grievous defeat when attacked on December 7 by Japan at Pearl Harbor, Hawaii and other strategic points in the Pacific. Soon after the surprise Japanese attacks, the President announced the Victory Program of war production to increase dramatically American military output. The program had been in preparation for months by a presidential team headed by Hopkins and aided by Nathan and Monnet.

Even by mid-1941, the American mood was changing. The Battle of Britain for air control preceding what seemed a certain Nazi invasion had inspired Britain's supporters. Passage of the lend lease act in early 1941 was, in fact, a referendum on full support of Britain short of actual American participation.

Monnet's key role in the group is clear. According to Nathan, "...Jean Monnet should be given credit for getting the Victory Program through by getting the production requirements from the military branches." [40]

Soon after the program became public, Monnet wrote Hopkins to say "how much I admire the decision taken by the President in setting the goal of this country's armament production.... No country at war has taken such fundamental decisions in such a decisive manner. I know how much we owe to you...." Hopkins replied that "there are great and heroic days ahead. I think we have laid the groundwork for final victory." In describing Monnet's own role, the presidential advisor added: "You have played a great part in the past as you will in the future."

Hopkins was more than an advisor to the President. He was his friend and confident, and Winston Churchill's ambassador to Roosevelt. Later he was acting secretary of state at the Teheran and Cairo conferences of 1943. Hopkins now became Monnet's most influential link to the President and to American decision-making.[41]

One should not exaggerate Monnet's wartime role. Writers sometimes call him one of the most trusted advisors to Churchill and Roosevelt, certainly an overstatement. Monnet is barely mentioned in Churchill's history of the war nor was he prominent in the President's small circle of advisors. Monnet met Roosevelt in 1938 and 1939 while buying planes for France and at least twice during the war but it was not a close relationship. Nor was Monnet the originator of the lend lease idea or its facilitator. He was a persuasive advocate, a prod and sometimes a burr under a complacent Washington. He moved carefully, chose his targets precisely and developed a capital network of friends which worked well during the war, in postwar France and in building a united Europe.

Just as the crucial year of 1941 was closing, the distrust of Monnet by treasury secretary Henry Morgenthau moved beyond murmurings to his staff. Morgenthau went to British Ambassador Halifax with his suspicions about Monnet's past. Halifax turned to Felix Frankfurter, now one of Monnet's closest friends, for an evaluation "of the view taken here of Jean Monnet and his services." Frankfurter replied:

> I have heard no higher praise of an official entrusted with British interests than what has been accorded Monnet.... I have heard Harry Hopkins, Secretary Stimson, the two Assistant Secretaries of War, McCloy and Lovett, leading men in the army, in the Lend Lease Administration and in OPM [Office of Production Management] speak of Monnet in terms of the highest esteem.... He has been a creative and energizing force in the development of our defense program [and] ...he possesses the rarest of talents: the power of self-abnegation. British victory and what makes for it are the complete absorption of his life. I might add that everyone to whom I have spoken who has worked on close and intimate terms with Monnet has absolute confidence in him....[42]

But a few months later Monnet had to defend himself against a direct attack by Morgenthau. In May 1942, the treasury secretary told Halifax and visiting Minister of Production Oliver Lyttleton that

Monnet, and his business partner, George Murnane, had engaged in various prewar transactions with German firms including efforts to hide German ownership from the U.S. government. These actions were taken, Morganthau suggested, because in World War I the U.S. government had taken over American subsidiaries as alien property. Monnet, Murnane was trying, he said, to prevent new takeovers through the creation of "voting trusts."

Furthermore, Morgenthau noted in his diary, the treasury department "may have a criminal case against Monnet on his tax returns." But he did not tell Halifax this because "I could not tell him anything I did not want repeated.... It would serve these English big businessmen and high nobility like Halifax right if, having warned them about Monnet, this criminal case breaks." Morgenthau had a clear phobia against private bankers and was determined to keep war profits now to an absolute minimum. But was this the only basis of his accusations against Monnet?

These Morgenthau charges were neither casual nor unexplored. Before the conversation with Halifax, Morgenthau presented some suspicions directly to Monnet. Twice in May 1942 he asked Monnet about Murnane's role with the American Bosch Corporation which had been owned by the German parent firm. After the first talk, Monnet said he would discuss the matter with Murnane who was still running the partnership in New York. Several days later, Monnet confirmed his initial impression that his partner had no knowledge than any German control existed over shares of the American company.[43]

But Morganthau was not convinced "that Monnet was telling all he knew." He summarized his conversations with Monnet in a May 7 memo to Roosevelt which also included a response to a question the President had raised about whether dividends of the American Bosch firm could still reach the putative German owners. Morgenthau also told the President that Monnet said "until the latter part of 1938 he was a believer in rapproachment between France and Germany."

This final insinuation flavored the Morganthau suspicions which previously were based only on business transactions; now he suggested that misguided political judgments, at least, were also involved, as well as alleged criminal tax violations. Such were the thoughts on Monnet planted by Morgenthau in the minds of the two highest officials of the American and British governments in Washington. As late as mid-1944, Morgenthau was still pursuing the connections between Monnet, Murnane and the American Bosch firm.[44]

After Morgenthau's May 7 1942 memo to the President but
before the June meetings with Halifax, Monnet started to prepare a
defense. He drafted a long letter which reviewed his service in London
and Washington on behalf of allied defense efforts. The draft
continued:

> Mr. Monnet is a citizen of France bearing a French
> diplomatic passport. At the same time he is one of the most
> senior British officials in the United States. In the exercise of
> his functions, he is responsible only to His Majesty (sic)
> government whose confidence he completely enjoys.
> In the difficult circumstances now prevailing, it is
> thought that the unique situation in which Mr. Monnet stands
> should receive at least the informal recognition of the United
> States and British governments. It is, therefore, suggested that
> Mr. Monnet might be regarded by the United States Government
> in all respects as an official of the British Government and that
> in matters concerning him the State Department might look to
> His Majesty's Government. [45]

Were these "difficult circumstances" only those created by
Morgenthau? This is not clear nor is it known whether this letter was
ever sent but its tone indicates Monnet took seriously the Morgenthau
threat.

Earlier, at the end of 1941, Tommy Brand had written from
London that he had heard Monnet was "depressed and pessimistic"
which Brand hoped was only due to Washington's weather. More
likely Monnet's state of mind was affected by Morgenthau persistent
attacks and threats.[46]

The December 1941 attack on Pearl Harbor by Hitler's ally,
Japan had dramatically induced the entrance of the United States into
the war. This had removed all legal obstacles to full cooperation with
the British. Although the military news was mostly bad throughout
1942, the full force of the American nation entering the war effort meant
that victory, while still far off, was only a matter of time.
Competition for supplies had to be regulated among the allies but this
too fell into a routine.

By the late spring of 1942, the major work on production goals
was underway. Monnet undoubtedly judged that the Victory Program no
longer needed his attention. But the success of that program itself
created new difficulties. The American military leadership was about
to receive both arms and responsibilities unimaginable in the republic's
150 year history. Sharing both with the British, and then with the

Soviet Union as well, was a task that had to be learned, step by painful step.

The creation of the Combined Production and Resources Board in Washington helped build Anglo-American cooperation but the predominance of strong American military leaders in Washington required occasional balancing by a strong imported British presence. Twice in 1942 Oliver Lyttleton, the British Minister of Production, came to Washington at Monnet's instigation to improve the common effort. Balancing the allies' interests remained a delicate undertaking and one engaging Monnet's direct attention and most delicate negotiating talents.

Not long after America entered the war in December 1941, and certainly by mid-1942, Monnet's supply council work, while still hectic, was becoming more routine. Much of the routine did not even involve Monnet. One of his secretaries during the 1940-43 period recalls that his schedule seemed to have little to do with the supply council itself. Monnet conferred with few members of the BSC or its staff. He was also somewhat mysterious, she recalled; he kept his inner doors closed, made his own appointments, and kept his files locked whenever he left the room. His few visitors were mostly friends from earlier days who were passing through Washington and an occasional French journalist. Much of the time he was out of the office but without telling his secretary where he was going. Several times he wrote Tommy Brand urging that letters be marked for his personal attention only, further insuring that his secretary did not know much of his activities.[47]

The other major task Monnet faced in 1942 --- aside from rebutting Morgenthau --- was to refocus on the problems of France and to get the American government's attention on those issues, chief of which was insuring that the French people reassert their political rights promptly after the war. The Vichy government under Marshall Petain had become less and less a counter-force to Hitler and much more his clumsy accomplice. De Gaulle's efforts in London to rally the Free French against both Berlin and Vichy made him a traitor to Petain but also suspect to those, including Monnet, who thought the general excessively interested in his own political power. In North Africa, site of important French military assets, several senior French military leaders competed to lead a third French presence, neither collaborationist nor Gaullist. It was into this three-cornered contest that Monnet descended.

Monnet's relations with General de Gaulle were now to become more complicated. When the two had parted in the summer of 1940, Monnet recalled fears that the political ambitions of the general might interfere with the war against Hitler. Roosevelt shared, and then magnified these suspicions. Monnet was asked to help end the divisions among the French which threatened the Allied role in regaining North Africa from the Germans. His apparent anti-Gaullist attitude undoubtedly influenced his selection for this task.

The Allies had decided on a landing in North Africa as their first step toward rolling back Hitler from western Europe. Putting troops ashore in North Africa raised, however, the question of whether the French forces there, which were not under de Gaulle's command, would fight with or against the American and British forces.

The Allied landing on November 8 1942 met sharp initial resistance from French forces. Eventually the resistance ended but the divisions among the French civilian and military elements in North Africa remained. To complicate matters further, General Dwight Eisenhower, commander of Allied forces in North Africa, had entered into talks with Admiral Darlan, the senior French official in North Africa, who had been part of the Vichy regime. In the midst of delicate negotiaticns with the allies, Darlan was assassinated on Christmas Eve.

Darlan's death forced postponement of de Gaulle's long-discussed trip to Washington. The festering relationship between the General and the Roosevelt administration might have been cleansed by the visit. Instead a series of incidents, some between de Gaulle and Churchill, others involving Roosevelt, aggravated the highly suspicious general who sensed slights from the Anglo-Americans even when none was intended.

Some were minor episodes, as when Churchill's staff once attempted to censor a de Gaulle speech to occupied France made over the BBC. Others were more serious. The Free French raid on the French islands of St. Pierre and Miquelon off Canada on Christmas Eve 1942 particularly provoked Secretary of State Hull who never forgave de Gaulle for the wartime histronics of an attack on a pitiful Vichy outpost in North America.

When Roosevelt and Churchill met in Casablanca, Morocco in January 1943 to plan strategy, the confused situation in French North Africa, which included de Gaulle's role, was on their agenda. It was also on Monnet's mind as he shifted from war supplies to French unity in the fight against Hitler.[48]

The Casablanca conference, which Monnet followed from Washington, provided him another occasion to help influence an important Roosevelt speech. Monnet had written Hopkins a long memorandum just before Christmas 1942 to focus the President's attention on France as he was to leave for Casablanca. Monnet revised the memo on December 27, taking into account the death of Darlan. In both versions, Monnet stressed that "the sovereignty of the French people must be safeguarded" and not usurped by any pretender to political authority inside or outside France. Monnet's approach here matched perfectly the hostility of both the Secretary of State, Cordell Hull, and the President himself to the pretention that de Gaulle spoke with political authority for all those Frenchmen opposed to the Nazi occupation of their country and, implicitly, that he would assume a central role within France after its liberation.

Monnet seemed to refer specifically to such pretentions by de Gaulle when his memo warned that "any French organization outside [should be] precluded from having a shadow of a right to claim the leadership of the French people." Roosevelt eventually incorporated, in his February 12, 1943 speech to the White House correspondents, the basic remark about safeguarding French sovereignty and the right of the French people to self-determination after the war.[49]

Despite this successful effort by Monnet to support Roosevelt's skepticism about de Gaulle, the crusty Hull, who was the principal supporter in Washington of Marshall Petain's Vichy regime, was suspicious. He saw in Monnet a covert spokesman for de Gaulle instead of an independent pragmatist who despised the capitulation of Vichy and would support de Gaulle to the extent the general worked for the Allied cause.

Hull raised his suspicions about Monnet several times, initially at a December 1942 meeting with navy secretary Frank Knox and war secretary Henry Stimson after Monnet had accompanied General Bethouart, a de Gaulle aide, on his Washington rounds. Hull said Bethouart was trying to get the administration to recognize de Gaulle as the "civil leader of all occupied provinces of France and of French territories." According to Hull, Monnet claimed that the American diplomat, Robert Murphy, accepted this arrangement over a year before on instructions from Roosevelt. Hull was upset on hearing this until his deputy Sumner Welles came into the meeting with a message that the President denied making any such agreement. This was another hint that Monnet's enemies suspected him of playing with the truth at times.[50]

Monnet's attitude toward de Gaulle was more complicated than Hull imagined. In his memoirs, Monnet says, he maintained "good personal relations" with de Gaulle but with a separate determination, from the fall of France in 1940, for each man to go his own way in supporting French resistance. American diplomat Robert Murphy said flatly that Monnet "was no Gaullist. He was as critical of de Gaulle as he was of [General Henri] Giraud." Monnet was above personalities, Murphy concluded.[51]

In a move to end this fiasco of French fighting each other and occasionally fighting the Allies and to consolidate the French land and naval units into the Allied armies, the United States brought a distinguished French war hero, General Henri Giraud, out of France by submarine. Giraud, who fought the Germans in both world wars with distinction, had escaped from a German prison camp not long before his flight to Algiers.

Once in the French possession, Giraud became less an asset and more a political liability to the allies. He seemed powerless to assume political control of Algeria and rid it of Vichy influences. Yet he resented the political aggrandizement he saw in de Gaulle's London committee.

De Gaulle saw the landings as underlining the Anglo-American tendency to deal with France as a defeated power whose leaders in exile need not be consulted. Churchill was aware "of the gravity of the affront offered to de Gaulle" by excluding him from the North African landing operation and then concealing it from him. But bringing de Gaulle into the operation, Churchill added, would have been "deeply injurious" to the North African affair since de Gaulle would have undoubtedly demanded the central military and political leadership of the landings.[52]

Roosevelt and Churchill planned their Casablanca sessions in mid-January to devise further Allied strategy in the war to roll back Nazi forces, of which the North African landings were the first step. Solving the divisions among the French in North Africa was only a small part of the strategy but politically it was important that the Americans and the British not appear to stumble over France, a former ally. Churchill helped persuade de Gaulle to fly to Casablanca for a brief, pro-forma meeting with Giraud.

The meeting showed Roosevelt that Giraud clearly needed help if he was to play a useful role for the allied north African operation. Monnet proposed himself to Harry Hopkins, who travelled with Roosevelt to the Casablanca conference, as a person who could assist Giraud. While still at the conference, Hopkins passed on the suggestion. Roosevelt knew Monnet from earlier meetings and was aware of his role in Washington on the British Supply Council. Since a mediator had to be found between Giraud, who succeeeded Darlan, and de Gaulle, who insisted that his committee was the supreme French authority in resisting Hitler, Monnet seemed to be the right one.

General Giraud is usually pictured as a brave soldier but hopelessly incompetent in the political role the Allies wanted him to play as leader among the French in North Africa. But Harry Hopkins saw good prospects for the general from the meetings both attended after the Casablanca conference.

> I gained a very favorable impression of Giraud. I know he is a royalist and is probably a right winger in all his economic biases but I have a feeling that he is willing to fight. He is about six feet, two inches and a man about 63 or 64. He has the appearance of health and vigor. He spoke with a good deal of modesty but with confidence. [I] had the feeling he had made up his mind that he was going to do whatever the President wanted in Africa. Apart from fighting in the war, it is impossible to tell whether or not he has political ambitions.

Monnet who had never met Giraud must have heard this descriptions from Hopkins for he met with the presidential aide just before departing Washington in late February.[53]

Roosevelt had cabled Hopkins' proposal to the state department asking that Monnet be sent to get some civilian strength into the "administrative picture here." The President described Monnet as one "who has kept his skirts clear of political entaglements in recent years and my impression of him is very favorable." Employing some curious presidential license with the facts, Roosevelt added that "I believe that Morgenthau knows and trusts Monnet." Hull tried to veto the suggestion (perhaps after conferring with Morgenthau), saying Monnet was "closer than anyone suspected" to de Gaulle.

But neither Hopkins nor Monnet would not be so easily thwarted; Monnet arranged a cabled invitation from Giraud. When

Hull still refused, Hopkins, in frustration, asked Monnet to travel to Algiers on behalf of the Munitions Assignment Board which he chaired since giving up the Lend Lease Administration. Monnet was to look into equipping the French troops in North Africa, acquaint General Giraud with the situation in Washington and keep in touch with General Eisenhower whose headquarters was now in French North Africa. He flew by U.S. military plane on a circuitous route to Brazil, west Africa and finally, Algiers, arriving in late February 1943.

Roosevelt had cabled Eisenhower about Monnet and then gave him a letter for the commander. In both, Roosevelt said that Giraud had asked Monnet to visit. No announcement was to be made by Eisenhower of the visit which was to be covered in Washington, the President noted, by the "formal reasons" given in Hopkins' letter to Monnet about the munitions board. Roosevelt added that Monnet "understands my views completely," a further indication that Monnet, Hopkins and perhaps Roosevelt himself were in close touch on this assignment.[54]

Monnet spent nearly eight months in Algiers where he was integrated into the French political system in a more complete way than when he represented the French government in London in 1939-40. He helped mediate the dispute between de Gaulle and Giraud. He also worked closely with Robert Murphy, the senior U.S. diplomat assigned to Eisenhower's headquarters, with Harold Macmillan, Murphy's British counterpart, and with many other important Allied figures.[55]

Shortly after arriving in Algiers, Monnet sent a long letter and a cable to Hopkins about his talks with General Giraud. Hopkins was now Monnet's principal contact in Washington and within the administration. Monnet described Giraud's good character and his excellent relations with the general. (The letter's salutation was "Dear Mr. Hopkins;" by May, the greeting would be "Dear Harry" and remain so in all of his subsequent letters to Hopkins.) [56]

A week later Monnet drafted a speech for Giraud, who had now been thrust by the "Imperial Council" of the Vichy proconsuls in North Africa to the front role of both military and civilian leadership. This was, Giraud later noted, "the first democratic speech of my life." It was also the start of Monnet's efforts to bring Giraud into a relationship with the Allies, and later, with de Gaulle, which would make France once again a force operating effectively against Hitler.[57]

Monnet spent considerable time in his first months in Algiers conferring with Murphy and with Macmillan, Churchill's political representative. Macmillan found ways to keep his perspective on the Gallic political confusion by getting out of town for quiet conversation, sightseeing and bathing in remote spots. He often took Monnet and, later, de Gaulle, with him. Macmillan lists more than a dozen private meetings with Monnet, in and out of Algiers, from March through June 1943.

In early May, de Gaulle made a speech in London which drew considerable attention to his self-proclaimed role as leader of the French forces opposed to Hitler. In a letter to Hopkins, Monnet called the speech "a straight bid for arbitrary power" which reminded him (and Macmillan, he added) of Hitler's speech on Czechoslovakia. But in the same letter, Monnet registered frustration with Giraud's "constitutional" difficulty in making decisions on people. His letter reflected a judgment that the importance of Petain and the Vichy government is fading but the contest between de Gaulle and Giraud, and their respective supporters, is growing. He detected an increasing willingness by de Gaulle to confront Giraud on ultimate authority.

Giraud, for example, wrote de Gaulle on April 27 with an approach to power-sharing. The only response, Monnet noted, is de Gaulle's proud London speech which "disregards all past negotiations." Harold Macmillan's diary records his amusement at the fuss over de Gaulle's speech which attacked Giraud and threatened negotiations between the generals. "I told them [Giraud, Monnet and others] that when... one politician made an offensive speech about another in my country... this was the almost recognized procedure preliminary to forming a coalition government." [58]

Monnet concluded by describing de Gaulle's goal of power now: "De Gaulle stands for arbitrary action with all the risks of Fascism; Giraud stands for the preservation of the right of the people and democratic process." Considering Giraud's limited experience with democratic theories as a career army officer and Monnet's renown abilities to persuade, it is likely that what Monnet admired in Giraud's approach was his own view of democratic versus authoritarian approaches which he tried to instill into the fledgling ruler. Monnet may also have sought to ingratiate himself with both the President and the state department by supporting Washington's resolute anti-Gaullism.

The split between de Gaulle and Giraud, Monnet concluded, was over what happens after liberation: democracy or personal rule; "...there can be no compromise...the issue must be fought through to the end and fought out NOW." [Monnet's emphasis.] [59]

This heated rhetoric is not typical of Monnet either in North Africa or elsewhere in his life. Perhaps the weather, absence from his family, or this tensions of the work provoked this outburst. His frustrating work in Algiers in 1943 reflected a man committed to bring together the contentious factions of the French military and political remnants which escaped the Nazis. His theme was, in fact, expressed by the title General Giraud later gave his own memoirs of the Algiers period: "Un Seul But --- La Victoire!" (A Single Goal--Victory!)

A revealing letter about Monnet in Algiers was written in July by Murphy. Describing Monnet's work as seeking unity among French resistance leaders, the American diplomat wrote:

> Monnet respects the United States and Britain and, I am sure, will avoid giving offense to us but he is definitely out to gain every advantage for the French he possibly can. He knows our methods so well that he will profit from every opportunity we offer him to seize advantage. He counts greatly on the support of Jack McCloy and Felix Frankfurter. Monnet is loyal neither to Giraud nor to de Gaulle but he is loyal to France and to Monnet.... [60]

Murphy's letter, cautious in tone and hedging in trust, if not suspicious, underlines Monnet's importance in 1943 for the allies and the key transitional role which that year played in his life. Until he went to Algiers, his life from 1938 through 1943 had been devoted to procuring military equipment for Britain and France. Those five years, in turn, broke Monnet's life pattern which, for his first 50 years, had been that of a private businessman pressed into extraordinary war and postwar service. Until 1938, Monnet had spent 25 of his 34 working years in private business, either his father's or his own. For the rest of his long life, he was to concentrate on public issues without any thought of returning to private life.

Other American diplomats were more critical of Monnet's Algiers role. One of Murphy's staff officers wrote a book at the end of war which devoted several chapters to the American role in North Africa in 1942-3. In it, he accused Monnet of coming to Algiers under false pretences by espousing the official American position of not choosing between rival French leaders while actually favoring de Gaulle over Giraud. The diplomat called Monnet "a great disillusionment to his Washington backers" whose "misplaced faith in Monnet was one of our major mistakes."

Yet these charges did not seem to affect Monnet's credibility importantly with Hopkins, McCloy or his other Washington backers. Even Giraud's own account of his Algiers experience is generally complimentary to Monnet although the general is quoted in state department dispatches from North Africa as saying Monnet betrayed him. Giraud was, no doubt, his own worst enemy; he was also no political match for de Gaulle who emerged by the end of the summer the undisputed head of the French resistance overseas.[61]

The eight months in Algiers marked another transition for Monnet: He arrived as an American envoy, nominally of Hopkins, actually, of Roosevelt, detached from his anomalous status as a Frenchman working for the British in wartime Washington. He would return to Washington at the end of the year, as an official of the new French Committee on National Liberation (FCNL). He would devote his remaining days in America to French matters, including supply and lend-lease.

Until now, his wartime service concentrated on helping fight the war against Nazi Germany. Now, Monnet began to focus on France in the postwar world. It was clear in 1943 that the long-awaited invasion of western Europe would come the next year. With that invasion would come the liberation of France. What was Monnet's role to be in his home country? What was France's role to be in Europe?

On August 5, in Algiers, Monnet wrote a long memorandum reflecting on this last point. Addressed to the FCNL, Monnet's memo saw France at the heart of Europe, different from Britain and Russia, and from the United States. It had therefore both an opportunity and responsibility to make a new and different peace from that negative one which followed the first World War.

Europe must now see itself as a force larger that its nation-states, he wrote. Protectionism, the quest for national sovereignty, and the division of Europe into small, inefficient national markets must end. Whether the replacement will be a "Federation or a European entity" was not clear, he said, nor was the distinction Monnet had in mind with those words.

The memo gropes for ideas and cannot be held to later standards of clarity in defining the European ideal. Yet it differs interestingly from Monnet's views during or even at the end of World War I. Then he only sensed the problem of the nation-state and its tendency to dominate although he soon learned, at the League of Nations, of this domination in full detail, especially by watching his own country and Britain control the League. He also witnessed in 1920-22 the full force of French revenge in its attempt to control Germany through reparations and denial of league membership.[62]

The year 1943 marked the culmination of Monnet's friendship with Harry Hopkins. The flurry of telegrams and letters from Algiers to Hopkins ended by mid-summer when the French political leadership had been sorted out by Monnet, Macmillan, Murphy and, of course, the principals, Generals de Gaulle and Giraud. Monnet felt close to Hopkins long after the crisis of the generals subsided. Monnet often used Hopkins' White House office to pass messages to and from Silvia during his absence. But by the end of the year, Hopkins' health was so bad that he needed extended hospitalization. His illness coincided with Monnet's return to Washington in November. Hopkins spent seven months to July 1944 recuperating from more surgery and from the debilitation of trying to be everything to the demanding Roosevelt. When Hopkins returned to limited duty in Washington, the final push against Hitler had begun on the western front, starting from the Normandy landings on June 6. During Hopkins' convalescence at the Mayo Clinic in Minnesota,and while Monnet was beginning his new role in Washington as an agent for the now-unified French resistance, Hopkins' youngest son, Stephen, was killed in the in the south Pacific. Monnet must have wondered how Hopkins could stand this new blow.

Soon after returning to the capital, Monnet was given a dinner by Supreme Court Justice Frankfurter where Stimson, McCloy and others heard about the situation in North Africa. Almost immediately Monnet then left the city to attend the first United Nations plenary meeting in Atlantic City, as France's principal representative.

The Atlantic City conference established the U.N. Relief and Rehabilitation Agency (UNRRA). While Monnet represented France during the two week meeting, his old friend, Dean Acheson, was chief U.S. delegate. The conference elected Acheson as permanent chairman and Herbert Lehman, former U.S. Senator from New York, as the first head of UNRRA. Monnet was quoted in the NY Times for characterizing Lehman's election as "the first act of the United Nations in organizing peace." Monnet also declared that the conference's start "was a warning to the United Nations that speed and cooperation were essential to see that the reoccupied areas get enough food and other supplies in the first few months after victory to prevent the spread of chaos." [63]

Back in Washington a few days after the conference ended, Monnet was quickly immersed in the details of shipping quotas for French supplies, the form of currency to be used by the allied forces in liberated France, the still tense relations between the Roosevelt administration and de Gaulle and with his own status as a French government official.

The currency question became a test of wills and of symbols for both de Gaulle and the Roosevelt administration, with Monnet uncomfortably positioned between the adversaries. Roosevelt had come away from the North Africa settlement between de Gaulle and Giraud convinced that reason and cooperation were impossible with the French exiles and he would have to wait for France's liberation, as Monnet as earlier suggested, for the French people to sort out their leadership. Meanwhile, the President believed, the United States should treat France like a country freed by force from enemy occupation and to be ruled by allied military government teams.[64]

This approach appalled de Gaulle who saw himself as the liberator and his forces as the natural heirs of democratic forces now that the Nazis were losing. He insisted, through Monnet, that the FNCL symbol appear on the military currency which the military government would use in liberated France. An uneasy compromise was finally produced by the treasury and Monnet with three French flags but no FNCL symbol on the currency. But the treasury officials refused to use the phrase "Republique Francaise" which de Gaulle wanted. Thus one of Monnet's last major negotiations in Washington was a losing one on behalf of de Gaulle.[65]

In the summer of 1944, while being interviewed by Fortune magazine, Monnet returned to the question of postwar Europe. But here the focus was not on the vague themes of the Algiers memo but on the problem of Germany. According to John Davenport, the profile's author, Monnet wanted "to see Germany shocked and stripped of part of her industrial potential, with possibly the great Rhine coal and iron fields run by a European authority for the benefit of all participating nations, including, eventually, a demilitarized Germany."

If this sounds more drastic than the Monnet of Algiers, or, later, of the Schuman Plan, the temper of 1944 must be understood. Germany was a desperate and vicious enemy. Henry Morgenthau, again becoming active in foreign policy, was pressing the President with an eponymous "plan" to strip Germany of her industrial assets and divide it in such a way as to make a single German force an impossibility forever.[66]

Before the interview appeared, Monnet slipped away to North Africa for a trip which seemed to have no purpose except being away from the U.S. capital during de Gaulle's first visit to Washington. Churchill had finally prevailed on the general to visit the United States but de Gaulle did not want a man as close to the Americans as Monnet present to serve as his guide through enemy fields.

Monnet was also more free to take a trip like this on short notice. Silvia and the children had left Washington for a small house in Narragansett, Rhode Island, principally a cost-saving measure to give up the expensive house in an exclusive Washington neighborhood which he had rented since 1940. He was now dependent entirely on the income from the French national committee since his partnership with Murnane was dissolved in 1944. A large U.S bill for back taxes was another reason to cut expenses.[67]

Nothing explicitly records Monnet's view on the Morgenthau plan but he was certainly not sympathetic to the extreme views of the treasury secretary who wanted to flood Germany's mines and destroy its forges. Morgenthau also suggested that thousands of German military and civilian leaders be shot on sight by advancing allied troops.[68]

Secretary of War Stimson favorably quoted a Monnet approach for an internationalized Ruhr to the treasury secretary as part of the larger Stimson strategy of blocking Morgenthau's attempt to create a "pastoral" Germany. Monnet never referred to this apparently unwritten plan in his memoirs, perhaps because it was still in incomplete form in 1944 and was presented as a tactical move to block Morgenthau. But both the President and Thomas E. Dewey, his 1944 presidential opponent, quoted favorably the Monnet idea of economic rehabilitation of Europe by making the Ruhr an international area.[69]

It can be assumed that Monnet quietly opposed the treasury secretary's extreme approach to Germany but Monnet's own views, as recorded in Fortune and in a public address the same year were severe compared to his later goal of French-German reconciliation. In his memoirs, Monnet refers critically to his compatriots' vindictiveness toward Germany after both the first and second World Wars. He does not repeat his own harsh words of 1944 of the same spirit.

There were, in that year, conflicting views and strong emotions within both Britain and the United States on Germany. Many centered on the Saar and the Ruhr, the heart of industrial Germany's strength. Morgenthau and his supporters wanted to destroy the industrial capacity of Germany by dividing the land, giving away parts of it and dynamiting, flooding or otherwise wrecking the rest. The other side, in this case, Stimson, McCloy and especially Monnet, wanted to use the strength of these mining and industrial areas and convert them to something else. Not surprisingly these opposing tendencies were sometimes in conflict within a single mind.

Monnet once elaborated on his plan for a Saar-Ruhr area under international trustees, even including the USSR. He told McCloy and Stimson that many of his compatriots would oppose the plan because they wanted these areas incorporated into France, as a mid-century version of the reparations forced on Germany a quarter century earlier.

Perhaps Monnet could not be more explicitly critical of the Morgenthau plan in 1944 since the President himself seemed inclined to punish Germany when he called, for example, for feeding its civilians in soup kitchens to show them they lost the war. War secretary Stimson once commented to General George C. Marshall on the incongruity of being both the man responsible for directing the killing of the enemy and the man least inclined to vindictiveness. Stimson and Monnet were alike in this dislike of violence and revenge, which the General of the Army also seemed to share.[70]

Monnet's public role in this later war period in the United States also included a nation-wide radio address on war aims at a large victory rally in New York's Metropolitan Opera House in spring 1944. He was no orator so this appearance is especially unusual but its prominent coverage in the New York Times was due more to the striking setting and its prestigious audience than to Monnet as a speaker. Perhaps the need to appear to be an active and public representative of the FCNL was part of the explanation for his appearance.

Press accounts of the speech noted his view that Germany was the center of the problem in Europe and must also be the central issue in finding a solution to European tension. Monnet spoke of the need to "transform" Germany "not only in its governmental institutions but also in its military traditions and its material strength." Monnet was also cited extensively in news accounts in 1943-45 in Algiers, in Washington and, eventually, in France. In contrast he is scarcely mentioned in the preceding three years in the American press.[71]

Harry Hopkins' precarious health undoubtedly limited his contacts with Monnet and correspondingly, Monnet's contacts with the White House, in the final year of the war. The "deputy president" was somewhat removed from the inner Roosevelt circle by 1945 and was, in fact, in the Mayo Clinic in April 1945 when the President was fatally stricken at Warm Springs, Georgia. An American acquaintance who was with Monnet on April 12 at a lend-lease meeting relates the distress he showed when he heard of Roosevelt's death. "This is a sad, sad day for Europe," Monnet said. "It's a sad day for the world," Will Clayton added as they looked out the state department window as the marines lowered the flag to half mast.[72]

Although Monnet had actually talked with Roosevelt only four times--three of them quite brief--he clearly felt a great affection for the wartime President whose picture, framed in black, he kept on his bedside table in his home outside Paris for many years. At this time of personal distress, coming just as the war in Europe was ending, Monnet must have shared his feelings with Felix Frankfurter who was, of his three principal Roosevelt links, now to be one of his closest ties to the administration in his remaining months in Washington.

With Frankfurter, who was "Felix" to both Jean and Silvia Monnet almost from the start, and with Hopkins, who was "Dear Harry" by 1943, Monnet had succeeded in bridging the gap of independent Frenchman and top-level presidential advisers. Morgenthau with whom Monnet had worked the closest and over the longest period, was still "Mr. Secretary" and he was addressed, in turn, as "Mr. Monnet" as they discussed the currency to be used in liberated France. With Morgenthau, the intellectual approaches and the personal chemistries differed so much that even the wartime urgencies and seven years of cooperation were never sufficient to create a genuine bond.

Monnet expanded his Washington network in 1944-45, aware undoubtedly that America would be the key to Europe's restoration in the postwar world. He met George Ball, a lend lease official; Edward Stettinius, administrator of the lend lease program, Will Clayton, assistant and later undersecretary of state, and many others. He also deepened his friendship with Acheson, Stimson and McCloy and with Katherine and Phillip Graham, the daughter and son-in-law of Washington Post publisher, Eugene Meyer.

In 1945, as it became clear that total victory over the Axis powers was imminent, Monnet made plans for his future. He talked with Charles de Gaulle in August 1945 while the general was again visiting Washington about the need for modernizing France. Their country, Monnet said, could never again thrive without hard work and sacrifice. Those who believed that the war's end would magically bring peace and prosperity had to be educated, he believed. De Gaulle accepted the Monnet approach and asked him to return to France to construct a plan to rebuild the country.[73]

But the American experience, the flexibility and vitality of American life in wartime, and the friends he made were to remain with him. He found, in the six years when he made Washington his home, that he was somehow partly American, at least in his outlook, his work habits and his pragmatism. He was aware, he noted, that as a young man he had found an affinity with the rugged experiences of the Canadian and American west early in the century. He also admired the largeness of purpose of the people he met there and with their sense of challenge and their belief in equality through common hardship. His Washington experience conditioned him for the next three decades of work in France and Europe, areas he had to learn about once again.

Endnotes.

[1] For the meetings with Dulles and Bruening, Jean Monnet, *Memoirs,* New York, 1978 (hereafter JMM)p.116; The French also sent Baron de La Grange, a member of the French Senate and a friend of Roosevelt, in the winter of 1937-38 to explore aircraft purchases with the state department and the President. Later, but before Monnet's first trip, a naval air mission came in September 1938 and an army study group in the spring of 1939. The latter two groups were cleared by Admiral William Leahy, the President's chief of staff, according to his papers in LC.

[2] HMD 158, 27 Dec 1938.

[3] HMD 172, 31 Dec 1938.

[4] HMD 27 Dec 1938. Where Monnet could raise such a sum is not clear since his partnership with Murnane still owed $37,500 borrowed from John Foster Dulles only three years earlier, and partnership income was limited both by Monnet's absence and the failure of China investments to produce any profit

[5] F. Fontaine, "Forward with Jean Monnet," *JM:PEU* p.63.

[6] Anne Morrow Lindbergh, *The Rose and the Nettle,,* New York, 1980, p.355.

[7] Charles A Lindbergh, *War Journals,* New York, 1970 , *passim* (after p. 204)

[8] There is some confusion about how many trips Monnet undertook to America in 1938-39 for the French government. After the October trip, he returned to Paris in early November then came back to Washington in December for a second mission. The trip in May 1939 was his third although his memoirs mention only two trips. Other writers mention a Monnet trip in spring 1938 but this seems a confusion with a Bullitt trip then. See Orville Bullitt,*For the President: Personal and Secret Correspondence between Franklin D Roosevelt and William C Bullitt*, Boston, 1972, pp.297, 303, 318, 326, 334-6, 353.

9 Ibid pp.318,326,334-6,353.
10 FJM AMD Oct, Nov 1939 contains details of Monnet's financial status at the time; JMM , pp.123-8
11 FJM AMD; author's interview with Anna Giannini, Monnet's stepdaughter.
12 Bullitt, *For the President;*, pp370-1.
13 PRO Avia 38, File "Jean Monnet's Pay." JMM, pp.12.
14 The diplomat was Oliver Harvey, minister at the British embassy, Paris and later Anthony Eden's private secretary, whose comments are in *The Diplomatic Diaries of Oliver Harvey, 1937-1940* , London, 1970, p.396. The Phillips' comment is in PRO Cab 26 Oct 1939. On the Morgenthau suspicions, John Morton Blum, *From the Morgenthau Diaries*, Boston, 1965, p.67 and HMD 27 Dec 1938 . John McVicker Haight, in *American Aid to France 1938-1940*, New York, 1970 p.81 summarizes the Morgenthau suspicions and gives an excellent account of the French US aircraft story in the prewar period.
15 The story of the Anglo-French Union plan is told most completely by Max Beloff in "The Anglo-French Union Project of June 1940" in *Intellectual in Politics* , London, 1970 pp72-199; for Monnet's account, JMM pp.24-35. On the shift in plane orders from France to Britain, JMM p.148 and an interview given by Tom Childs, the American lawyer and counsel for the BPC to John McVickar Haight and provided to the author; on the importance of these orders for the war effort, WSC, Vol II *Finest Hour,* p.89 where Churchill praises Monnet's role; Monnet's interviews with John McVickar Haight in 1971 which were given the author in note form by Haight and Duncan Hall, *North American Supply*, London,1955 pp.146-55. This book gives an excellent and detailled account of the entire British supply relation with the U.S. during the war.
16 WSC Vol II, *Finest Hour* pp.175-96 on the fall of France. For the work with Purvis, see Hall, *North American Supply* pp.159-60.
17 For the Churchill-Monnet exchange, JMM pp.147-8.
18 William L. Langer and S. Everett Gleason, *Challenge to Isolation,* Boston, 1972 Ch XXII; WSC, Vol II *Finest Hour* pp. 404,414; RES: *R&H* pp.174-6 on the political and legal climate FDR faced on the destroyer deal and on the support he got from Interior Secretary Harold Ickes.
19 Monnet may have met Frankfurter first at the Versailles Peace Conference when both men were in close touch with Colonel Edward M House, President Wilson's chief aide at the conference. Family relations of the Frankfurters and Monnets are suggested in Personal Files, FF.
20 Letter to author from Phillip Elman and phone conversations with him in Aug-Sep 1991. Elman was Frankfurter's law clerk from Jul 1941-Jul 1943. The letter from Anna Monnet to Roosevelt is in FDRL, PPF 7365 with the President's reply of 7 Feb 1941.
21 Nathan article "The Unsung Hero of World War II" in *JM:PEU,* pp71-80.
22 Overall British aid figures cited in Langer and Gleason,*The Undeclared War,* p.264. The U.S. budget figure is from *US Historical Statistics* , Washington, 1976, p.1105. Morgenthau's reflections are in HMD 3 Mar 1941.
23 HLSD, 2 Dec 1940, 29 Dec 1942.
24 The Monnet memo is in FJM AME 18 Dec 1940 and HLSD 2 Dec 1940. The President's statement was in his message to Congress, 1 Jan 1941.
25 For the "arsenal of democracy" phrase, RES:*R&H* p.826; *JMM*, p.160; and Samuel I Rosenman, *Working with Roosevelt* , NY 1952 pp.261-2.
26 HLSD 29 Dec 1942.
27 The Brand letter of 15 Jan 1941 to Monnet is in FJM AME.

[28]　For Stimson's insistence on War Department authority in foreign arms sales, see HLSD 10 Sept 1940. For Morgenthau's reflections in foreign arms sales, see HMD Mar 3 1941. For more on the resistance from the Army Air Corps' viewpoint, see H.H. (Hap) Arnold *Global Mission* , New York, 1949,Ch. 11; for Morgenthau's efforts see HMD vols 172-4.

[29]　For Monnet's office life in Washington, his memoirs are of little help. I have relied on interviews and correspondence with Allison Carroll, who was one of Monnet's secretaries at the BSC and on interviews with Robert Nathan.

[30]　JMM pp.161-3. His work patterns are derived from his memoirs, and from the Carroll and Nathan interviews cited in preceding note.

[31]　Nathan article "The Unsung Hero of World War II," in *JM:PEU* pp.83-4.

[32]　HMD 3 Jun 1942. Monnet's lifestyle is from his memoirs and interviews with Fontaine, Nathan and Jacques Van Helmont and their articles in *JM:PEU*. His income and money problems, are from letter by Robert B. Brand to Lord Kindersley, 18 Jun 1943, Brand Papers, Filebox 198, Bodleian Library, Oxford University. Silvia Monnet's lifestyle is based on an undated profile in a Washington newspaper in 1944 or 1945 in FJM AME.

[33]　Purvis' note is in President's Personal File, 19 Mar 1941, FDRL.

[34]　Monnet's note is in FJM AME 30 Dec 1940. Monnet's salary details are in PRO Avia 38, File "Jean Monnet"s Pay." His balance sheet concept is discussed in many papers by him and others. See JMM pp.126-7 and Francois Duchene, "Jean Monnet's Methods." in JM:PEU p206.

[35]　Nathan, in JM:PEU pp.75-6;

[36]　Ibid;*Felix Frankfurter Reminisces: An Intimate Portrait as Recorded in Talks with Dr. Harlan B. Phillips* New York, 1960 p.184.

[37]　Nathan in JM:PEU , *loc.cit* and interviews with him. Isaiah Berlin discusses these meetings *passim* in *Washington Despatches 1941-45*, London, 1981. Monnet discussed the study group in a 1961 interview with John McVicker Haight who shared his notes with the author.

[38]　RES:R&H 262.

[39]　For Hopkins personality and character, Ibid *passim*; for Hopkins interest in literature, see undated letter from Ethel Hopkins, his first wife, to Sherwood in RES, personal papers, Series II, in the Georgetown University Library, Washington; for Monnet's original underestimate of Hopkins, see notes Sherwood made for his book on his 24 May 1946 interview with Monnet in RES, Houghton Library, Harvard University; for Monnet's account of meeting Hopkins, JMM,p. 166; for Sherwood's account *R&H* ,p.28. The optimism of the two men as a bonding agent was pointed out to me by Sidney Hyman, who helped organize Hopkin's papers and who worked with Sherwood on his Hopkins biography.

[40]　1992 interview with Nathan.

[41]　The exchange between Hopkins and Monnet is in the Correspondence File, 14-15 Jan, 1942, in Hopkins Personal Papers, Georgetown University Library. The importance of Hopkins to Roosevelt and Monnet is also noted by RES:*R&H* , pp.765, 777.

[42]　FF, 14 Nov 1941.

[43]　HMD, 3,1,17Jun 1942.

[44]　HMD 7 May 1942, 19 May 1944.

[45]　FJM AME 14 May 194

[46]　FJM AME 12 Dec 1941.

[47] The Lyttleton visits are mentioned in JMM p.176 and in RES:*R&H*, pp.578-81. Monnet's work with the British Supply Council was described by a secretary, Allison Carroll in a 1990 interview and in subsequent correspondence.

[48] JMM pp. 141-7 covers the Monnet-de Gaulle relationship in London before 1943; JMM pp.178-80 indicates Monnet's view of events in North Africa immediately before his 1943 arrival there.

[49] Sherwood has an interesting but incomplete account of the "French sovereignty" memo. He refers to an unsigned memo which, in fact, Monnet wrote on 24 Dec, as constituting "an admirable statement of Roosevelt's fundamental point of view in dealing with the French problem." Sherwood also quotes the White House correspondents speech where the President summarized the Casablanca meeting and discussed French sovereignty and self-determination. RES:*R&H*, pp.680-81,702. What is not clear is whether Monnet influenced Roosevelt on the postwar French sovereignty question, or Roosevelt's position influenced Monnet toward these conclusions, or whether the two men simply thought along the same lines. Whatever the interaction, de Gaulle was the object of the warning that "no French political authority can exist or be allowed to attempt to create itself outside of France" as the Monnet memo contended. What is also clear is that Roosevelt persisted in this anti-de Gaulle mode long after Monnet accepted that the French general was the best one to lead the French resistance movement.

[50] HLSD 29 Dec 1942.

[51] JMM, p. 141-7; 178-801 Robert Murphy, *Diplomat Among Warriors*, Garden City, NY,1964, p.182.

[52] WSC Vol IV, *Hinge of Fate*, p.542

[53] For Monnet's role, JMM , pp.183-5. For the American view of North African events, RES:*R&H* , pp.667-697 and Murphy, *Diplomat Among Warriors* pp.178-80. Monnet said he asked Hopkins to send him to Algiers,(JMM, p.183) but in Feb 1943 he showed Hopkins a cable from Giraud asking Monnet to visit Algiers (Hopkins memo to Roosevelt, 5 Feb 1943, HH, FDRL). Perhaps Hopkins instigated the cable (at Monnet's suggestion) when he accompanied Roosevelt to the Casablanca conference. For Roosevelt's telegram to Hull and Hopkins authorization for Monnet to travel to Algiers, which bypassed Hull's objection, see HH, FDRL post-Casablanca file 22 Feb 1943.

[54] This chapter cannot cover the entire story of Monnet's work in Algiers which is the subject of Andre Kaspi's excellent work, *La Mission Jean Monnet a Alger, Mars-Octobre 1943*, Paris, 1971.

[55] Hopkins view of Giraud is quoted in RES: *R&H* 683-4. Later, Hopkins changed his mind and called Giraud "dumb" in an 28 Oct 1943 interview with journalist Raymond Clapper. Clapper Papers, LC.

[56] HH FDRL 11 Mar 1943.

[57] JMM, pp.186-88.

[58] For Monnet's letter of 6 May 1943 to Hopkins on de Gaulle's speech, see HH, Box 330, Book 7; for Macmillan's 1943 meetings with Monnet, see HM, *passim* for his amused comments on the uproar over de Gaulle speech, HM, p.80.

[59] 6 May and 9 May letters from Monnet to Hopkins in Box 330, Book 7 in HH FDRL.

[60] Murphy's letter 6 Jul 1943, HH FDRL, post-Casablanca file.

[61] Kenneth Pendar, *Adventures in Diplomacy* New York, 1945 163-175, and Henri Giraud, *Un Seul But--La Victoire* , Paris, 1948, p.121; *FRUS*, 1943, II, pp.152-7.

[62] The Monnet memo is quoted in JMM p.222; longer extracts(in the original French) in *L'Europe, une longue marche* Lausanne, 1985, pp.12-16.

63 See NY Times 12,17, Nov 1943 for the UNRRA conference including speeches by Monnet and others;

64 See Raoul Aglion, *Roosevelt and De Gaulle* , New York, 1988 ,pp.73 *passim* for Monnet's new relations with de Gaulle. For Roosevelt's views on postwar France, James MacGregor Burns, *Roosevelt, Soldier of Freedom*, New York, 1970, pp.480-2; JMM ,pp.215-220.

65 The Monnet-Morgenthau exchange in Mar-Jun 1944 on US-printed script for use in liberated France, FJM AME. "Accretions to the Morgenthau Diary" in HMD has a file on 1944 currency problems involving France and other countries.

66 Fortune, Aug 1944, p.120.

67 JMM pp.219-220; HM 482. The family's move to Narragansett, which may have started while he was still in Algiers, is described in a letter to a London friend from Robert H. Brand, Monnet's close friend and financial adviser. Monnet owed $45,000 in back U.S. taxes from the Murnane partnership whose assets were worth only $35-40,000 to Monnet. His pay from the French committee was only about $6000 annually, less than the $7500 he still earned from the Hong Kong partnership branch. File box 148, Brand papers, Bodleian Library, Oxford.

68 HMD, 4 Sept 1944.

69 Blum, *op.cit.* Vol III. 1941-1945   344, HLSD 28 Aug 1944 and Berlin, *Washington Despatches*, pp.365,419.

70 HLSD Sept 5,6 1944. Marshall's view of 1940 is from Ed Cray, *General of the Army*, NY 1990, p.730.

71 NY Times 12 Mar 1944 for the war rally speech and NY Times files 1940-45 where, before the 1943 Atlantic City conference, the only mention of Monnet was when he went to the airport to meet Arthur Salter.

72 Interview in 1968 with Emilio Collado, a US banker with the lendlease program, in COHP.

73 JMM, pp.228,234.

4

Dean Acheson and Jean Monnet: On the Path to Atlantic Partnership

Douglas Brinkley

Historians tend to focus primarily on the achievements of Jean Monnet and Dean Acheson in the decade following World War II, when both were at the pinnacle of their power and prestige. This chapter explores their experiences during wartime (as foundational for these achievements) and their final joint project in the 1960's, John F. Kennedy's promulgation of the Atlantic Partnership, an initiative that was sidetracked by the president's assassination, U.S. involvement in Vietnam, and Charles de Gaulle's obstructionism.

While the documentary record of the Acheson-Monnet relationship during the Truman years is largely complete, there is no record of how often Acheson and Monnet met after the secretary of state left office in 1953. The written exchanges after 1953 were friendly and frank, but sporadic. Acheson was a prodigious letter writer yet Monnet was not one of his more frequent correspondents. Monnet, on the other hand, rarely wrote letters, preferring to rely on his unique gift of oral persuasion.

Monnet's uncanny influence was largely based on his ineffable charisma exercised in face-to-face encounters with American policy-makers. In Henry Kissinger's words, Monnet "mesmerized" America's leading statesmen into seeing the world from his own unique perspective.[1]

Kissinger's description may itself contain a clue to Monnet's powers by implying that Monnet was dealing with men open to suggestion, primed to hear his message by their own ideas and beliefs. As Alfred Grosser concluded: "The work and friendship ties [Monnet] had with men from the most diverse countries were so intense that even historians given to explaining everything in infrastructure and profound trends find themselves obliged to take account of them." [2]

Monnet was always attuned to change and never permitted his notions of the state of the American psyche to become stale or outdated. "To understand America, its people and its leaders, one has to go back regularly and form some general notions about America and the Americans, acquired over the decades of friendly contact; but when it comes to action I rely on my judgment at the time," he wrote in his *Memoirs*. "That was the real reason for my regular visits, which always began with calls on well informed friends." Monnet's interest, though, was not the poll-taker's cross-section of America. His focus was on New York and Washington. There, he always called on "men who cannot afford to make mistakes -- bankers, industrialists, lawyers, and newspapermen. What others say may be colored by imagination, ambition or doctrine. I certainly respect their influence; but I base my judgment on the wisdom of practical men." [3] Or, to be more precise, powerful, practical men.

By almost anyone's definition, Dean Acheson was a powerful, practical man. Trained as an international lawyer, Acheson's public life was dedicated to creating order out of chaos, collective institutions out of previously disparate structures, and Western unity out of anachronistic Euronationalism. Both as secretary of state (1949-53) and elder statesman (1953-71), Acheson anchored his political philosophy in the classical notion of balance of power and strong alliances. One of NATO's founding fathers and an early advocate of European integration measures, he passionately believed that maintaining and strengthening the political, military and economic ties within the Atlantic Community -- the linkages and balance between North America and Western Europe --was the cornerstone on which post-WWII American foreign policy rested. [4]

Monnet is generally regarded as the individual who did more than any other statesman or lobbying organization to advance the concept of European integration in the United States. It was Monnet who was responsible for garnering American support for the European Coal and Steel Community (ECSC), European Defense Community (EDC), Euratom, the Common Market (once it was created), and the Atlantic partnership idea. He did so by using his captivating personality, time-honored American friendships (many cultivated during World War I), vast international experience, instinct for the *loci* of power, mastery of English and American colloquialisms, and tireless dedication to a single idea -- European unity. Historian John Gillingham captures the essence of Monnet's long career: "The United States was both the most decisive influence of Monnet's life and the main source of his power." [5] Even after he stepped down as President of the ECSC's High Authority in 1955 and to form the Action Committee for the United States of Europe (1955-75), Jean Monnet remained one of Europe's most respected voices in America; and Dean Acheson was one of his most devoted listeners.

The question usually asked about Monnet is how did an ostensibly shy and reticent Frenchman who never held public office position himself as the unofficial liaison for the European Community movement in America. This essay focuses on a narrower question: How did Monnet, with his unshakable vision of the United States of Europe, motored by his trademark perspicacity, use his American contacts -- Dean Acheson and the other Eurocentric diplomats of the state department sometimes known as "the Club" -- to further his integration crusade. [6]

On one Washington excursion shortly after John F. Kennedy became President, Monnet, in a single afternoon, met separately with Acheson, Walter Lippmann, McGeorge Bundy, Joseph Alsop, and Ted Sorenson.[7] Leonard Tennyson, an American working for the European Community in Washington, met Monnet at Union Station on a March 1961 visit. His first words as he got off the train were, " I don't know how long I'm going to stay here, perhaps several weeks," followed by "Who is the most important man next to Kennedy?" Tennyson, taken aback by the bluntness of the question, answered, "Oh, it's probably Arthur Schlesinger Jr." Monnet looked straight at him and said, "It is not. It's a young man by the name of Sorenson." Tennyson, telling the story in a 1981 oral history interview with Katherine Graham, the publisher of the Washington Post, added the clincher: "He was, of course, quite right. But the interesting thing is, that although he'd never met Kennedy, within two weeks he'd lunched with the new President several times, and dined with him at least once." [8]

How did a private citizen of France manage to spend so much time with a newly inaugurated American president? A partial answer is Dean Acheson with whom Monnet held meetings on March 3, 6, 13 and 18. He would fly back from Paris to visit Acheson again on June 12 and 15.[9] Acheson and Monnet were working together again to launch a new institutional initiative: the Atlantic Partnership. Their joint efforts, along with those of Walt Rostow, George Ball, Henry Owen and J. Robert Schaetzel, would culminate in JFK's historic July 4, 1962 Independence Hall speech where the young President called for the creation of just such an "Atlantic Partnership," soon known under the administration slogan "The Grand Design." Converting the American President was to be one of Monnet's last great achievements, for Kennedy's assassination,

American involvement in Vietnam and Charles de Gaulle aborted the Grand Design.

The history of the European integration movement during the Cold War could not be fully appreciated or explained without recognizing the immense influence that the Acheson-Monnet relationship had on the formation of U.S. foreign policy attitudes toward Europe, and therefore Europe itself. Monnet's World War II years in Washington, concerned with the conversion of the U.S. civilian economy to armament production, taught him the precise locus of institutional power in America and who controlled that power; during the Cold War he used that knowledge to maintain Dean Acheson's support of the European integration movement in all of its various guises. The story begins in the institution building years of post-Versailles Europe.

Jean Monnet first met Dean Acheson in 1927 at a small Washington dinner party hosted by a mutual friend, lawyer George Rublee. Acheson arrived with Felix Frankfurter, his mentor at Harvard Law School and his "enthusiastic door-opener" in Washington and who first introduced Acheson to Monnet.[10] The 34-year-old Acheson was already known around Washington as an international lawyer with a dazzling wit and a budding future. His Washington firm, Covington, Burling and Rublee was one of America's leading international law firms, with many European clients.

One of Acheson's first major cases for his firm was his skillful and successful defense of the Kingdom of Norway in a 1921 reparations claim against the U.S. government before the Permanent Court of Arbitration at The Hague. His reputation as a lawyer eventually brought him to Monnet's attention.[11]

Acheson, the son of an Episcopalian bishop who attended Groton, Yale and Harvard Law, had been groomed for a life of public service. In the early 1920's he cultivated a vast array of influential European -- especially British -- friends, often through letters of introduction by Frankfurter. But in 1927, while Acheson was just becoming known in international circles, Jean Monnet had already established an international reputation as a shrewd banker and financial manager.

Jean Monnet made a transformative journey to North America in 1906 at the age of 18, traveling mainly in the rugged Rocky Mountains region selling his family's brandy to trading posts and saloons. The young Monnet marveled at the wide open spaces and sturdy frontier folk he encountered who, through sheer will and determination, had transformed a wilderness into disciplined communities yet felt compelled by the need for new challenge to push even further West.[12]

It was American optimism that Monnet found most congenial. "One personality trait of Jean Monnet which many students of the Monnet method have noted is his persistent, perhaps even therapeutic, optimism," Monnet scholar Clifford Hackett has written. "He seemed to require optimism as a form of oxygen for his mental processes. His metaphors about prevailing over obstacles by using them, about even using one's enemies to overcome them, about the need to change the context when problems seem insolvable -- all these point toward this optimism. Those who knew Monnet well often saw in him an exemplar of that optimism which is seen as a peculiarly American cast of mind." [13] But in the 1920's Monnet's mind was not focused on North America but on the economic dislocation in Europe.

During World War I, the young Monnet persuaded French Prime Minister René Viviani of the need to end Anglo-French competition for scarce war supplies. He was subsequently sent to London as a member of the French Liaison Committee and played a major role in Anglo-French joint efforts. Following the war, Monnet was an enthusiastic supporter of the League of Nations, where as assistant secretary-general (1919-23) he led negotiations on Silesia and the Saar, and the economic rehabilitation of Austria. Disappointed by French President Raymond Poincaré's attempt to keep the nations defeated in World War I under Allied domination, Monnet resigned, returning to Cognac to help his ailing father save the family brandy business, which was verging on bankruptcy.[14] By 1923 Monnet's enthusiasm for the League faltered, a process Acheson had also undergone; initial enthusiasm followed by disillusion. Acheson came to regard the League as a "universal plumb plan," while for Monnet it was only useful as a "switchboard," a secondary diplomatic channel for dialogue among nations.[15]

Throughout the 1920's Monnet traveled the world advising governments and building his reputation as an international banker to be reckoned with: in Sweden he helped to liquidate the Kreuger match empire; on Wall Street, where he made and then lost a small fortune in the 1929 crash, he advised the likes of John J. McCloy, Donald Swatland, James Forrestal and John Foster Dulles on European investment opportunities; [16] in Shanghai he worked closely with Chiang Kai-Shek; in Warsaw (with Dulles as his lawyer) he advised the Polish Government on how to refloat the Polish zloty; and in Bucharest he stabilized the Rumanian currency.[17] He also became vice-president (European partner) of Blair & Co., investment bankers, became involved with the Bank of America and set up a small investment firm with George Murnane called Monnet-Murnane and Co.[18]

By 1939 with war in Europe imminent both Monnet and Acheson were putting their deep-rooted internationalist convictions to work. In concrete terms this meant providing Britain with air and naval aid. The French Air Ministry, which wanted to purchase American aircraft, sent Monnet on confidential missions to the United States in October and December 1938, and again in January 1939. Monnet, as chairman of the Anglo-French Coordination Committee in 1939-40, persuaded de Gaulle and Churchill to back his abortive plan for a Franco-British political union and joint citizenship. Soon after this failed attempt, after France fell and with his French passport endorsed by Churchill, Monnet went to Washington as a civil servant in the British Ministry of Supply; he remained there for the next five years.[19]

It is natural for historians to focus on Monnet and Acheson's accomplishments in the decade following World War II. But both men made crucial contributions to the Allied war effort, and in their joint and separate experiences lay the seeds of their later achievements. Both men spent World War II in Washington, where two programs brought them together in a working relationship: Lend-Lease and UNRRA. They not only worked together, but often socialized together during this period.

Acheson had not been in the public sector since 1933 when he resigned as undersecretary of the treasury in a policy disagreement with President Franklin D. Roosevelt. Though not viewed as a friend of the New Deal, Acheson nevertheless made himself useful to FDR in the summer of 1940, when as a prominent Washington lawyer with Covington & Burling he helped devise a legal arrangement by which the President could transfer 50 old destroyers to the British Government in exchange for the leasing of British naval and air bases off the Atlantic coast of Canada and in the Caribbean --- without obtaining Congressional approval. Monnet reconnected with Acheson in Washington after Acheson articulated their position publicly in a long letter to the New York Times on August 11, 1940 co-signed with three other prominent lawyers.[20]

The destroyer-base deal proved an unmitigated Rooseveltian triumph over the isolationist forces in Congress. After he was re-elected President in November 1940 for an unprecedented third term, FDR repaid Acheson for his legalistic legerdemain by appointing him to an important position as assistant secretary of state for economic affairs, on February 1, 1941.[21]

During World War II, Acheson served with distinction in Cordell Hull's otherwise mediocre state department. There he participated in all the significant lend-lease arrangements that ultimately poured $39 billion in U.S. military and civilian matériel into countries resisting fascism in both the East and West, chaired the United Nations Relief and Rehabilitation Agency (UNRRA) planning committee and represented the state department at the Bretton Woods conference of 1944. This work brought Acheson into contact with many of Europe's best economic minds: John Maynard Keynes, Lord Halifax and Jean Monnet.[22]

As a member of the British Supply Council during World War II, Monnet, whom Robert Nathan calls "the unsung hero" of the war because of his innovative contributions to stimulating war production, hoped the war program would evolve into a system whereby resources were pooled cooperatively for a common end.[23] Monnet believed that American armament production was the most critical requirement for winning the war. He visited FDR at Hyde Park, and with the help of Harry Hopkins, persuaded the President to announce in his 1941 State of the Union message the incredible production goal of 50,000 airplanes a year. According to Robert Sherwood, Roosevelt's famous phrase "America will be the great arsenal of democracy," was coined by Monnet.[24] "Monnet was a minor legend in Washington," George Ball has noted of his French friend's years with the British Supply Council. "I grew accustomed to the idea that Monnet was not like other people; he was *sui generis* ." [25]

While administering lend lease and working for the "Victory Program," Monnet was sent to Algiers in 1943 at FDR's personal intervention where he helped to reconcile the feuding generals de Gaulle and Giraud. He then became a member of the French National Liberation Committee headed by de Gaulle. From then on, Monnet, who foresaw the obsolescence of national sovereignty, and de Gaulle, the embodiment of French nationalism, would be at loggerheads. From World War II onward Acheson, who reluctantly conceded that de Gaulle was "a great man" but regretted "the havoc he wreaked on European unity," relied on Monnet's experience and expertise to discover how best to overcome the French nationalist's notorious obstinacy.[26]

Monnet and Acheson often swapped ideas over dinner at the home of Felix Frankfurter, Philip Graham of the Washington Post or at the British Embassy.[27] Monnet, an early riser who took long walks in

Rock Creek Park to help think through problems, occasionally ran into Frankfurter and Acheson walking together to work. "With their two bowler hats, the two friends were the incarnation of Law and the Constitution," Monnet recorded in his *Memoirs*.[28] It was during these war years that Monnet and Acheson became intimates and developed a mutual, life-long respect for the other's discipline, dedication and ideas. Both shared a profound and single-minded devotion to international cooperation. Katherine Graham characterized Monnet during the war years as having "no power base at that time except the power of his brains and his personality and his ability to get things done. The little circle of personal friends with whom Jean and [his wife] Silvia were close included the Frankfurters, the Archibald Macleishs and the Dean Achesons." [29]   Monnet must have been an inspiration to Acheson as to what could be accomplished by sheer dint of personality, persuasion, and connections, for once he stepped down as secretary of state, Acheson never ceased to work to achieve the implementation of foreign policy objectives he believed in.

Although in the 1990's Monnet is commonly cited as a visionary, Acheson never saw him as such. Monnet, whom Acheson called "one of the brilliant men of his generation," could wax philosophical, but this is not what Acheson valued.[30]   It was Monnet's action-oriented, no-nonsense, tireless get-the-job done approach to every assignment or project he undertook that Acheson treasured in his French friend. To Acheson, the greatness of men like Jean Monnet, Harry Truman, George Marshall and Louis Brandeis lay in their compassionate realism -- utilitarians who were not callous to those less fortunate, decisive men who dealt in the concrete and disdained utopian panaceas, and were devoted to the truth. Acheson often compared Marshall and Monnet, because each was viewed as virtuous and wise by his countrymen, each had a global reputation as a prestigious statesman of great consequence while usually managing to remain above the fray of partisan politics.[31]

Monnet, like Acheson, revered innovative and contributive action. In fact, as former U.S. Ambassador to the European Economic Community John Tuthill noted, Monnet's word was "action," evident in the organization he founded in 1955 to "propel Europe to unity": the Action Committee for the United States of Europe.[32] This observation was recently stressed by former state department advisor Henry Owen: Monnet's "optimism, his dedication to action, were in a way more American than European." [33]

The other great forum in which the two men operated was the first United Nations institution--- the Relief and Rehabilitation Agency

(UNRRA). During wartime, Acheson had remained in the United States except for a trip to Montreal. But in his domestic travels, Acheson by 1945, had rung up a record for international conferences within the country.

It was at the important UNRRA Conference in 1943 in Atlantic City where Acheson first became acquainted with the power of his friend Jean Monnet's singular vision for the postwar world.[34] Although Acheson was well aware of Monnet's prodigious reputation as a planner or, as Theodore White characterized him, a "broker of ideas," [35] nothing prepared him for Monnet's wide-ranging barrage of reconstruction concepts at the first UNRRA meeting.

Formally created on November 9, 1943 in Washington, UNRRA grew out of various suggestions from the United States, Britain, and the Soviet Union for a humanitarian postwar relief organization to administer "food, fuel, clothing, shelter and other basic necessities, medical and other essential services." [36] The first session of the UNRRA Council met in Atlantic City from November 10 to December 1, 1943, with forty-four nations participating. Monnet represented France. The delegates elected Acheson chairman of the council meeting and former New York Senator Herbert Lehman as director general, settled budgetary questions, and agreed on procedures of working with military authorities and nations that could not pay. Throughout these weeks Acheson and Monnet often dined together and took early morning walks on boardwalk, often accompanied by Sir Oliver Franks and Sir Owen Dixon, the Australian Minister in Washington. Acheson wrote that "Monnet gave me fascinating glimpses into General de Gaulle, who is yet only a controversial mystery to me, and into Monnet's own pragmatic view of Europe's need to escape its historical parochialism." [37]

Following the UNRRA conference, Acheson became convinced that after the allied victory over Germany, Europe would again be left economically impoverished, politically enfeebled, and brimming with hatred. A cable of thanks Acheson received from Monnet is indicative of Acheson's activities on behalf of European rebuilding and integration in the decade following Atlantic City.

The 1953 cable, which arrived a month after Acheson stepped down as Harry Truman's secretary of state, was stimulated by the opening of the European common market for coal, the institutional predecessor of the European Common Market.[38] In the wake of the destruction and dislocation of World War II, their "great enterprise" had been nothing less than the international restructuring of the European economic order. Fearing the dislocations of the war would lead to a dangerous power vacuum, Acheson make their elimination an overarching concern of American foreign policy. Even as the Cold War intensified, Acheson thought that once the West had halted Moscow's political and military expansionism the rebuilding and restructuring of Europe must be America's foremost priority.

Monnet's cable and Acheson's reply seem surprisingly devoid of the ebullience both must have felt. "You were more than kind to think of me on the day the common market [of coal] went into effect," Acheson replied on March 4. "Certainly this step gives every indication of being the most significant, hopeful economic step in Europe in any of our memories. I hope it will have the environment to succeed and that it will succeed and lead to other developments as full of promise. It is good to look back on the work we engaged in together, and I am deeply touched that you should have sent me a cable including me in those who have had a hand in shaping this plan." [39]

Acheson was being uncharacteristically modest and self-effacing, for he did not merely lend a hand in the making of the ECSC but worked assiduously to help create it, in the process becoming the leading American proponent of a new, integrated Europe. He was the dynamic foreign-policy thinker who helped lead the United States out of its prewar isolationism to postwar internationalism. Throughout the cold war period, it was Jean Monnet, perhaps more than any other catalyst, who influenced the way Acheson perceived the rebuilding and restructuring process for postwar Europe.

By 1946 it was apparent to Acheson and Monnet that they had underestimated the economic chaos in Europe and overestimated UNRRA's ability to rebuild it. The eventual answer was the Marshall Plan, which both Acheson and Monnet viewed as a needed tonic for Europe's economic ills. After persuading Congress to approve aid to Greece and Turkey in March 1947, Acheson began a campaign of interdepartmental memo-writing focusing on European integration as a means of stimulating recovery and solving the problem of a divided Germany. Perhaps Acheson's most significant contribution to European economic recovery was the trial balloon he sent aloft in his May 8, 1947 speech before the Delta Council in Cleveland, Mississippi. President Truman had been scheduled to deliver the address but sent Acheson instead. In the speech, a precursor of General Marshall's historic June 5 Harvard commencement address, Acheson proposed a massive economic aid program to Europe.[40]

While Acheson worked on initiating Marshall Plan aid, Monnet was working to rebuild a war-torn France. After the liberation of France, railroads, mines, and electric power companies were nationalized. In January 1946, Monnet was chosen to head the newly created *Commissariat du Plan*, which was charged with preparing a comprehensive blueprint for the reconstruction and modernization of the French economy (later to be known as the "Monnet Plan"). In January 1947, the plan was adopted by the French government and Monnet himself was appointed Commissioner General of the Plan. Acheson thought the Monnet Plan "brilliant" and gave it his wholehearted support. The plan is generally viewed as the first step toward creating economic stability in France, which created an environment conducive to the pooling of coal and steel with Germany.[41]

In July 1947, shortly after the initiation of the Marshall Plan, Acheson left the state department to return to private law practice; in January 1949 he was summoned back into government service as President Truman's secretary of state. Even in his brief tenure as a private citizen in 1948, Acheson continued to write to many of his friends praising integrationist steps.

Shortly after Acheson's return to State, a simple handwritten note from Monnet -- "When you have a minute free I should love to see you" -- initiated what would become a four-year joint pursuit of European integration.[42] Monnet and Acheson had much to talk about. While Acheson was out of government, a crucial step toward safeguarding the continent against a rearmed Germany had been taken. On March 17, 1948, representatives of Belgium, France, Luxembourg, The Netherlands and Britain met in the Belgian capital to sign the Brussels Treaty, providing not only for collective self-defense but also for the Western European Union (WEU) in the fields of cultural and economic collaboration. The WEU was the forerunner of the next and much larger stage of military confederation that Acheson labored to create -- the North Atlantic Treaty Organization (NATO).

Although Acheson and Monnet conceived of NATO primarily as a military alliance for "joint determination of the participating nations to resist armed attack from any country," it is also apparent that both had larger strategic aims. By 1952, they had come to regard NATO as a springboard for launching a broader Atlantic Community. On March 10, 1952 Acheson spoke of NATO in terms beyond its military significance: "There must be economic and social and moral strength. Future hope lies in the development of a community of free peoples, strong in their minds and hearts as in their resources -- resources strong enough to meet any challenge that may be offered by those who still hold the ancient doctrine that might makes right and who regard the fundamental human aspirations and sympathies of our peoples as weaknesses to be despised." [43] Neither Acheson nor Monnet ever believed the military, political or economic aspects of the alliance could, in Acheson's words, be kept apart in the "intellectual equivalent of a cream separator." [44]

In a series of notable speeches from 1949 to 1953, Acheson lectured what then was coming to be called the Free World on how to build a deterrent to war through unity and strength. From the moment he took the chair in London at the First Working Session of the North Atlantic Council in May 1949 until his December 1952 farewell as secretary of state calling for progress toward integration and the Atlantic partnership, he never tired of promoting unity in the West. "Unity in Europe required the continuing association and support of the United States," Acheson insisted. "Without it Free Europe would split apart." [45] Before Acheson delivered his December farewell he had a long talk with Monnet on the progress of integration, and Acheson's speech reflects Monnet's conviction that the farewell should use the phrase "unity of Europe." Acheson's efforts were undergirded not only by the working support of Jean Monnet, but also other like-minded European statesmen: Konrad Adenauer, Alcide de Gasperi, Dirk Stikker, Paul-Henri Spaak, and Robert Schuman. "Their innovations of political ideas and methods were as startling as those taking place in physics," Acheson effused in 1963. "Their conception of supranational and irrevocable rules administered by common institutions empowered to make decisions binding upon individuals and member countries was as far-reaching as the conception of nationalism in the fifteenth century." [46]

While secretary of state, Acheson generally approved most European-initiated integration programs that pointed in the direction of ultimate political federation. But, in 1950, when Senator J. William Fulbright, who chaired the American Committee for a United Europe, spoke of a Europe moving away from economic dependence on the United States and toward political federation, Acheson balked. Since Europe was not yet economically on its feet, Acheson said in rebuttal, it was thus incapable of meaningful political unification. "While there is growing popular debate in Europe on the problem of federation, neither the people nor their governments appear ready for this step," Acheson asserted on March 13, 1950.[47]

Europe had not yet reached the level of stability and development necessary for a sound federation, nor had Europeans yet psychologically overcome their firmly rooted attachment to unbridled national sovereignty. Although acknowledging the European "right to decide democratically, as our founding fathers did when, how and whether they will federate," he frowned on Washington Pan-Europeanists like Fulbright (who had passionately embraced Winston Churchill's 1946 call for the establishment of a United States of Europe) whose overheated rhetoric demanded political federation for Europe now.[48] Acheson thought Europe had to set its own pace, without pressure from Washington, It would take the combined efforts of Jean Monnet and Robert Schuman to turn Acheson into an outright believer in a united Europe.

When Monnet proposed that France take the lead in establishing an international authority to regulate coal and steel production, Acheson was initially taken aback. It sounded like "the damnedest cartel I have ever heard in my life." [49] But the more he thought about it, the more he realized Monnet's inspired scheme might be the solution to overcoming the persistent dollar gap while ending Germany's "pariah status" as well.[50] The Schuman Plan called for combining all of the Western European coal and steel industries into a single market. On May 7, 1950, Schuman informed Acheson in Paris, prior to informing his own cabinet colleagues, of his plan to announce the concept of a coal and steel community in two days. The secretary of state was delighted by Monnet's cunning and Schuman's nerve, despite the tongue lashing he received a few days later from British foreign minister Ernest Bevin for not telling London of Schuman's proposal. Acheson made it unmistakably clear to Bevin, a man he thought would rank with Castlereigh, Canning and Palmerston "as one of the great British foreign secretaries" that the United States was trying to develop a European policy and that the so-called special relationship with Britain ran counter to this continental approach. Acheson let it be known that he was disappointed at the British government's refusal to participate in discussions for the ECSC, as the Schuman Plan became known. Bevin remained unconvinced.[51]

"The genius of the Schuman-Monnet plan," Acheson wrote, "lay in its practical, commonsense approach, its avoidance of limitations upon sovereignty and touchy political problems. What could be more earthy than coal and steel, or more desirable than pooling a common direction of France and Germany's coal and steel industries?" [52]

Although Acheson acknowledged Monnet as the father of ECSC, he never underestimated the crucial role Schuman played in its genesis. In *Sketches from Life of Men I Have Known* (1961), Acheson devotes an effusive chapter to Schuman's postwar tenacity, although Acheson never cultivated the same warm personal relationship with Schuman that he had with Monnet.[53]   Nevertheless, Schuman and Acheson enjoyed a productive, professional rapport. Acheson saw Monnet as a citizen of Europe, a man who thought in terms of what is best for Europe. Schuman, he saw, as a Frenchman first and a European second. Although Acheson believed European unity would never become a reality unless "the French [did] something about their constitutional system," he was in fact won over to the European integration monument partly because of his admiration for French ingenuity as exemplified by Jean Monnet and Robert Schuman.

Yet Acheson's admiration was ambivalent. "I think the inherent, deep-seated weakness of the whole alliance of the West is France," Acheson told colleagues at the Princeton seminars in 1953, "but at the same time there is the greatest inventiveness and ingenuity coming out of France, and [the Schuman Plan] was a brilliant idea." Acheson, speaking of the Schuman Plan, wittily remarked that "the most terrible preparation for diplomatic life is the training in Anglo-Saxon law. That gives you the spurious idea to be specific: you try to find out categorically what things mean.   People who have really great constructive ideas don't really know what they mean." [54]

In the months following the start of the Korean War in June 1950, Monnet tried to deflect American pressure for a rearmed Germany by suggesting to French Prime Minister René Pleven a plan to allow for gradual German rearmament within a larger European army. The Pleven Plan, or the European Defense Community (EDC) as it came to be known, was received from its birth with hostility by the French public for allowing Germans to parade once more, now in uniforms alongside Frenchmen. It was seen as granting the Germans a form of moral equivalency. Although France had signed a Bonn peace contract on May 26, 1952 and the EDC treaty a day later, the treaty would not take effect without ratification by the six European parliaments. The ratification process, Monnet knew, would be long and its outcome doubtful.[55]

Shortly before Acheson's farewell address to the NATO Council meeting in December 1952, he received Monnet. Concerned about French Socialist and British roadblocks to the EDC, Monnet urged Acheson to stress American commitment to the Euroarmy approach in his NATO speech, but warned that the ratification process "would take time, but that it probably would come out all right in the end." [56] Acheson was put off by Monnet's insistence that it was up to Washington to apply pressure on Europe to accept EDC. "Sometimes it seemed to me that Monnet forgot -- as do the rest of us -- Justice Holmes' admonition that certainty is not the test of certitude," Acheson wrote in *Present at the Creation.* "The trouble seemed to me to run far deeper and to lie at the very root of popular acceptance of European unity. I pointed out to him the amazing distance the United States has gone, often in cooperation with European initiatives as brilliant as they were novel.... Now momentum in Europe was being lost and retrogression had set in to the point of threatening disaster.... It would be quixotic [for America] to struggle [pushing EDC] if the Europeans were giving up the struggle. If the European Defense Community went to pieces, I foresaw great difficulties for the new administration. What was hard for me to understand was how the Germans and French, who had seen us go to great lengths to respond to statesmanlike efforts on their part, could risk their own defense and future, as they were now doing, in petty political squabbling." [57]

Although Acheson's NATO speech did not strike the united Europe tone Monnet had wanted, his January 14, 1953, farewell state department news conference did focus specifically on the need for EDC.[58] Acknowledging that getting the French to ratify the treaty was an uphill battle, he pointed to the Schuman Plan, which had also faced formidable obstacles. It would devolve upon President-elect Dwight D. Eisenhower to see to it that the EDC and European political unity became realities.

When a year and a half later on August 30, 1954, under the government of Pierre-Mendès France, the French National Assembly finally rejected the EDC treaty, Acheson was livid, viewing the rejection as a severe setback to European integration and Western military cooperation. With rejection, came the collapse of the proposed European political community. To a deeply disappointed Acheson, the ECSC now appeared an isolated outpost of integration in a Europe reverting to nationalist lines. Acheson, with uncharacteristic tunnel vision, placed the blame for the treaty's failure squarely on Eisenhower and Dulles. Acheson saw their condescending attitude toward the French before, during, and after the fall of Dienbienphu in Indochina as having caused America's oldest ally to reject the treaty. Common sense, he thought, demanded that Washington deal tactfully with France; instead they only got Dulles's "agonizing reappraisal" threat.

For the eight years of Eisenhower's presidency, Monnet, for the most part, ignored Acheson. Although Monnet did send Acheson a telegram when he stepped down as secretary of state, not once during these years did he write Acheson to solicit his advice. The two met twice -- once in Paris and once in Washington a day before Monnet spoke to

President Eisenhower in January 1958, but now that Acheson was no longer a player in the European integration process Monnet focused his energies on the American decision makers who mattered: David K.E. Bruce, Douglas Dillon, Robert Bowie, and in particular, John Foster Dulles.

Monnet's acquaintance with Dulles predated his meeting of Acheson by nearly eight years. Monnet first met Dulles at the Paris Peace Conference of 1919, where Dulles was serving as an advisor to President Woodrow Wilson. Monnet could not have been more pleased with Eisenhower's choice, for he was closer to Dulles than to Acheson and knew from previous conversations that Dulles was strongly committed to the ratification of the EDC and the movement behind a united Europe. When Dulles died of cancer on May 24, 1959, Monnet was the only foreigner among the pallbearers.[59]

In early February 1953, less than a month after Eisenhower's inauguration, Dulles flew to Luxembourg to observe firsthand the inauguration of the ECSC. There, during the course of their extended conversations, Monnet asked Dulles to name an American ambassador to the ECSC. Dulles honored the request and nominated David K.E. Bruce, a long time proponent of European integration and an originator of the concept of the European army. Monnet's strong recommendation of Bruce appears to have been determinative in Dulles's choice, for Monnet thought Bruce bright, eager and loyal thereby representing the "highest tradition of [an] American [diplomat]." [60]

Bruce, a Democrat, was a wealthy Baltimore lawyer and career foreign-service officer with close ties to Dean Acheson, at a time when Wisconsin Senator Joe McCarthy's "positive loyalty" campaign was guillotining some of the best heads in the state department. Dulles was likewise reluctant to risk negative political repercussions from the equally venomous Republican isolationist wing of Congress by appointing a liberal Democrat like Bruce to the ECSC, a concept that reeked of collectivism. Monnet reminded Dulles that he himself had served the state department when the Republicans were out of power and that Bruce was the best man for the job. It is a tribute to Monnet's persuasion that he convinced Dulles to put politics aside and appoint Bruce.

The appointment of Bruce came as a relief to Acheson. From 1953 to 1960 Bruce became Acheson's American source on European happenings. Constantly bolstering Acheson's sagging morale with optimistic reports of integration advancements, Bruce also updated his former boss on Monnet's maneuverings. In 1958, while France was involved in colonial problems in North Africa, Bruce wrote Acheson of his pessimism over the situation, saying "Jean Monnet ought to be employed to develop a Confederation there." [61]

Under Eisenhower's stewardship, Acheson believed, the momentum of the entire postwar European unity movement was slowly grinding to a halt because of weaknesses and mistakes by a Republican administration. Acheson decided it was time to pick up the integration baton for the Democrats, and putting aside his private law practice, he began pouring his energy into articles and speeches on the need for a new European unity program. Although Acheson was never again to hold government office, when the Democrats recaptured the White House in 1960 Acheson's views would be heard in the corridors of power. Meanwhile in Europe, Monnet's mandate as President of the ECSC High Authority was due to expire on February 10, 1955. On November 11, 1954, Monnet surprised many by unexpectedly announcing he would not put himself up for re-election. Eleven months later, on October 13, 1955, Monnet launched a new European unity program: the Action Committee for the United States of Europe.[62]

Monnet knew that the very name -- Action Committee for a United States of Europe -- would have a reflexive appeal to his influential American friends, friends he needed more than ever if his goal of a united Europe were to advance. Since the Action Committee got much of its financial backing from the Ford Foundation, and its officials like Shepard Stone, and Joe Slater and from other American establishment institutions and individuals, de Gaulle saw the Action Committee as "almost a subversive organization." [63] With American help and the EDC setback behind him, Monnet immediately began organizing this political lobby that had neither official standing nor power -- only a vision of a United Europe and a lifetime commitment to build a network of like-minded thinkers.

To Monnet, there was no alternative for the people of Europe but unity. The "Europeanists" themselves, Monnet charged, were partially to blame for EDC's rejection, because they had failed to win the support of the working class. To correct that oversight, Monnet invited the directors of European labor unions, heads of socialist political parties and important business elites from the six ECSC members to participate in the relaunching of Europe. He gained important socialist, non-Communist support in Germany, no small achievement considering that the German Social Democrats had voted in the German Parliament against both ECSC and the EDC. In France, Monnet brought non-

Gaullist political parties, the trade unions and socialist party leader Guy Mollet into the united Europe movement. The immediate goal Monnet had in mind was to broaden the ECSC by putting the production of petroleum and electricity under the jurisdiction of the High Authority. A unicameral legislative assembly would continue to serve the expanded community.[64]

In mid-January 1956, Monnet had announced his Action Committee's intention to lobby for an atomic energy community modeled after the coal and steel community. From then on, until the Treaties of Rome were signed in March, 1957, Monnet ironically disassociated himself from the European Economic Community (EEC), instead using his Action Committee to promote Euratom. Monnet claims he refused to support the EEC because his political instincts told him that the French Parliament would reject this challenge to their protectionist traditions as it had the EDC. He felt the European integration movement could not survive another EDC-like setback. Instead, Monnet argued that European integrationists should concentrate on promoting Euratom to bolster Europe's nuclear energy industry while simultaneously renouncing nuclear weapons on behalf of all the member states. Once the Rome treaties had been signed Monnet, of course, fully supported them. But by doggedly showcasing the supposed virtues of Euratom to his American friends while simultaneously downplaying the EEC, Monnet had lent his powers of persuasion to the secondary cause.[65]

The EEC and Euratom were created when the Six signed the Treaties of Rome of March 25, 1957. The EEC's objectives for its member states were the establishment of a customs union with free movement of goods, the dismantling of quotas and barriers to trade, a common external tariff and the introduction of free movement of people, services and capital. "Even without American help, the unification of Europe has picked up," an enthusiastic Acheson wrote a close friend. What he found most encouraging, however, was that the treaty provided for common policies on agriculture and transportation, a social policy, an external trade policy, and taxation authority.[66] Euratom sounded to Acheson an ideal next step. His assessment was incorrect, for France soon turned away from Euratom, opting for its own nuclear force. Nevertheless, Acheson remained a staunch supporter of Euratom well into the 1960's, mainly at Monnet's urging.

"The success of the movement toward unity in the West of Europe is no longer in doubt," a buoyed Acheson wrote shortly after the Treaties of Rome had been signed. "Only the rate of progress is undecided. The Coal and Steel Community, Euratom, and the Common

Market have been accepted. A common community and political community are on the way." [67] Acheson's optimism over European integration was soon to be tested by events: Europe's loss of confidence in U.S. leadership following the Suez debacle and its loss of prestige when the Soviets launched Sputnik, the first artificial earth satellite, in October 1957.

Acheson always viewed U.S. leadership as an essential ingredient to European integration. As a Democrat, not in control of the White House in the 1950's, Acheson's approach was two-fold: attacking Republican military spending cuts and the Eisenhower-Dulles doctrine of massive retaliation and working through the Democratic party to capture the White House for a presidential candidate who would promote European unity and Atlantic partnership. During this period Acheson also worked assiduously to reassure America's allies of Washington's continuing commitment to Europe.

When John F. Kennedy defeated Richard Nixon in the 1960 presidential election, leading Europeans such as de Gaulle and Adenauer made their disappointment known. These statesmen wanted continuity and experience in international affairs from Washington, not fashionable rhetoric from a relatively unknown geopolitical novice. But Jean Monnet seemed not to mind. Monnet always managed to maintain close American friends in both political parties. If Nixon had won, Monnet would have continued high-level consultations with the Eisenhower administration holdovers. When Kennedy won, Monnet simply resurrected his fallow friendships with the old Truman administration gang -- particularly George Ball, John McCloy and Paul Nitze, and their younger disciples like Walt Rostow, Henry Owen and J. Robert Schaetzel. That Monnet regarded relationships as instruments to achieve his objectives is clearly illustrated in his friendship with Dean Acheson.[68]

During the Kennedy era Dean Acheson was Monnet's most useful Washington asset, with the notable exception of George Ball. This revival contrasted with the Eisenhower years when Monnet seldom corresponded or met with his old friend and working colleague of the Truman period, meeting only twice, once in 1957 and once in 1958. But after Kennedy won the election and appointed Acheson to serve as chairman of the Advisory Committee on NATO, Monnet immediately wrote Acheson a rare personal letter on his plan for "Atlantic Partnership" which would unite the West between two separate powers of the United States and the United Europe. Acheson, a staunch believer in European integration, was back in government -- if only in an unofficial capacity -- and Monnet was going to use him and every other sounding board he could find to bring his Action Committee's ideas (namely the Atlantic Partnership) to the young President's attention.[69]

Jean Monnet not only sought to influence the new President; he was also advocating Atlantic partnership in the state department. The EEC's creation in 1957 had forced the state department to reconsider what they had meant by an "Atlantic Community." From 1958 to 1962 Christian Herter's "dumbbell plan," depicting Europe and the United States as equal weights on two sides of the Atlantic was the metaphor used to describe Atlantic relations. By the summer of 1962, the new Democratic administration, seeking its own metaphor, could not fall back on the notion of a giant Atlantic Community, which like NATO would be formed of one superpower and smaller friends. Jean Monnet was able to convince the state department to scrap the Atlantic Community concept, which rested on American supremacy, and adopt a policy of equal partnership with Europe to be called the Atlantic Partnership. No relation, Monnet argued, based on such inequality of power would be viable, and the creation of the EEC was making the notion passé. "Atlantic partnership" replaced "Atlantic community" on all department memorandums, speeches, and press releases.[70]

On February 8, 1961, President Kennedy had officially announced Acheson's new position as chairman of his advisory committee on NATO. In preparing his report for the President Acheson consulted with Jean Monnet at great length. Monnet's advice to Acheson was straightforward and direct: make sure the review "unequivocally" supported the EEC and British membership in it.[71]

Contained in the Acheson NATO report, which was approved by Kennedy on April 21 for dissemination throughout government and implementation, were the seeds of Kennedy's ambitious new approach to European affairs, the Grand Design. It translated into the general Monnet notion of a European union within an Atlantic partnership. The Grand Design had concrete objectives: facilitating British entry into the European Community, in part, by discrediting British perceptions of a "special relationship" between the U.K. and U.S.; increasing U.S. exports by reducing trans-Atlantic tariff barriers; convincing Europe to bolster its conventional forces; and persuading European nations to forego developing independent nuclear forces in favor of the multilateral force (MLF). Except for the MLF, which Acheson opposed until August 1963, his NATO policy review articulated how these Grand Design objectives could be realized. Much of the report focused on how to overcome de Gaulle's nascent nuclear *force de frappe* as a dangerous impediment to Atlantic Partnership.[72]

A week after Kennedy appointed Acheson to conduct the NATO review, Acheson received a phone call from Jean Monnet, the contents which Acheson retold to journalist Joseph Alsop: Monnet, Acheson said, told him he had "some new ideas he wanted to bounce off him soon. You are still receptive to new ideas, aren't you, Mr. Secretary?" Monnet bantered. "I'm still receptive to your sardine sandwiches and Christmas cognac," Acheson replied, "but spare me any bold new ideas, the Kennedy crowd has a monopoly on those and you'll end up broke ... stick to the one good idea you've already got [European unification] and let's work to expand it... but please let's use the words 'sound ideas' and avoid the word 'new'."

The two old friends agreed to meet soon in Washington. A few days later Acheson received a special delivery package from Monnet: a flashy Hawaiian-style necktie, the kind Acheson loved to wear while drinking martinis. A jovial Acheson told Alsop that "Monnet was the only man he enjoyed being bribed by... he knew how to do it with understated flair." Acheson also told Alsop he knew he was back in the White House fold "because Monnet was once again using him to advance his united Europe cause." Alsop concluded that Acheson did not mind Monnet's renewed overtures because he knew his friend was not trying to advance himself personally but advance his Action Committee integration ideas.[73]

In fact, Acheson became just one of many from the Truman administration to play prominent roles in Kennedy's administration, and whose friendships Monnet dusted off. As one commentator of the Kennedy administration put it, "The New Frontier fairly crawled with his (Acheson's) disciples and associates." [74] George Ball, C. Douglas Dillon, Will Clayton, McGeorge Bundy, Walt Rostow, J. Robert Schaetzel, Stanley Cleveland, Arthur Hartman, Tom Finletter, David Bruce, and a host of others, many of whom became architects of Kennedy's Grand Design program to renew military and economic cooperation between the United States and Western Europe, were making policy and Monnet wanted to get his ideas across to them. At one time or another since the 1940's, Monnet had influenced all of these men and many other Kennedy administration officials in the state, defense and treasury departments into favoring and creating institutions and policies that would promote the unification of Europe and a trans-Atlantic partnership between a united Europe and the United States. When one looked below the top rank of officials, Monnet's influence was even stronger, a phenomenon acknowledged by The Economist's Washington correspondent: "It is perhaps even more important that in the lower levels of the Administration, where cables are drafted and commanded, there are enthusiasts for the pure milk of M. Monnet's doctrine who make even Mr. Ball -- and perhaps M. Monnet himself -- appear as moderating influences." [75]

Of the New Frontiersmen only McGeorge Bundy distanced himself from Monnet's grand visions. At first, Bundy viewed the Atlanticists with a mixture of mild derision but as the MLF debate grew, Bundy pejoratively dubbed these Eurocentric statesmen "theologians" for mindlessly preaching the Monnet gospel of Atlantic Partnership that included nuclear sharing.[76]

Kennedy had surrounded himself with bright young minds, most of whom favored European unity. George Ball, who had first met Monnet on the wartime supply matters, later gave legal advice on spending France's Marshall Plan money in the U.S. He was not only well-suited to serve as Kennedy's undersecretary of state, but for Monnet provided a channel through which to lobby the President for American support of British entry into an enlarged EEC and a new Atlantic partnership.[77] Buttressed by recommendations to Ball from Acheson and Philip Graham, Monnet was invited to the first of three luncheons at the Kennedy White House on March 6, 1961 to discuss NATO, the Algerian crisis and the Common Market.[78] Kennedy was intrigued by the Action Committee and Monnet's ideas on European unification. (In 1963 Kennedy would note the receipt by Monnet, the father of the European Community, of the Freedom Medal.)[79] Monnet was likewise impressed with Kennedy, and his *Memoirs* are filled with praise of JFK the man, his creative vision of the world and his strides toward achieving "an equal partnership between the United States and a united Europe." [80] Acheson realized that the mere presence of Monnet in the White House would help Kennedy remember that de Gaulle only spoke for a fraction of Europeans and that the majority of the continent's citizens still supported a united Europe.

Monnet returned to Washington in April 1962 for a three week visit, and began lining up appointments with highly placed friends in the Kennedy circle: Secretary of State Dean Rusk, Secretary of the Treasury C. Douglas Dillon, Chief Policy Planner Walt Rostow, White House Advisor McGeorge Bundy, and, of course, Dean Acheson and George Ball. Monnet was on the circuit trying to sell his vision of partnership between the United States and a united Europe in which united Europe would never be the rival of the United States but rather a partner, joined by the indissoluble bond of common interest.[81] James Reston of The New York Times, wrote of Monnet on April 11: "He knows that there are immediate difficulties but he assumes their solution and asks: What is the next step?   And with the question he has at least started a quiet debate among some of the most powerful officials in Washington."[82] Working with Acheson at his P St. home in Georgetown, Monnet reworked a draft of a new Action Committee Resolution which, given to Rostow, Ball, Owen and Schaetzel, resurfaced in a slightly revised form in a major policy speech Kennedy delivered a week later.[83]

In his famous July 4, 1962 Declaration of Independence speech, which was delivered from the steps of Independence Hall in Philadelphia, and which was worked on at various stages by Acheson, Ball, Rostow, Schaetzel, and Owen, Kennedy called for a true "Atlantic partnership" between the United States and the "uniting of Europe." [84]   A week before Monnet's Action Committee, on June 26, 1962, issued a resolution in some ways closely resembles the economic section of Acheson's NATO Policy Review.   Kennedy had called for an Atlantic Partnership, stating that: "the economic political unity of Europe, including Britain (which had applied for entry into the EEC) and the establishment of relations of equal partnership with the United States, alone will make it possible to consolidate the West and so create conditions for lasting peace between East and West." [85]

Acheson liked both Monnet's Action Committee resolution and Kennedy's Philadelphia speech but cringed at their use of the phrase "equal partnership;" his experience as a lawyer led him to insist that he had seen and been engaged in numerous partnerships, but never one that was equal.[86]   Still, for a brief moment, he saw hope that the West might finally work together in tandem instead of falling into petty squabbling.

Throughout his brief presidency, Kennedy constantly sought counsel from Acheson on all aspects of U.S.-European affairs.   In White House debates over U.S. policy toward Africa, it was Acheson more than any other advisor who was able to convince JFK that his "Africa for Africans" advisors -- Adlai Stevenson, Chester Bowles, Soapy Williams and John Kenneth Galbraith -- were "wooly-headed liberals" who understood nothing about the delicate transition America's European allies were experiencing in their efforts to disengage from colonial rule.[87] Acheson constantly warned Kennedy that if his administration continued to vote against European allies in the U.N., NATO would be weakened, the European movement for greater political unification would be stalled and any possibility of a new Atlantic Partnership would collapse.   For the sake of a United Europe, Acheson incessantly and vociferously applied pressure on the administration to once and for all scrap the notion of a "special relationship" with Britain.

On the six visits to Europe Acheson made from 1961 to 1963, most on Kennedy's behalf, he visited Monnet each time, except when a planned visit was canceled because Kennedy asked Acheson to meet Adenauer for an emergency briefing during the Cuban missile crises. "The day I had hoped to see you I was sent on to talk with the Chancellor in Bonn." Acheson wrote Monnet. "It was useful ... but not as pleasant or informative (to me) as an hour or two with you would have been." [88] Acheson told his former personal assistant Luke Battle that no European trip was worthwhile unless he go in at least an hour "jaw session" on current affairs with Jean Monnet.[89] Besides his 1961 and 1962 sessions, Monnet held lengthy meetings with Acheson four times in 1963 on May 14 and May 16 and on November 27 and December 5, only days after Kennedy was assassinated. Monnet hoped Acheson would be able to keep the new President Lyndon Johnson on the path to partnership.[90]

Shortly after the Cuban missile crises of October 1962, Acheson wrote Monnet complaining about weakness in the West, de Gaulle's continuing anti-British bias, the mediocrity of world leadership, the "slowness" of the whole European integration process and the seemingly endless crisis in the Atlantic Alliance that made a broader "Atlantic Community" appear unrealistic. Monnet challenged Acheson's bleak assessment. "I am not pessimistic as to the conditions of the world," Monnet wrote back. "It is inevitable that Europe and the United States move on different wavelengths. They are different .... The way to get this [Atlantic] partnership is for Europe first to get unified and for this, England should be part of it; then Europe and the United States should deal jointly with problems that neither of them can solve by themselves, such as monetary stability, aid to under-developed countries or agricultural surpluses. As the interests will become more and more unified, the political view will become more and more common. This may be a cynical view, but I think that if we want men to unite, we must unite their interest first and for this it is necessary that they accept to act according to the same rules administered by common institutions. I know that this may appear to be a long process, but a change in the attitude of men is necessarily a slow process. I think this is what we are doing and in fact this is what is happening." [91]

Acheson thought it was easy for his friend Monnet to be optimistic. Was not the purpose of the Action Committee to promote all aspects of the European integration movement, to prod the leadership in the Western capitals to think broadly and boldly? While approving of the Action Committee's public relations activities, Acheson also saw the organization as weak and handcuffed by de Gaulle's obstructionist efforts. The general had power, Monnet had only channels to like-minded people with limited power, of no consequence in preventing de Gaulle from vetoing British entry into the Common Market. "Monnet and his people can help: they are good at organizing support for a new idea when the opponent is ignorance or inertia," Acheson wrote Schaetzel on April 1, 1963. "But they cannot lead against de Gaulle. They have no power base." Acheson, however, could not and did not, dismiss Monnet and his ideas. In this very same letter to Schaetzel, Acheson quoted extensively from a speech Monnet had recently delivered in New York, recommending that Schaetzel, who was deputy assistant secretary of State for Atlantic affairs, carefully study Monnet's ideas on the importance of monetary stability to the West.[92]

When de Gaulle shocked the West on January 14, 1963 by announcing he would veto British entry into the Common Market, many in the Kennedy administration were alarmed. Acheson seemed to take the long view, casually noting it was to be expected of de Gaulle and was no cause for Western anxiety. But soon after Acheson's unflappability was temporarily tested when de Gaulle and Adenauer signed the Franco-German cooperation treaty on January 23, 1963. "Chancellor Adenauer made a mistake -- and I think a serious one -- in signing the French treaty when he did," Acheson wrote German industrialist Dr. Kurt Birrenbach. "The Chancellor has never understood General de Gaulle's design [of French leadership in Europe] nor the undignified and demeaning role designed for him and for Germany. He has believed that his place in history would be that of the reconciler of France and Germany -- a place long since occupied by Messieurs Schuman and Monnet. Neither nation has today the power, interest, or inclination to return to the futile hostilities of the past. His real role, if he but knew it, was to cement together Western Europe and North America." [93]

As the sixties progressed, Acheson the advocate grew disillusioned with both American and European leadership, and found Monnet's unrelenting optimism grating. De Gaulle's two vetoes of British entry to the EEC, the failure of MLF, French withdrawal from the NATO integrated military command structure, France's wooing of the Soviet Union behind America's back and U.S. absorption with Vietnam depressed the aging Acheson. He feared the "great enterprise" was slowly dissolving, with the Common Market turning into more of a bureaucratic paper mill than the forward-moving supranational organization of Jean Monnet's dreams. In a 1970 letter to Shepard Stone, the director of the Aspen Institute in Berlin, Acheson reaffirmed his long-standing affection for Monnet, while also expressing his doubts on the likelihood of the Common Market advancing economically or politically in the near future: "I am delighted to hear that le grand Jean is well and can still handle his wines and vittles. I am sure that when I see him next he will tell me, as he always does, that the unification of Europe is just around the corner, although it does seem to me that that corner is a receding one." [94] On Monnet's part, a stomach operation had caused him to slow down and he came less frequently to the States.[95]

Throughout the 1960's, Monnet and Acheson seemed to overestimate the possibilities of the Grand Design and the Atlantic partnership and deluded themselves about the realities of MLF and British entry into the Common Market. At the same time they underestimated their rival Charles de Gaulle. But to say this is not to indict either, for the two aging statesmen saw their mission as promoting, in fact, inspiring interest in the notion of a united Europe. From the signing of the treaties of Rome, well into the 1970's a period many historian refer to as the second wave of European integration, there was no shortage of nationalistic cynics and obstructionists, both in Europe and America. Even as Acheson's optimism dwindled, Monnet saw it as his duty to never lose sight of his ultimate goal, to remain an optimist when the cards were stacked against him, even when his enthusiastic but temperamentally less optimistic disciple of European unity faltered. The combined strength of an Atlantic Community, both Acheson and Monnet believed, would render global war obsolete, lead to the collapse of the Soviet totalitarian system, and allow a "free world" federated system modeled after the United States to flourish in Europe.

Even as late as 1972, a year after Acheson had died, James Reston was writing of Monnet in The New York Times marveling at the ability of "Mr. Europe" at 83 years of age to continue his special role as European advisor to the United States: "The other day when Henry Kissinger was in Paris, he had a talk about the money, trade and security problems of the United States and Europe with Jean Monnet. Ever since Colonel House and Harry Hopkins, White House aides have been turning to him for help, and while they don't always take his advice, he always has something sensible to say." [96]

By constantly renewing, cultivating and prodding his Washington connections from the days of Woodrow Wilson to Richard Nixon, usually working behind the scenes with small coteries of decision makers, Jean Monnet kept the United States committed to the concept of European unity and Atlantic Partnership. Throughout these years Dean Acheson was an important and productive convert.

Endnotes

1 Henry Kissinger, *Years of Upheaval*. Boston, 1982, p. 138.

2 For a good brief overview on Monnet's relationship to the United States see Alfred Grosser, *The Western Alliance: European-American Relations Since 1945*. New York, 1982, Chapter 4, "Jean Monnet's Europe During the Cold War," pp. 101-28.

3 Jean Monnet, *Memoirs*, translated by Richard Mayne. Garden City, NY, 1978, p. 271, (JMM hereafter).

4 For Acheson's views of what constituted an Atlantic community see, Larry Kaplan, "Dean Acheson and the Atlantic Community" in Douglas Brinkley (ed.) *Dean Acheson and the Making of U.S. Foreign Policy*. New York, 1992 pp. 28-54; and Douglas Brinkley, "Dean Acheson and European Unity" in Francis Heller and John Gillingham, Eds., *NATO and the Founding of the Atlantic Alliance* New York, 1992. Most of Acheson's papers pertaining to postwar U.S.-European relations are located at the Harry S. Truman Library, Independence, MO. and the Sterling Memorial Library, Yale University, New Haven, CT, (DGA-HST and DGA-Yale, respectively, hereafter).

5 John Gillingham, "Solving the Ruhr Problem: German Heavy Industry and the Schuman Plan," in Klaus Schwabe Ed. *The Beginnings of the Schuman Plan* Baden-Baden, 1988, p. 402.

6 The answer to this question may come in part from a study of the Monnet travel diaries now underway at the Foundation Jean Monnet Pour l'Europe, Lausanne, Switzerland (FJM, hereafter).

7 Ibid Mar 18, 1961.

8 Leonard Tennyson oral history interview with Katherine Graham, Jul 28, 1981, Washington, DC (transcript), FJM.

9 Monnet travel diaries, FJM.

10 Louis J. Halle, "Acheson: Birth of a Statesman." The New Republic, Vol. 153, Number 20 (Nov 13, 1965), p.23.

11 Howard C. Westwood, *Covington & Burling 1919-1984*. Washington, DC, 1986, pp. 44-45. Also see, Walter Isaacson and Evan Thomas, *The Wise Men: Six Friends and the World They Made* , New York, 1986, pp. 129-30.

12 JMM, p. 45.

13 Clifford P. Hackett, "Jean Monnet, Europe, and the United States," in Giandomenico Majone, Emile Noël and Peter Van den Bossche (Eds.) *Jean Monnet et l'Europe d'aujourd'hui*. Baden, 1989, pp. 168-69.

14 For Monnet's work during the First World War see JMM Chapter 3 , pp.53-77.

15 For Acheson's view of the League of Nations see Dean Acheson, *Morning and Noon: A Memoir*. Boston, 1965, pp. 121-22. Monnet discusses his role with the League in JMM, pp. 78-99.

16 Leonard Tennyson interview with George Ball, Jul 15, 1981 (transcript), FJM.

17 JMM, pp. 99-115.

18 Ibid, p. 115. Also Tennyson interview with Ball, *op. cit.*

19 JMM, pp. 116-149.

20 For Acheson's account of the destroyer-base deal see Acheson,*Morning and Noon*, pp. 161-194; DGA to J.D. Alexander, Jr., Nov 2, 1966; DGA to Philip Goodhart, Feb 15, 1960; and DGA to Quincey Wright, Aug 29, 1940, Series II, Box 38, Folder 1, DGA-Yale.

21 David S. McLellan, *Dean Acheson: The State Department Years*, New York, 1976, p.43.

22 Ibid, pp. 44-46. Also see Dean Acheson, *Present at the Creation: My Years in the State Department*. New York, 1969, pp. 36-86.

23 Robert Nathan, "An Unsung Hero of World War II" in Douglas Brinkley and Clifford Hackett Eds. *Jean Monnet: The Path to European Unity*. New York, 1991, pp. 67-85 (*JM:PEU* hereafter); and Leonard Tennyson oral history interview with Robert Nathan, Dec 18, 1981, Washington, D.C. (transcript), FJM.

24 Robert E. Sherwood, *Roosevelt and Hopkins*, New York, 1948, p. 226.

25 Tennyson interview with George Ball, *op.cit.*

26 For a detailed overview of Acheson's mixed feelings about de Gaulle, see Douglas Brinkley, *Dean Acheson and American Foreign Policy: The Cold War Years 1953-1971.* New Haven, CT, 1992, Chapters 6 and 7.

27 Interview with Joseph Alsop, Mar 12, 1988, Washington, DC.

28 JMM pp. 301-2.

29 Tennyson interview with Katherine Graham, *op. cit.*

30 Dean Acheson *Fragments of My Fleece.* New York, 1971, p. 126.

31 DGA to Michael Janeway, May 24, 1960, Series I. Box, Folder DGA-Yale.

32 John Wills Tuthill, "Jean Monnet: An American Ambassador Recalls a Friend and a Colleague," France Magazine, Winter 1989, pp. 38-40.

33 Leonard Tennyson, interview with Henry Owen, Jun 30, 1981, Washington DC (transcript), FJM.

34 McLellan, *Dean Acheson: The State Department Years*, pp. 44-56; and Acheson *Present at the Creation*, pp. 68-80.

35 Theodore H. White, *In Search of History: A Personal Adventure*, New York, 1979, p. 333.

36 Acheson, *Present at the Creation*, pp. 76-77.

37 Quoted in George Woodbridge et al. in *The Story of the United Nations Relief and Rehabilitation Administration* , New York, 1950, 3 vols., I, p.4.

38 Jean Monnet to DGA (telegram) Feb 11, 1953, Series I, Box 23, Folder 288. DGA-Yale.

39 DGA to Jean Monnet, Mar 4, 1953, Series I, Box 23, Folder 288, DGA-Yale.

40 Dean Acheson, "The Requirements of Reconstruction," address before the Delta Council at Cleveland, Mississippi, May 8, 1947 (transcript), Accession 89-M-44, Box 1, Folder 5, DGA-Yale. For an evaluation of Acheson's speech on the European integration movement, see Ernst H Van Der Beugel, *From Marshall Aid to Atlantic Partnership.* Amsterdam, 1966, pp. 40-49.

41 Irwin Wall, "Jean Monnet, the United States and the French Economic Plan in Brinkley and Hackett , *JM:PEU* pp. 86-113.

42 Jean Monnet to DGA, May 21, 1949, Series I, Box 23, Folder 288, DGA-Yale. For an understanding of the Acheson-Monnet relationship during the Truman era see Richard J. Barnet, *The Alliance.* New York, 1983, Chapter 3: "Atlantic Civilization and Its Discontents: Mr. Acheson and M. Monnet Rebuild Europe," pp. 95-143.

43 Dean Acheson, "Statement by Acheson," Department of State Bulletin, vol. 24, No. 663 (Mar 10, 1951).

44 Dean Acheson, *Sketches From Life of Men I Have Known* , New York, 1961 p. 103.

45 Quoted in McGeorge Bundy, Ed. *The Pattern of Responsibility: Speeches and Statements of Dean Acheson* , Cambridge, OH, 1951, p. 55.

46 Quoted from Dean Acheson, "The Dilemma of Our Times," address at the University of Connecticut, Nov 18, 1963, Series III, Box 51, Folder 6, DGA-Yale. For Acheson's gratitude to the European statesman who worked with him on integration problems, see Dean Acheson, "Europe Decision or Drift,"

Foreign Affairs, vol. 44 (1966), pp. 198-205; and "Germany in the New Europe," address to the German American Club, Oct 18, 1963, DGA-Yale.

47   Dean Acheson, "Economic Collaboration Basic to Our National Policy," Department of State Bulletin, vol. 22, No. 558, Mar 13, 1950, pp. 403-405.

48   Lawrence S. Kaplan, "Dean Acheson and the Atlantic Community" in Douglas Brinkley (ed.). Dean Acheson and the Making of U.S. Foreign Policy New York, 1992.

49   Dean Acheson, "Princeton Seminar," Oct 10, 1953, Reel 3, Track 2, quoted from Kaplan, "Dean Acheson and the Atlantic Community," op. cit., p.17.

50   Lloyd C. Gardner, "Economic Foreign Policy and the Quest for Security," in Norman A. Graebner, Ed., The National Security: Its Theory and Practice 1945-1960 , New York,1986, pp. 88-89.

51   Acheson, Present at the Creation, p. 382; JMM, p. 301 and Alan Bullock, Ernest Bevin: Foreign Secretary 1945-1954 , New York, 1983, Chapter 21, pp. 766-790.

52   Dean Acheson, Present at the Creation, p. 304, for the role Monnet played in influencing Acheson's attitude toward the Schuman Plan see interview with Acheson, Jun 30, 1971 (by Theodore A. Wilson and Richard McKinzie), HST Library.

53   Acheson, Sketches from Life of Men I Have Known, Ch. 2,. Also see Schuman-Acheson Correspondence, particularly Schuman to DGA, Mar 5, 1953, Series I, Box 28, Folder 359 DGA-Yale.

54   Dean Acheson, "Princeton Seminar," Oct 10, 1953, Reel 3, Track 2, (transcript), DGA-HST.

55   JMM, pp. 349-371; and "Memorandum of Conversation with Mr. Jean Monnet." May 6, 1952, Monnet File, DGA-HST.

56   Memorandum of Conversation (Monnet-Acheson), Dec 15, 1952, DGA-HST.

57   Acheson, Present at Creation, pp. 707-708.

58   Acheson, State Department Farewell Address, Jan 14, 1953, Accession 89-m-44, Box 1, Folder 6, DGA-Yale.

59   Grosser, Western Alliance: p. 104.

60   JMM, p. 270.

61   David K.E. Bruce to DGA, Mar 4, 1958, Series I, Box 3, Folder 50, DGA-Yale.

62   For reason's why EDC failed and why he refused to seek re-election to the presidency of the ECSC, see JMM pp. 275-76.

63   Lennard Tennyson interview with John Tuthill, Apr 15, 1981. Washington, DC (transcript), FJM.

64   JMM, pp. 405-416. See also memorandum of conversation (Dulles-Monnet), Oct 25, 1955, Department of State, Central Files, 400. 119/3-2855, FRUS: 1955-57, pp. 275-76.

65   For Monnet on Euratom see JMM, pp. 418-27; Lawrence Scheinman, Atomic Energy Policy in France Under the Fourth Republic , Princeton, 1965, and Jonathan E. Helmreich, "The United States and the Formation of Euratom," Diplomatic History, vol. 15, No. 3 (Summer 1991), pp. 387-410: and J. Robert Schaetzel, in Temoinage a La Memoire de Jean Monnet, Lausanne, 1989, p. 483.

66   DGA to Frank M. Shea, Feb 4, 1958, Series I, Box 28, Folder 364. DGA-Yale.

67   Dean Acheson, "The Illusion of Disengagement," Foreign Affairs, vol. 36 (1958), p. 379.

68   For Monnet's relationship with members of the Kennedy Administration see Arthur Schlesinger, Jr. A Thousand Days: John F. Kennedy in the White House, Boston, 1965, pp. 842-66; Grosser, The Western Alliance, pp. 101-128; George W. Ball, The Past Has Another Pattern: Memoirs, New York,1982, pp. 208-222;

and Brinkley, *Dean Acheson:*, Chapter 6.; and Name Index and other files, Kennedy Library, Cambridge, MA (hereafter, JFKL).

[69] Monnet letter to DGA 1961.

[70] George M. Taber, *John F. Kennedy and A Uniting Europe* , Bruges, 1969, pp. 96-98.

[71] Dean Acheson interview, Apr 27 1964, JFKL, pp. 10-11; Dana Adams Schmidt, "Kennedy Pledges More Aid to NATO-Acheson to Help," New York Times, Feb 9, 1961, p. 1; and JMM pp. 462-472.

[72] Dean Acheson, NATO Report, "A Review of North Atlantic Problems for the Future." Mar 1961, National Security File, Box 220, JFKL.

[73] Interview with Joseph W. Alsop, Mar 11, 1988, Washington, D.C.

[74] Joseph Kraft, *The Grand Design* , New York, 1962, p.24.

[75] Economist, Jan 27 1962, p. 324. For other Monnet friendships in Kennedy Administration see Taber, *John F. Kennedy and A Uniting Europe,* pp. 40-43.

[76] Interviews with J. Robert Schaetzel, Oct 16, 1987, Bethesda, MD; and McGeorge Bundy Apr 7, 1988, New York, NY.

[77] Ball, *The Past Has Another Pattern*, pp. 69-99; and Ball, "Introduction" in Brinkley and Hackett *JM:PEU*, pp. xix.

[78] Memorandum for the President, Subject: Luncheon with Jean Monnet, Mar 6, 1961, National Security Files, Box 321, JFKL.

[79] See Kennedy letter to Monnet reprinted in JMM p. 472. A transcript of Monnet's Freedom Award address can be found in the Acheson Papers, Post-Secretarial Papers 1953-1971, DGA-HST.

[80] Ibid, pp. 471-473.

[81] Jean Monnet travel diary, FJM.

[82] James Reston, New York Times, Apr 11, 1962.

[83] Interview with Joseph W. Alsop, Mar 11, 1988.

[84] Interview with J. Robert Schaetzel, Apr 11, 1990.

[85] Kennedy's Philadelphia, speech, as well as a later one in Naples , Italy on European unity, are in *The Burden and the Glory: President Kennedy's Public Statements and Speeches*, Allan Nevins, ed., New York, 1969, pp. 136-140.

[86] Quoted in J. Robert Schaetzel, *The Unhinged Alliance: America and the European Community* , New York, 1975, p. 41.

[87] For Acheson-JFK policy discussions see Douglas Brinkley and G.E. Thomas, "Dean Achson's Opposition to Liberation in Africa," *TransAfrica Forum*, Vol. 5, No. 4 (Summer 1988), pp. 62-81.

[88] DGA to Jean Monnet, Nov 23, 1962, Series I, Box 23, Folder 288, DGA-Yale.

[89] Interview with Lucius Battle, Mar 14, 1988, Washington, D.C.

[90] Monnet travel diaries, *FJM*. For Monnet's efforts to keep LBJ on the path to Atlantic Partnership see JMM pp. 473. After Monnet sent President Johnson a copy of recent Action Committee for the United States of Europe declaration, LBJ thanked him and added: "I can assure you that the integration of Europe and her partnership with the United States remain fundamental principles of the foreign policy of the United States," President Lyndon Johnson to Jean Monnet, Jun 24, 1964. Papers of LBJ, IT 5-4, Box 2, Economic Community, Johnson Library, Austin, Texas.

[91] DGA to Jean Monnet, Nov 1962, Series I, Box 23, Folder 288; Monnet to DGA, Nov 23 1962, Series I Box 28, Folder 356, DGA-Yale.

[92] DGA to J. Robert Schaetzel, Apr 1, 1963, Series I, Box 28, Folder 356, DGA-Yale.

[93] DGA to Dr. Kurt Birrenbach, Feb 19, 1963, Series I, Box 3, Folder 36, DGA-Yale.

94 DGA to Shepard Stone, Jan 3, 1970, Series I, Box 29, Folder 376, DGA-Yale. For another example of Acheson's growing Common Market skepticism see, Dean Acheson testimony, Senate Subcommittee on National Security and International Operations, *Hearings on the Atlantic Alliance,* 1966, pp. 18-20.

95 Monnet travel diaries, FJM.

96 James Reston, New York Times, Dec 18, 1972.

5
Eisenhower, Dulles, Monnet and the Uniting of Europe

Pascaline Winand

On July 3, 1951, General Dwight D. Eisenhower made a strong plea for European economic and political integration before the English Speaking Union in the great ballroom of Grosvenor Place, Park Lane; nearly one thousand dinner guests were present, among them, Winston S. Churchill. The newly appointed allied commander in Europe had quite recently spoken with Jean Monnet. The Frenchman could not but feel some satisfaction in recognizing echoes of his conversation with Eisenhower in the language and substance of his London speech. Going as far as advocating the establishment of a European federation, Eisenhower defended the merits of European unity on the grounds that it would allow for a more efficient division of labor and resources and ease the flow of trade between Western European nations. The benefits to NATO would be incalculable: a united Europe would have the political and psychological self-confidence, the economic health and hence the resources to assist the United States in furthering the objectives of the Atlantic Pact, no longer merely as a recipient of American aid but as a full-fledged partner.[1]

Already as chief of staff of the United States Army from 1945 until 1948, then as president of Columbia University from 1948 until 1951, Eisenhower had been preoccupied with the prospects for a united Europe. As Supreme Allied Commander in Europe (SACEUR), the general came to believe that a United States of Europe was a *sine qua non* for finding a satisfactory solution to the problem of European security. The united Europe he envisaged encompassed all of those countries which were part of NATO at the time plus Germany, with Sweden, Spain, Greece and Yugoslavia as strong potential candidates for joining a united Europe; the United Kingdom could be omitted "if necessary." A divided Europe, he felt, stood to lose much from shortages of manpower in some countries, excess productive capacity in others, and most of all from Franco-German dissension, all of which posed problems for the viability of the organization of an effective defense mechanism for the West. A single government for Europe, on the other hand, would have the advantage of rationalizing European efforts towards Western defense, while at the same time allowing for a reduction of American help to European defense "both in amount and duration." [2]

Yet Eisenhower's speech did not go so far as to support the supranational European army concept put forward by the French in the fall of 1950, mainly as a counterproposal to German rearmament within NATO. Similarly to President Truman, Dean Acheson and George Marshall, Eisenhower initially shirked from being associated with the project which seemed "almost inherently, to include every kind of obstacle, difficulty, and fantastic notion that misguided humans could put together in one package." Eisenhower believed the plan would most likely encourage division rather than unity in Western Europe, and was militarily unsound and ineffective. Above all, Eisenhower strongly suspected the French to have put forward the proposal for a European army on the assumption that the plan would never be adopted, and that German rearmament if contingent upon the realization of a European army, would topple down with it, or at the very least be considerably delayed.[3] Despite these initial misgivings, Eisenhower shifted his position on the European army during the summer of 1951 and became one of its staunchest proponents in its successive avatars, first as a European Defense Force, then as the ill-fated European Defense Community.

A lunch appointment with Jean Monnet at twelve thirty on Thursday, June 21, 1951, at the Hotel Astoria in Paris was apparently determinant for this change of heart.[4] The meeting had been instigated thanks to the adroit efforts of the United States High Commissioner for Germany John McCloy, and Ambassador to France David K. E. Bruce, both long-time friends of Jean Monnet. Earlier in June McCloy had written to Eisenhower to urge him to talk with Jean Monnet, whom he presented as one of the individuals most likely to influence the French position on the European army.[5] For if McCloy was a fervent advocate of European integration, he held strong reservations about the scheme of a European army as it then stood on the French agenda. In its current form, he told Monnet, the plan seemed to be nothing but a device to delay or avoid a German contribution to NATO. In addition the European army did not make much sense from a military point of view. Could the French perhaps drop off "such excrescencies as non-divisional units?" [6] He would be glad to support the European army scheme, he later wrote Eisenhower, but only if the plan were militarily effective.

Eisenhower thought much along the same lines, but doubted that the scheme could be made viable from a military viewpoint. During his meeting with Eisenhower and some of his collaborators[7] at the Hotel Astoria where the SHAPE (Supreme Headquarters Allied Powers, Europe) planning group had set up shop, Monnet convinced Eisenhower that the crux of the matter was not so much military effectiveness as rather political soundness. Essential were not the size of the divisions or other technicalities, but the creation of a common European outlook, a "solidarity of destiny." Eisenhower understood the point well. What Monnet proposed to him was to have "the Germans and the French serve under the same uniform"; the real issue was to organize relations between men, thus the problem was "more a human problem than a military one." [8]   Reassured as to the motivations of the European army scheme, Eisenhower decided to support it.

But the Eisenhower-Monnet cooperation was a two way street. If Monnet succeeded in convincing Eisenhower that the plan for a European army should be viewed within the larger framework of European integration, without which no viable solution could be found to the German problem, Eisenhower and his collaborators in turn put pressure on the French to integrate the European army strictly within NATO, so that there would in fact be no autonomous European command. In other words: the United States would support the creation of a European army only if it were organized within the safe compounds of the Atlantic Community. This would have the advantage of deflecting the fears of the French and other European nations as to the potential domination of one of the members of the European army over the others, particularly Germany. It would also provide the United States with a means of controlling the evolution of the European army. In addition, top-echelon American policy-makers, including Acheson, insisted that there should be no second-class status for the Germans. The European army would be formed on the basis of a full equality of rights for all member nations, or it would not see the day. Such was the "constructive and vigorous leadership" which Eisenhower felt the United States must exert to bring about an acceptable version of the European army.

By the end of July 1951, about one month after the Eisenhower-Monnet meeting at the Astoria, President Truman approved a policy of support for German rearmament within the context of the European defense force. Support for the European army concept, although considerably watered down to the taste of some, had now become American policy. Eisenhower's shift of position in favor of the

European army proved to be decisive in overcoming Acheson's and Truman's strong initial reservations on the matter.

In the fall of 1951, Monnet's association with Eisenhower resumed when the Frenchman was asked to be one of the "Three Wise Men" of the newly created Temporary Council Committee (TCC). The task of the three-man committee mainly consisted in matching NATO military needs with the economic capacities of the member nations. Chairman was Averell Harriman, President's Truman Special Adviser on Foreign Affairs, with Hugh Gaitskell, the British Chancellor of the Exchequer, and Jean Monnet acting as vice-chairmen.[9]

On the morning of November 24, 1951, Monnet came to see Eisenhower. He could not go to the Rome meeting where the North Atlantic Council (NAC) was holding its eighth session and would consider preliminary reports of the TCC. Would Eisenhower please stress "the need for European amalgamation -- political as well as the earlier steps involved in the Schuman Plan and the European army ?" Eisenhower obliged. That same day Eisenhower wrote in his diary that he would do so since he believed "implicitly in the idea...even if some of the politicos present" resented his "intrusion into their field." Unless "Denmark, Holland, Belgium, Luxembourg, France, Italy and western Germany" formed "one Federated State", wrote the General, the millions of dollars the United States had spent on the Economic Cooperation Administration (ECA) would be wasted. On the other hand the United States could "afford to spend a lot", to encourage the development of a unified Europe because they would "get something successful, strong, sturdy." [10] During his presidency, Eisenhower would repeatedly emphasize the distinct link he perceived between American fiscal responsibility and economic viability on the one hand, and national security on the other. His support for European integration stemmed in part from his belief that it would increase the economic strength of Western European nations, which would then combine their resources to foot most of the bill to insure their own security, thereby freeing American resources.

On November 26, the general addressed members of the NAC in terms that showed him to be a faithful spokesman of Jean Monnet. Not only did he emphasize the advantages of Western European unification---economic, military and political---but he also un-equivocally voiced his support for the creation of a European Defense Force. Such a force, he said, would incorporate German strength without having it pose a threat to the alliance. "German help," said Eisenhower, "will be tremendously important if freely given; and it can be so given, I believe, through a European Defense Force. It would stand alongside the Schuman Plan---which must be successful---and the two would constitute great steps toward the goal of complete European unity!" [11]   In mid-December the General testified before Harriman and the TCC. Commending the results of the work of the TCC, to which Monnet had largely contributed,[12]   Eisenhower also took this opportunity to reaffirm his strong support for the European army concept.[13]

Monnet's method of developing an idea and then seeking the man who had the power to apply it was successful.[14] Not only did Eisenhower agree to be Monnet's spokesman when he was still serving as SACEUR, but the General later continued to be a staunch supporter of European integration in its various guises, when serving in the high office of President of the United States. Jean Monnet thus made his ideas known where they had a good chance of being effective: SACEUR and, opportunely, the presidential office. He sought the advice of his friend John McCloy who identified for him the man in whose hands the power to gather official American support for the European army lay.[15]

But while Monnet's influence was key in Eisenhower's decision eventually to support the EDC, Monnet's exchange of views with Eisenhower and other American leaders in turn prompted Jean Monnet and Hervé Alphand to transform their first version of a European army into a European Defense Community. The new EDC heeded American concerns for German participation on the basis of equality and strictly integrated the European Defense Community within NATO.

By the end of 1951, Eisenhower and Monnet, who until then did not know each other well, were on a friendship basis. Shortly after Christmas, Eisenhower sent Monnet a letter in which he thanked him for his New Year's present, most likely some bottles of the delectable Monnet cognac which the Frenchman used to send to his best friends and associates once a year. The letter showed Eisenhower's esteem and friendship for Jean Monnet. "[I was] Touched by [your] kindly thoughtfulness", Eisenhower wrote. "Although the assignment to this post brought to my wife and to me many disappointments due to the severance of ties that seem to grow more valuable as the years pass, yet we have been compensated by the opportunity of forming new friend-ships among people that we admire and esteem. Among these we are bold enough, and most certainly exceedingly proud, to number you." [16]

When Eisenhower was elected U.S. President one year later, Monnet sent him the following message: "May I offer you, Mr

Eisenhower, my most sincere congratulations on your election for the great office of President of the United States. I would add my very best wishes for the attainment in these years which can prove decisive for the unity of Europe, the prosperity of our countries and for peace of the momentous objectives which we have all set before us and which I know are so close to your heart." [17]   Eisenhower's answer was short and to the point: "Thank you for your message and look forward to continuing coop[eration] for the great goals ahead." [18]

Eisenhower knew Monnet from the war years, although the Monnet/Eisenhower connection was not close at the time. In 1943, General Eisenhower was in Algiers to prepare a peripheral attack on the Axis, and organize French Africa both politically and militarily to make it a safe basis for subsequent operations. On February 23 Jean Monnet left Washington where he had been active since August 1940 in mobilizing American production for the war effort, and arrived in Algiers four days later. Harry Hopkins, with the approval of President Roosevelt, had sent him to Algiers to supervise the equipment of French forces in North Africa. Through this assignment, Monnet was in contact with Eisenhower, in whom he could already perceive "the human and moral qualities that were to make him a great statesman." [19]   The two men might very well have exchanged views on the future of Europe. On December 31 1943, now back in Washington, Monnet sent the general his best wishes for the New Year and "the great enterprise he [was] going to lead." Always the practical man, he took this opportunity to arrange to meet with him "on the first day in Paris soon." [20]

During his time in Algiers Monnet was not only active in reconciling the two "prima donna" French generals Henri Giraud and Charles de Gaulle, but also gave considerable thought to the organization of post-war Europe. Monnet reflected "there would be no peace in Europe if the States were reconstituted on the basis of national sovereignty with its corollaries of political prestige and economic protectionism." European countries needed larger markets to insure prosperity for their people, but such prosperity was beyond reach unless "European States formed a Federation or a 'European entity' which transformed them into a common economic unity." [21]

In a conversation with General de Gaulle, in October 1943, Monnet told his interlocutor that he could envisage a political division of Germany only if each German state were part of a European whole, and shared the same advantages as the non-German elements of this European entity. Monnet also advocated the creation of "a European industrial land notably encompassing the Ruhr, the Saar, the Rhineland, Luxembourg, and in which the iron and steel industries would be exploited to the benefit of Europe as a whole by European nations themselves." [22]   In doing this, Monnet hoped to excise Germany of its main war making industries, coal and steel, and to channel German energies towards the larger goal of European economic unification.   In other words, Monnet was already thinking of the antecedants to the coal and steel community.

John Foster Dulles was thinking along much the same lines as Jean Monnet, with whom he often discussed his own ideas for European unification.   During the Second World War Monnet worked in the British Supply Council in Washington which Dulles advised as legal counsel; this facilitated frequent contacts between the two men, whose association dated back to the bustling days of 1920's Wall Street.[23]   In the immediate years following the First World War, a young Dulles then serving as adviser at the Versailles peace conference had fought hard to prevent the war victors from forcing huge reparation payments on Germany that would undermine its economy and lead her to resort once again to warfare, with dismal consequences for the prosperity of Europe.

Throughout the 1920s Dulles expressed deep concern for European economic viability and political stability, upon which much of American prosperity depended, and emphasized the need for the removal of trade barriers and the dilution of sovereignty in Europe and in the world at large.[24]   Dulles later pursued and refined this line of thought, and spoke of a European federation. As early as September 1941 he claimed that the solution to the war-breeding political divisions of the old continent lay in "the political reorganization of continental Europe as a federated commonwealth." [25] In January 1942 Dulles, now president of the foreign affairs commission of the Federal Council of Churches of Christ, wrote in Fortune that the United States would serve its own interests by fostering the federation of Europe in the post-war years.[26]   Dulles lunched with Jean Monnet about two years later and agreed with his friend that "if Europe remains as twenty five or twenty eight separate states with two great Powers (U.S. and Russia, with Britain as a possible third power) they will be merely torn apart by rival jealousies and maneuverings." [27]

What preoccupied Dulles most was to find a viable solution to the German problem; a European federation seemed to be part of the answer. "Germany ought to be integrated into a unified Europe," [28] he wrote in 1942. During the summer and fall of 1946, more and more

convinced of the need for European economic and political unity, Dulles
doubted it would ever see the day if "a central German government
ha[d] exclusive control of the resources which constitute[d] the economic
heart of Europe [particularly the Ruhr and Rhine areas.]" [29]
Addressing the National Publishers Association on January 17, 1947 he
then advised the war victors to think of Western Europe as a single
economic unit of which the "basin of the Rhine, with its coal and
industrious man power" constituted "the natural economic heart."
"From that area", said Dulles, "ought to flow vitality not merely for
Germans but for Germany's western neighbors. If that happens Western
Europe , at least, with its 200 million people, could develop into a more
prosperous and stable land." To him the German problem called "for
some application of the federal solution" to Europe much after the
pattern of the United States.[30]

      In March 1947 Dulles, now a member of the American team at
the Moscow foreign ministers conference, proposed the creation of a
Ruhr commission to his American colleagues, who did not, however,
respond with the enthusiasm he had anticipated and merely chose to
make a vague proposal to develop some international control of the
Ruhr. The commission Dulles proposed would have possessed the
authority to allocate "coal and other heavy products (to be defined)"
and would have been responsible for the "equitable distribution as
between domestic use and export to one or another place." [31] Members of
this commission were to be France, the Netherlands, Belgium,
Switzerland, Czechoslovakia, Poland, Denmark and Italy; which gave
it an essentially European character. One year later, during a meeting
of the Council on Foreign Relations in New York, in which his brother
Allen held a prominent position, Foster again emphasized that solving
the problem of the Ruhr was a key to building the new Europe.[32]

      By a curious coincidence, a few weeks later, in February 1948,
Lewis Douglas, with whom Monnet frequently met at the time, made
the suggestion to create a European authority that would control the
Ruhr as well as other European regions and be one of the milestones on
the road towards European economic integration.[33] This was nothing
less than the Schuman Plan in its infancy. Had he and Monnet
discussed this proposal? Whatever the case may be it did not arouse
any great enthusiasm in French quarters, while the American
administration did not think it viable in the current international
situation. On the whole it is safe to say that the idea of the necessity
of the internationalization or perhaps of the Europeanization of the
Ruhr was very much part of the thinking of Dulles as well as other
American policy-makers at the time. Yet while Dulles advocated the

integration of Germany and the Ruhr area within a unified Europe, he did not clearly propose to submit European regions beyond the German ones to the authority of the Ruhr Commission he envisaged as did some of his colleagues and Jean Monnet, who had already outlined such a solution as early as 1943. Monnet and Dulles were united in their deep commitment to the goal of European unity as an essential element of peace, although this did not mean an agreement on the means to reach this common goal.

John Foster Dulles had met Jean Monnet at the Versailles peace conference of 1919, where Dulles was acting as legal counsel to Bernard Baruch, the United States representative on the reparations commission. John Maynard Keynes and Jean Monnet were serving on the British and French delegations, respectively.[34] Foster Dulles and Jean Monnet were of the same vintage year of 1888 and soon became close friends,[35] as too did Jean Monnet and Allen Dulles. Following the peace conference, after a short passage as deputy secretary-general to the League of Nations in Geneva, and spending some time in Cognac to reorganize the family business in order to save it from ruin, Monnet became the vice president of the Société française Blair and Co. Foreign Corp, which he and Elisha Walker, the director general of Blair, had just created in Paris in August of 1926.[36] From that moment until his death over fifty years later, Monnet was in touch with many of the movers and shakers of Wall Street. John McCloy, Donald Swatland and Foster Dulles, to name only a few, soon numbered among his friends. In early 1927 Jean Monnet left for Warsaw, where he and his young collaborator, René Pleven, endeavored to stabilize the zloty. In this instance, as in many others, Monnet enlisted the services of Foster Dulles, whom he respected as an associate and valued as a friend.[37]

In the wake of the chaos that followed the suicide of Ivar Kreuger, the Swedish "Match King" in March 1932, Foster Dulles, then acting as legal counsel to a committee of bankers holding several millions in debentures of Kreuger and Toll, managed to have his friend appointed as the foreign liquidator of Kreuger and Toll. Later on, Dulles, then head of Sullivan and Cromwell, convinced his titular superior William Nelson Cromwell, to support a partnership between George Murnane, one of his old friends and business associates, and Jean Monnet. The two of them proposed to organize a New York firm that would help various enterprises get a fresh start by acting as their financial agent. Dulles' recommendation to Cromwell indicated he had full confidence in Monnet's and Murnane's business talents: "I have long felt that they would make an ideal combination, and the fact that they are apparently coming together is largely due to my efforts in the belief that if they did so they would be exceedingly successful in becoming engaged in enterprises which in turn would produce a large amount of legal business." Dulles showed he was prepared to back his words with a material contribution when he proposed that Sullivan and Cromwell put up $50,000 in support of the plan, half of which he would supply himself.[38]

Jean Monnet frequently visited Dulles in his New York home, and a deep friendship ensued between their two wives: Janet Dulles and Silvia Monnet. Many years later, when Foster lay on his hospital bed, dying of cancer, Monnet wrote to him fondly remembering the years before he joined the United States Government, their friendship, and Foster's "kindness to [him] in New York." [39]

Jean Monnet's portrait of Foster Dulles in his memoirs bears testimony to his lasting admiration and affection for him:

> I had met him at the Peace Conference, and we had become friends. I appreciated his great ability, which proved useful to us in Warsaw and elsewhere. But above all I admired his great strength of character and the moral authority that he already commanded outside his professional sphere.... [He] was deeply religious and profoundly convinced that liberty is essential to civilization. I have always known him as decisive and inflexibly determined, just as history paints him, and at the same time warm, fond of good living, and an affectionate friend. One day the world will come to see him, alongside Eisenhower, as a man of great stature, a symbol of willpower that aroused conflicting passions. But this was not Foster Dulles the man. The Dulles I knew and loved was like many other men, but greater and more upright than most.[40]

Foster Dulles, the friend, and the associate who believed in European integration as one of the key elements of post-war peace, was a rather sympathetic and courageous character, yet Foster Dulles, the public figure, was rather clumsy in his public statements and was the object of much criticism and dislike both at home and abroad. Dulles' biographer Townsend Hoopes has noted that "in the bosom of his family or with close and trusted associates, he could be warm, sentimental, occasionally jocular, exhibiting a hearty, even bubbly Victorian humor." This description comes close to the warm and generous character Monnet remembered. On the other hand "in all other groups he was notable for a flat hardness and a striking insensitivity to people at large." Much of this attitude was the result of his upbringing which had "denied him a normal young manhood." [41] Dulles' friendship with Monnet and his dedication to the cause of European integration do not of course excuse clumsiness and insensitivity in presenting his ideas, which showed nothing but bad statesmanship, but they do uncover another perspective on the man, which will perhaps help rehabilitate him somewhat to his critics.

In 1949 Governor Thomas Dewey appointed Foster Dulles to fill an unexpired U.S. Senate term. Yet Foster's term as New York Senator (R-NY) was short-lived. After his November 1950 defeat when he ran for a full-term mandate, Dulles served as special consultant and adviser for the state department and helped negotiate the Japanese peace treaty from spring, 1950 into 1951. Although Dulles spent most of his time educating himself about the Asian situation and negotiating the treaty, he still found time to correspond with Monnet, and occasionally to see him. When Dulles' book *War or Peace* was published in 1950, Foster sent an advance copy of it to Monnet.[42] Monnet, who then served as Commissaire Général of the French Modernization and Equipment Plan, immediately wrote him back on April 4 thanking him. That same day Monnet read in the papers that the administration might enable his friend "to enter again actively in the direction of foreign policy." Monnet quickly added a handwritten note to the typed letter he had already prepared: "I do hope that if this really happens you will not hesitate. Now is the time where clear views expressed with courage will determine our destinies. I wish that I may read soon that you have accepted to be 'harnessed' again." [43]

Later on that month Dulles received another letter from 18, rue de Martignac. It was a letter of introduction for a young friend of Monnet, Jean Servan Schreiber, whom Monnet said was "the first Frenchman to receive a state department grant for travel and study in the United States under the Smith-Mundt bill." Monnet hoped Dulles would see him so that he could "bring back with him a complete picture of the conditions in your country, and thus be more able to inform French public opinion." [44] It was indeed part of the Monnet method not only to identify sources of power, but also to bring in contact with these sources associates or friends whom he esteemed and could serve the cause of European integration. The journalistic skills of a young man with a promising future like Servan Schreiber were of course not to be neglected. In this case as in many, Monnet demonstrated one of his greatest talents: networking.[45]

On May 23, 1950, a few weeks after the announcement of the Schuman plan, Foster Dulles, who was about to leave for Japan in a few days, wrote Monnet a long letter. Foster Dulles was not part of the co-conspirors who evolved the Schuman plan, and Jean Monnet does not seem to have put him in the confidence, but the plan espoused much of Dulles' own preoccupations. Dulles had long been convinced that integrating Germany within Western Europe and the West and encouraging a French-German rapprochement were the keys to any lasting European peace settlement. He had also thought of Europeanizing German coal and Steel production, so that it would benefit not only Germany but other European nations. In *War or Peace* Dulles wrote that it was the "enlightened self-interest" of the United States to encourage European unity; this, he felt, would not happen without the United States exerting "strong pressure" on the Europeans.[46]

Monnet and Dulles differed on this point: there was a substantial difference between American hegemonic pressure, that is outright demands, and American encouragement and support, which Monnet viewed as essential for the success of European unification. With the Schuman plan initiative, strong pressure from the United States was not needed for it was, without doubt, a European initiative. The Schuman plan offered a chance to put an end to the age-old Franco-German conflict, integrate Germany within the West and use the coal and steel community as a stepping stone towards more far-reaching steps on the road towards European federation. Dulles was quick to see the political implications which seemed to him "even more important than the economic." "A genuine union of interest between Germany and France is an enormous insurance for a peaceful future," he wrote Monnet. "The proposal brings a new spirit into a western world which has so far not been able to imagine anything better than going down the rather dreary road which in the past has usually led to war." [47]

Dulles' enthusiasm did not match the initial reaction of Dean Acheson who first saw the Schuman plan as the worst cartel ever. Fears were also expressed in various quarters in the United States that the plan was nothing more than a new and larger governmental cartel. The danger that the Schuman Plan would impede free trade and encourage the recrudescence of national and international cartels appeared real. Monnet quickly moved to reassure Acheson that the Schuman Plan was anything but a cartel.[48] He was much aided in his efforts by John McCloy and David Bruce, who had been a close collaborator of his since the Marshall Plan days, and was now ambassador to France.[49]

Bruce immediately realized the importance of the Schuman proposal, even though he held some doubts about the complex motives of the French government. Overruling some subordinates, including his economic counselor, Robert Terrill, Bruce stressed the importance of the plan in a cable to the state department, which also included many skeptics, and flew to London where he met with Acheson convinced him that it was essential that the United States react positively to the Schuman Plan.[50] A little more than one week after the Schuman declaration, President Truman hailed the plan as a token of "French leadership in the solution of European problems." Yet this did not end the debate within the administration.

If some American officials were worried about the danger of cartelization, they were also preoccupied by the possible emergence of a "third force" Europe.[51] The Schuman Plan was open to "all countries that wanted to participate in it; " did this mean that a united Europe would adopt a neutral attitude towards the United States? The fear of an independent Europe, aloof from the United States was sufficiently real for Dulles to suggest that Monnet clarify this particular point: "As I understand it," wrote Dulles, "there is no desire to be 'neutral' except in the sense of not wanting a war, and we all want to be neutral in that sense. If building up new strength in Europe by ending the age-old rivalries between France and Germany will contribute a new strength against war and end the temptations of some to maneuver the Germans against the French, and vice versa, that is surely a good thing for peace." [52] Dulles also gave Monnet some advice on how to get the Schuman proposal through.   The plan had originally "gained momentum because it was not first haggled over by all sorts of committees," if Monnet kept up the momentum by continuing to stay away from committees Dulles felt "quite confident that no serious roadblocks" would be "thrown in" by the United States.[53]

Yet Dulles was far removed from the immediate Washington circles that might have had some impact on the fortunes of the Schuman Plan at the time. In January 1951 and again in December 1951, Dulles thanked his friend for the two bottles of special gift brandy which Jean Monnet had sent him and regretted he had not been able to follow "as closely as heretofore the European situation." [54] Had Dulles' assignment been in the west rather than in the east, he and Monnet "might have worked together." [55] Dulles nevertheless continued to correspond with Monnet, occasionally sending him press clippings and copies of his speeches.[56]

On March 21 1951, Dulles congratulated his friend for "initialing the Schuman Plan." [57] About one month later, just the day after the Paris Treaty had in fact been signed, Monnet thanked Dulles for his congratulations, and always thinking ahead, wrote him he was anxious to see him on his next trip to the United States. When that would be he did not know for much depended on whether elections

would be held in France in June.[58]   Dulles later wrote him that he
might himself be in Europe in June and hoped their trips would not
conflict.[59] The two friends did in fact meet in June, twice at the
American Embassy residence in France, and once at Monnet's country
home at Houjarray.[60] This was about ten days before Monnet's meeting
with Eisenhower, which was decisive in convincing the general to go
along with the EDC. Dulles and Monnet most likely discussed the EDC
and the Schuman Plan on this occasion, although the details of their
conversations are not known.

By March 1952, the American Senate had ratified the Japanese
Peace Treaty and the Pacific Security Treaties. Foster Dulles'
association with the Truman administration was thus finished.
Without any apparent bitterness Dulles wrote Monnet that he now
expected "primarily to resume private life." "The separation from the
Administration" was "entirely normal and as contemplated on both
sides", and as far as he could tell "in every respect friendly" despite
some efforts of the American Press "to play it up as a 'break.'" [61]
Monnet's well-publicized trip to the United States in April and May
unfortunately found Dulles away. The trip was a major publicity
success for "the father of Europe" and his brainchild, the European
Coal and Steel Community. Upon his arrival in the United States,
Monnet was hailed in the New York Times as "one of the main
architects of a new and unified Europe." [62]

Meanwhile Monnet kept in touch with Eisenhower whom he
hoped he would see in Europe before the general left France for the
United States. Thanking him for his contribution to the solution of
European problems, Monnet tried to keep the general informed of his
own thinking, thereby perhaps hoping to consolidate Eisenhower's
support for European integration and future contributions to this cause in
the future. In a letter to him on May 13, Monnet enclosed a copy of a
speech he had made in Washington D.C. before the National Press
Club. This major address saluted the Schuman and Pleven Plans as "the
beginning of a revolution in Europe's political, military, economic, and
institutional life."   That revolution, Monnet said, would "do away
with the causes of the conflicts of Europe, the greatest of which ha[d]
been the age-old opposition between Germany and France" and "must
now be carried forward towards complete unification." In a flight of
oratory Monnet suggested that the unification of Europe was "the most
important political and economic undertaking of our time." "Because
Americans understand this," he continued, "you have consistently
supported and encouraged our efforts to make a united Europe. I believe
this is the first time in history that a country with such a

preponderance of power as the United States is giving active and vital support to different peoples in their efforts to unite in a strong and free community."

Monnet also dealt with the European army and the German question. In doing so he directly launched a counter attack against the recent Soviet proposals which proposed the reconstituting of a German state and a German national army. Such a proposal, said Monnet, posed the threat of re-opening old wounds, it would revive nationalism in Germany and reawake "nationalistic feelings of Frenchman and other Europeans against the Germans." German unity, insisted Monnet, could only find place within a United Europe, only then would the errors of the past which had brought disaster to Europe and the world not be repeated. Always the optimist, Monnet adroitly cast his speech in an essentially positive mode. Rather than describing all the difficulties on the way towards European integration, he chose instead to describe to his audience the main milestones on the road to unification and presented his topic in terms of goals and achievements.[63]

The Monnet method of setting a goal, then moving towards that goal without thought that it might not be successful, had the advantage of captivating audiences and securing the undying support of friends and associates who had the impression of participating in "something exciting." Yet it also had its drawbacks. As in the case of the failure of the EDC, blind optimism posed the threat of having no fall-back positions. In the particular instance of Monnet's visit to the United States, it had the misfortune of being too successful. Enthused by Monnet's pronouncements, the American public as well as American officials found it hard to reconcile Monnet's optimism with the lack of concrete progress in Europe on the road to European unification. Although the EDC Treaty was signed in Paris on May 27, 1952, it was far from being ratified. As for the Schuman Plan, all of the signatories, including Italy, had ratified it by mid-June, yet concrete manifestations of its promises were lacking. Meanwhile Monnet maintained contact with his old friend Dulles, whom he sent a specially printed replica of the Schuman Plan treaty in late April.[64] When Eisenhower appointed Dulles as his secretary of state, an obviously elated Jean Monnet telegraphed him:

> My dear Foster the news of your nomination has moved me very deeply. It is a source of joy for me as your devoted friend but it is also a source of hope for all of us and for me particularly who know you well. The burden is heavy but the task ahead is great and the reward full of promise if peace can be not only kept but developed. To attain this goal I believe that the prompt creation of a United States of Europe is

essential and I know how much you share these convictions.
Good luck and God bless you. Jean" [65]

Dulles immediately cabled back: "Greatly appreciate your
cable and look forward eagerly to our continuing association. I share
your conviction that it is of the utmost importance promptly to create
greater unity politically, economically and militarily in Europe. This,
as you know, has been my conviction for many years." [66]

Shortly before the announcement of the Schuman Plan, Monnet
had written Dulles he felt "very sorry that the circumstances" had
taken him "momentarily out of the active direction of foreign policy,"
especially at a moment when "all contributions specially as [he could]
make, [were] vitally needed." [67]   The president of the High Authority
now could count on the cooperation of a friend in one of the highest
offices of the United States government. If Monnet enjoyed being close
to the sources of power, his friend Dulles was now right at the source.
Seeing mostly eye to eye on the necessity to promptly create a united
Europe for the peace of the world, the two men would frequently
function as "associates" during the years of the Eisenhower presidency.

The Eisenhower administration had barely taken office when
Foster Dulles and Mutual Security Agency Director Harold Stassen flew
to Luxembourg to see for themselves the first concrete steps of European
integration, and to push for the EDC. Obviously pleased by the news of
the impending visit, Monnet immediately wrote Dulles, underscoring
its special significance for the United States, since the visit coincided
with the opening of the European market for coal on February 10, "a
great date in European history."   Dulles answered it "would be a
pleasure to pay our respects to this functioning community which in so
important an area replaces the costly rivalries of the past." [68]
Monnet's welcoming address to his guests on a very cold winter day,
forty eight hours before the opening of the first common market, echoed
Dulles' words. "The European coal and steel community," said Monnet,
"is the beginning of this union of the peoples of Europe who, renouncing
at last their age-old divisions, will soon unite in a strong, prosperous
and peaceful community to the benefit of their populations, free
peoples and civilization as a whole." [69]

Even though Dulles left that same day for the United States,
Monnet had enough time to suggest the appointment of an ambassador
at large or a special United States representative, whose main task it
would be to push for European unification. He was deeply convinced
that the European venture would not succeed if it did not benefit from
the strong backing of the United States. Hence the importance of

appointing an American representative ranking above regular American representatives in Europe to underscore the significance the United States government attached to European integration.

Earlier in Bonn that winter Monnet had discussed a similar proposal with Adenauer , who had been thinking much along the same lines.[70] Alfred Gruenther, Eisenhower's former chief of staff at SHAPE, and a close friend of Monnet, had also been toying with the thought and had written his former boss in early January suggesting the name of David Bruce. Eisenhower had shown himself favorable to the idea of a roving ambassador who would "visit with all the appointed ambassadors in their own region and attempt to promote common understanding and viewpoint," yet he did not see how he could call on a prominent Democrat such as David Bruce at the very start of a Republican administration.[71]

During his conversations with Monnet in Luxembourg, Dulles voiced his own objections to Monnet's proposal. To begin with there were already too many ambassadors, and he felt adding another ambassador at large would be a great mistake. He did, however, sound more positive on the possibility of appointing a special representative. Would Lewis Douglas be all right? Monnet was noncommittal and boldly suggested that David Bruce might be more acceptable.[72] Dulles hesitated at first. David Bruce was close to Acheson; appointing a liberal Democrat like Bruce could mean anathema at a time when McCarthyism reigned supreme.[73] Yet Bruce was a close friend of Foster's brother, Allen, and had been associated with Foster during the negotiations for the Japanese Peace Treaty. He was also a friend of Monnet's from the Marshall Plan days, and Monnet held him in great esteem. Monnet's advice eventually prevailed, and Dulles decided to go along with his scheme.

Yet Jean Monnet did not put all of his eggs in one basket. Unsure at first whether Dulles would accept his proposal, Monnet telephoned his old friend Alfred Gruenther the day after Dulles had boarded his flying fortress to return to the United States. Would Gruenther please telephone Douglas MacArthur II so he would try to expedite Bruce's appointment? In doing this Monnet hoped to directly secure the agreement of the President, and put pressure on Dulles. Douglas MacArthur II enjoyed the confidence of Eisenhower as his former chief adviser in international affairs, while the general was SACEUR. He was serving as counselor in the Department of State,[74] being one of the few whom Dulles relied upon for advice in foreign affairs. Gruenther agreed to write to MacArthur, emphasizing that Eisenhower felt highly about Bruce's qualifications, although he would likely object to his being a Democrat. There was no need for MacArthur's good offices, though. Already in the plane, Dulles and his assistants had had a thorough discussion on the matter.[75]

Two days later, on February 10, after clearing with Eisenhower, the state department got in touch with Bruce who was shooting turkeys in the South. Bruce agreed to take on the job; he did not ask for any specific title. Dulles eventually recommended to the President that Bruce be designated not only as United States observer to the European Defense Community Interim Committee but also as United States representative to the ECSC. By doing this, he felt, the United States would be sending a clear signal that it was interested in the EDC "as part of a broader six-country development and not solely as a necessary arrangement for our mutual defense." [76] Both the spirit and the letter of Monnet's proposal had thus been respected.

Ten days after Monnet had shared his plans with Dulles, President Eisenhower announced that David Bruce would soon leave for Europe to serve in the two capacities Dulles had suggested, with the additional responsibility of observing the progress made towards the creation of a European Political Community.[77] The next day Dulles telegraphed Monnet, telling him the good news. "This appointment," he underscored, "is of course indicative of the great importance which the President and the US Government attach to the movements in Europe to develop a unified six nations Community." [78]

Soon Bruce presented his credentials to Jean Monnet, and rejoined his young co-worker from the Marshall Plan days, William ("Tommy") Tomlinson, who headed the United States Embassy group in Paris charged with supervising activity relating to the six members of the Common Market prior to Bruce's arrival. "Tommy" was already a very close friend of Jean Monnet, whom he would continue to meet extremely frequently during the Eisenhower years until his death in 1955.[79]

Monnet's lobbying efforts were thus successful in establishing privileged American channels in Europe through which he could communicate his views to Washington, knowing fully well that they had a good chance of reaching the secretary of state and the President. The communication channels Monnet could use to reach the main foreign policy decision centers in Washington were many. First of all, there was a direct link with both the President and his secretary of state. There were also privileged channels through Bruce and Tomlinson in

Europe, with Alfred Gruenther and others available. In private circles, McCloy, the former high commissioner for Germany, now Chairman of the Chase National Bank in New York, and particularly George Ball, to name only a few, were frequently helpful to Monnet. In addition, Monnet adroitly used appointees in the administration such as Douglas MacArthur II to lobby for his views.

Monnet's friends and sympathizers were many in an administration that counted many Europeanists. Familiars of the President and his Secretary of State included Robert Murphy, who had met Monnet in 1937-38 in Paris and then again in 1943 in Algiers, and was undersecretary of state for United Nations affairs[80] and Livingston Merchant, Dulles' deputy during the negotiations for the Japanese Treaty, and recently deputy to the special representative in Europe, William Draper, who was assistant secretary for European affairs.[81]

As for Robert Bowie, the new head of the policy planning staff in the State Department, he had first met Monnet in Paris shortly after the Schuman declaration. Bowie was then counsel to McCloy in the implementation of Law 27 to deconcentrate the coal and steel industry in Germany. He later coordinated that law with the Schuman Plan. He became very closely involved with Monnet in the preparation of the Schuman plan treaty itself.[82]

Another old friend of Monnet, Walter Bedell Smith, with close ties to his former boss Eisenhower, whom he had served as chief of staff during World War II, was appointed to undersecretary of state. An ex-director of the CIA, and a former director of the American Committee on United Europe, Smith now held the major responsibility for administering the State Department while Dulles busied himself with travelling and formulating American foreign policy. Bedell resigned in August 1954, but continued as an unofficial adviser.[83]

Monnet's American connections were put to good use during his lobbying efforts for a loan by the American government to the ECSC. An in-depth analysis of Monnet's role in these negotiations will serve to illustrate the mechanics of his association with Eisenhower and Dulles, and, also, his networking and negotiating skills.

The common market for steel opened on May 1, 1953 following shortly after the beginnings of the common market for coal in February. Impressed by these concrete achievements, American public opinion was largely favorable to Monnet, whom eulogistic profiles in key newspapers around the United States featured as "Mr. Europe." [84]

All the ECSC needed now was the official reaffirmation of the administration's support, which Monnet thought essential for the ultimate success of the ECSC and European unity. The Bruce/Dulles connection played a key role here. In late April David Bruce informed Foster Dulles that Jean Monnet would be coming to New York in the first week of June to receive an honorary degree from Columbia University. Why not invite Monnet to Washington as an official guest, suggested Bruce. Dulles readily acquiesced and wrote Eisenhower. On May 12, the White House issued a press release announcing the official visit of Monnet and explaining his role as one of the outstanding leaders of the movement for European unification.[85] On Dulles' suggestion Monnet met the President on June 3, while Dulles himself met with him several times during his visit to the United States.

Shortly after their arrival in the United States in late May, Monnet and vice-president of the ECSC Franz Etzel set out to enlighten American steel industrialists on the merits of the ECSC. They succeeded in neutralizing the skepticism, if not the outright opposition, of some key industrialists like Clarence Randall, chairman of the board of the Inland Steel Corporation, who had previously written a series of articles criticizing the ECSC as a giant cartel and an encouragement to *dirigisme*. This was no small achievement, given the great influence those industrialists could exert on the Republican Party and hence on the current government.

Monnet also met with General Donovan, chairman of the American Committee on United Europe, and had dinner on May 28 with Thomas Dewey, Governor of the State of New York and a key figure in the Republican Party with close ties to Dulles, whom he had appointed to fill an unexpired Senate term in 1949. Also present at the Brooks Club that night were important personalities of financial circles, some of whom were Monnet's friends. George Ball and Robert Bowie had been invited along with Monnet's dedicated friend, Justice Felix Frankfurter. Having thus insured his rearguard both in the political and economic spheres, Monnet was ready for Washington.

Ten thousand guests were present to watch Monnet receive his honorary degree from Columbia University on June 2. The next day Monnet met with President Eisenhower at nine o'clock in the morning. Their meeting lasted for about half an hour. Faithful to his own thinking, Eisenhower reaffirmed his support for European unity and was quite sympathetic to the efforts of Monnet and his peers to implement the Schuman Plan Treaty. The publication of a communiqué right after the meeting, a rare occurrence, gave some measure of the

President's sympathy. Later that day Monnet and the two vice-presidents of the ECSC met with Dulles and a group of high ranking policy-makers from the administration. Monnet then proceeded to convince Capitol Hill that the European movement was making great strides, perhaps in terms too optimistic for the facts.

On June 5, "Mr. Europe" told the senate foreign relations committee of his faith in the "inexorable development" of a United States of Europe. The draft treaty for a European political authority and a common parliament had just been published and now underwent the close scrutiny of the governments of the Six. If the governments approved it and ratification ensued in their respective parliaments, Monnet insisted, this would mean nothing less than the creation of a European federation. Steady progress on the political treaty was needed to legitimize the creation of a European army. Europe would not accept the creation of a European army if not controlled by a civilian authority: there would be no European army if there were no Europe.[86]

Although Monnet had devoted considerable effort in convincing key members of the American administration to support the EDC at the beginning of the project, he was now well aware of growing opposition to the EDC in France, not least by de Gaulle. Seeking to strenghten the chances of the EDC, Monnet proposed to move away from public ex-planations that presented the European army as "an entity in itself." [87] As part of this strategy, Monnet now focused his energy on making the ECSC a success. This was perhaps not so much a choice as a necessity: the new ECSC president had enough on his hands with the infant ECSC, and little time to devote to anything else. While in Washington Jean Monnet, and his two vice-presidents also made "vigorous efforts" [88] to show that the ratification of the EDC treaty was not the only decisive factor for the advancement of European unification, even though it remained an important factor.

The Monnet visit was successful in gathering support for the Schuman Plan both in Congress and in the administration. After testifying on Capitol Hill on June 4 and 5, and meeting with Senator Fulbright, Monnet wrote a "personal and confidential" letter to Dulles in which he recommended that he and the President write a letter to Senator Wiley, the Chairman of the Committee on Foreign Relations, in support of a loan to the ECSC. The moment to act was "exceptionally favorable," wrote Monnet. President Eisenhower was ready to support it; so too was the senate committee on foreign relations. Better still, the ECSC assembly would meet June 15 in its annual session. "It would make a profound impression on the Assembly, and indeed in Europe generally" if Monnet, Etzel and Dirk Spierenburg, another High Authority member, could show U.S. support for the ECSC program.

That American participation would be on a loan rather than a grant basis would "mark a break with the form in which most American aid to Europe ha[d] been furnished in the past few years, and would show the American people that, after such aid has served its purpose, the relations of the United States with Europe [would] be taking a new form. It would confirm the self-confidence and self-respect of the people of Europe by showing that the United States ha[d] confidence in them." Monnet enclosed a short memorandum outlining "points that may be useful in any communication that might be decided upon." [89]

A draft letter, mainly the work of Robert Bowie and Thruston B. Morton, the assistant secretary of state for congressional relations, circulated in the state department. The final output incorporated some of Monnet's suggestions. On June 15 Eisenhower sent a letter to both Senator Wiley, and to Representative Robert B. Chiperfield, chairman of the house committee on foreign affairs, confirming his commitment to European integration and strongly recommending that the United States government provide part of the financing of the development program of the ECSC as a "tangible and useful way" of fostering European unity. Heeding Monnet's advice, Eisenhower suggested June 15 might be an appropriate occasion to express the approval of both the house and the senate committees for the progress made so far and their "keen interest in the success of this and future steps towards European integration." The President received very favorable replies by Wiley and Chiperfield ar.d made the letters public in a White House press release the following day.[90]

After much lobbying Monnet had obtained part of what he wanted: official expressions of support by the President and Congress for the ECSC. Monnet proudly reported on the exchange of letters to the Common Assembly on June 19, thanking Dulles, Eisenhower and the Congress for their support.[91] Yet, despite auspicious beginnings, still more lobbying was needed to secure the loan and agreement on its terms. If made in a timely fashion, this commitment, calculated Monnet, would indirectly enhance the chances of the EDC by emphasizing American support to European unity.[92]

Monnet had helped put the Eisenhower administration clearly on record as strongly favoring the EDC. At the very beginning of his presidency, Eisenhower had reiterated not only his support for European unity but also for the EDC.[93] Dulles' exhortations further amplified the administration's commitment. Where he and Monnet differed was on the way to express that commitment. Monnet advocated encouragement of the EDC along with other manifestations of European unity, and thought of indirect ways of showing American support to the EDC, one of which would be a loan to the ECSC. By contrast, Dulles exhorted and threatened, perhaps endangering rather than helping the chances of the EDC.[94]

Upon his return from his mission to various European capitals in February, Dulles publicly deplored the slow ratification of the EDC treaty.[95] In late October, he threatened a thorough revision of American foreign policy if the EDC did not succeed.[96] Unhappily he also tied NATO to the success of the EDC and eventually culminated in a crescendo with his "agonizing reappraisal" speech before the North Atlantic Council on December 14, 1953.[97] Assistant secretary of state for European affairs Livingston Merchant, policy planning staff director Robert Bowie and Foster Dulles himself had all been involved in its preparation and the President endorsed it completely.[98] Many other members of the administration including Ambassador to France Douglas Dillon, state department counselor Douglas MacArthur II and, above all, David Bruce, encouraged Dulles' inclination to "get tough" with the French who, they reasoned, would ultimately comply for fear of being isolated from their allies. The results of these tactics were disappointing. Dulles' statement only succeeded in irritating the French prime minister and his foreign minister and in identifying the EDC as an American diktat, even though it was a French initiative.

Meanwhile, in mid-December 1953, Monnet had several conversations in Paris with Dulles, Secretary of the Treasury George Humphrey, foreign operations administrator Harold E. Stassen and their advisers on the proposed loan to the ECSC. Monnet suggested a public announcement by the United States Government asking Congress to approve a loan to the ECSC "of a certain amount, with terms and conditions to be determined by subsequent negotiations;" this would help the EDC by reaffirming US support of the European Community. United States support would in turn incite the British to make quick progress in their plans for association with the Community, which could mean a difference of at least 20 votes in favor of the EDC in the French Parliament. Chancellor Adenauer fully supported Monnet's plan. The intention was for the announcement of the approval of the loan by the United States to be made before the Common Assembly meeting convened on January 14, 1954.[99]

Dulles reaffirmed his support for the EDC, this time also underscoring the achievements of the ECSC. About a week after his agonizing reappraisal speech, Dulles made another statement dealing primarily with NATO and the EDC before the National Press Club and had two copies of it forwarded to Monnet through Bruce.[100] While the address to the North Atlantic Council had made no mention of the ECSC, Dulles now emphasized that "much progress" had already been made towards economic and political unity with the ECSC, heeding Monnet's advice. A White House press release on December 23 also underscored the achievements and reaffirmed Eisenhower's hope that a ECSC loan might soon be negotiated, without however officially asking Congress to approve the $500 million loan which Monnet had requested. By January 13, 1954, after numerous memoranda and telephone conversations in Washington, the administration submitted a proposal to Monnet. Yet Monnet found it unacceptable and had accordingly little to show the Common Assembly in mid-January.[101]

Even though Dulles pleaded Monnet's case with the secretary of the treasury and the director of the foreign operations administration, they insisted that a $100 million loan to the ECSC would be ample to demonstrate American support for European unification. Dulles insisted such a small amount could hardly "capture European imagination" and provide the political impetus needed to get the EDC through, yet he eventually had to concede to his colleagues. Monnet not only objected to the amount of the loan, but also to the suggestion that the United States government might conduct a project-by-project review of the loan funds. Such a proposal, argued Monnet, would jeopardize the high authority's independence and "might be the cause of considerable misunderstanding and thus be detrimental to relations between the United States and the Community." [102]

During the next few months Monnet repeatedly pressed Dulles to begin negotiations on a loan. When Dulles was in Berlin in early February to attend the meetings of the Berlin Conference, Monnet met with him three times. Personal diplomacy proved effective again. While Dulles tried to impress on his colleagues the urgency of starting negotiations on the loan, he and Monnet worked on a communiqué in which the US government would announce its agreement to open negotiations in Washington; the communiqué was subsequently released on February 20. About one month later David Bruce sent a formal letter to Monnet inviting him to send a delegation to Washington to start negotiations. Monnet replied immediately underscoring the special importance of his forthcoming visit to the United States at a time when European integration needed money, but even more so the "evidence of support of European integration by the United States." [103] EDC ratification was entering a crucial stage in France and the ECSC itself was having a hard time weathering the attacks of the EDC's critics.

Monnet arrived in the United States on April 6 and met with Dulles and Ben T. Moore, director of European regional affairs that afternoon. The next day Monnet called on Bowie in the state department and had a cocktail with Merchant at Blair House. The stage was set for another of Monnet's brilliantly persuasive performances. The first meeting on the loan negotiations took place at the state department on Thursday June 8. Dulles tried to give the key note of the meeting by reminding his colleagues from the treasury, the foreign operations administration (FOA), and state of its "historical significance since it was the first time the United States...had the opportunity to deal with a sovereign Community representing more than national states." Using as always a positive approach, Monnet pointed out that the ECSC was only the beginning of a united Europe. He outlined its achievements, while defusing potential critiques, notably the insufficient efforts of the ECSC to eliminate cartels. It was not an easy task. Secretary of the Treasury Humphrey was adamant that the loan should not exceed $100 million. The United States, he told Monnet, had not balanced its budget and American coal and steel industries were facing grave problems, which made them reluctant to condone a loan to the ECSC. Monnet encountered many other obstacles during subsequent meetings. Personal diplomacy came in handy.

With Foster Dulles, Monnet discussed the need for low interest rates. He arranged a meeting between Monnet and the President, who gave his blessing for the loan. Monnet's old friend Bedell Smith assured him he would help him get the loan no matter what difficulties his colleagues threw in his path. During the last stage of the negotiations, Monnet had dinner with his lawyer Donald Swatland and assistant secretary of state for economic affairs Samuel Waugh who agreed to launch a joint attack on Humphrey so he would stop insisting on a "closed mortgage" which precluded the Community from getting further loans in Europe. This they did three days later and thus removed one of the main stumbling blocks to the loan. One of Monnet's youngest collaborators, Jean Guyot, also played an important role in the negotiations. After more battles on the interest rate, the terms of payment and the wording of the communiqué, an agreement was finally reached on a $100 million loan to the ECSC for 25 years to be disbursed by the treasury and the FOA. The interest rate on the loan was a low 3.7%. The agreement was signed on April 23, 1954.[104] But it was too late to change the declining fortunes of the EDC.

On August 30, 1954, the French assembly rejected the EDC by 319 against 264 votes with 43 abstentions by a negative procedural vote. This was a tremendous blow to Monnet, but disappointment did not cripple him. He soon informed Dulles through Bruce that he viewed the British suggestion of transforming the Brussels Treaty and creating a Western European Union "as a camouflage and dangerous decoy because it would give [the] impression that European unity can be achieved without transferring powers of decision to common institutions." What was needed was a truly European solution, and a European initiative. Monnet also told Bruce confidentially that if no such solution were found and the situation should lead to a return of nationalism and dissensions in Europe, he would not seek a renewal of his mandate as president of the High Authority "in order to be able to act freely." [105] This he did on November 10 by sending a letter to each foreign minister of the six ECSC member states, and issuing a communiqué the following day in Luxembourg. On November 30, in a speech before the ECSC assembly, Monnet recognized that "the decision to transfer new powers to European institutions depended on parliaments and governments. The stimulus would thus have to come from outside." Hence his decision to work with forces on the outside, mainly political parties and unions, to advance European integration.

Monnet's unexpected announcement caused some turmoil in Europe. On December 1, the ECSC Assembly unanimously adopted a resolution that encouraged him to reconsider his decision, but Monnet persisted. In the United States, the secretary of state later expressed "deepest regret" at Monnet's decision for he believed that the "Community in this formative stage" would have benefited from Monnet's "wise leadership." [106]   Although by April 1955 Monnet had second thoughts about leaving the High Authority, it was then too late to reverse his decision. Monnet left his post on June 10, 1955. His replacement by René Mayer was interpreted in the United States as another set-back for European unity.

Meanwhile Monnet was pained by Bruce's decision in the fall to terminate his current assignment, and attempted to convince Dulles to put Tomlinson in his post. He also urged Dulles to maintain American representation to the High Authority separate from intergovernmental organizations such as NATO or the OEEC, as a confirmation of the American commitment to supranationality, as opposed to the intergovernmental approach. Foster Dulles did not immediately oblige: the administration, he wrote Monnet in December, had not yet reached a decision on whether to keep the American representation to the Community separate from intergovernmental organizations.[107]

David Bruce resigned in January 1955, and was not replaced until 1956 when Walton Butterworth succeeded him as representative to the ECSC, with the rank of ambassador. The departure of Bruce, without his being replaced, signalled a temporary discouragement with the cause of European unity. Dulles' hesitations on whether to keep a separate American mission to the community pointed to the problem of what was meant by "European integration."

Despite Dulles' initial noncommittal reaction to Monnet's plea for a clear recognition of the supranational approach, the secretary of state soon decided to back Monnet, as did many of his colleagues, and the President himself. Just prior to the Messina Conference in early June 1955, the state department and United States representatives abroad agreed that European integration meant "supranational authority and responsibility.... [A]rrangements less binding were merely cooperative." It was decided that the ECSC approach "pav[ed] the way for the truly integrated association, politically, economically and otherwise, of member countries, and especially Germany and France, upon which [the] long term welfare, strength, and security of [the] Atlantic Community may well depend." The Western European Union [WEU] did not "appear to [the] Department to offer promise of accelerating integration in this sense." As for the OEEC, it was an "institution designed [to] maximize effective cooperative arrangements, and only over [a] very extended period of time, if ever, [was] it apt to become [the] framework for arrangements involving waivers of sovereignty in favor of [an] authority such as now existed for [the] CSC." [108] Once again Monnet's arguments had found a receptive ear with Dulles and the state department. The decision to favor the six nations' approach to real European integration became a decisive factor in American reactions towards subsequent British "inter-governmental" proposals.

When British foreign minister Eden proposed to integrate the Schuman plan institutions and the European army with the Council of Europe in March of 1952, Monnet found the proposal unacceptable. To him the coal and steel assembly had effective powers, while the assembly of the Council of Europe was entirely consultative. In one case there was a real delegation of sovereignty, in the other participating countries retained their complete sovereignty. Clearly to differentiate the two approaches, Monnet thought the European Community must have an independent administrative organization of its own.[109] Monnet later tried to convince Dulles to oppose the Western European Union plan on the grounds that it was not sufficiently supranational.

After declining to join the Six in building either Euratom or the Common Market in November 1955, the British government suggested to the United States that it might be better to cooperate in the field of atomic energy within OEEC. A month later, in a letter to Harold Macmillan, Dulles was clear to the point of bluntness: the United States did not see any inherent conflicts between the cooperative and the supranational approaches towards European integration, but, he, and the President, would give their full support to the six-nation approach because it offered the greatest hope for European prosperity, security and influence in world affairs. "It may well be," Dulles wrote, "that a a six-nation community will evolve protectionist tendencies. It may well be that it will show a trend toward greater independence. In the long-run, however, I cannot but feel that the resultant increased unity would bring in its wake greater responsibility and devotion to the common welfare of Western Europe." [110]

Monnet later had a conversation with Dulles who was in Paris for the North Atlantic Council ministerial meeting. Monnet warned him of British efforts to torpedo the Common Market and Euratom, and expressed the hope that Dulles would speak to them at the time of Eden's visit. Dulles immediately cabled the President "Eyes only", faithfully transmitting Monnet's message and recommending a serious discussion with Eden and Macmillan in January.[111]

The American administration's reactions to the British proposal for a free trade area including the Six as a single unit and those OEEC countries that agreed to join, were similarly colored by a preference for the supranational approach. Eisenhower initially appeared to endorse both the common market and the free trade area proposals, but this was on the condition that the common market would be created first and the free trade area "thereafter", "gradually, over a period of years." When Macmillan introduced a set of proposals in December 1956 that called for the grouping of European regional organizations into one single assembly assisted by specialized commissions notably in the military, cultural and economic fields, Dulles and the state department immediately saw a threat in the "tendency [to] blur [the] vital distinction between merely cooperative arrangements (OEEC) and genuine integration (CSC)." The "sim- plification" proposed by the British appeared to threaten the very institutions of the coal and steel community, Euratom and the Common Market, especially since it included the economic dimension. The main concern was that the British proposal would dilute the movement of the Messina countries towards "genuine integration", thereby preventing them from acting as "a unit within Atlantic organizations."[112]   Another concern was the prospect of the free trade area coming into being and the common market never following. These fears were very much those of Monnet. Fortunately, the Common Market and Euratom treaties were signed in March of 1957. Yet Monnet's concern for maintaining the integrity of the Community continued during the discussion on the British proposals.

In October 1958, Monnet's Action Committee for the United States of Europe (ACUSE), while insisting that the Community of the Six was open to those European countries that were ready to delegate part of their sovereignty to common institutions, noted that the reality of the community "must be respected in the ongoing negotiations for a Free Trade Area." If it was "essential to reach the goal of associating England and other countries" with the community, it was "equally essential that this association respect the unity of the community itself." [113]

After the failure of the British negotiations, the primacy of the Six in American policy continued as the British Government initiated new negotiations which were to lead to the creation of the European Free Trade Area (EFTA) in January 1960. Despite some fears that the Common Market would discriminate against American exports and the declining economic fortunes of the United States from 1957, the cause of the Six continued to be championed by the Eisenhower administration, then under Kennedy. Monnet's friends in high places, including Dulles and the President, played no small role in this development.

Yet the misfortunes of the EDC moved "Europeanists" in the state department toward more caution. Encouragement for European unification did not mean pressure. Both Monnet and Spaak were adamant that the mistakes of the EDC not be repeated and were "most emphatic" in convincing their American colleagues to "remain entirely in the background" especially before the treaties were signed and ratified. Dulles also seemed to have learned his lesson, and to agree with Monnet. When German Foreign Minister von Brentano asked that the United States publicly indicate its support for the six nations approach and its clear opposition to other programs, Dulles told him that while the United States "could not exert pressure, it could use its influence." [114]

Meanwhile Monnet persuaded Ambassador Douglas Dillon, then Foster Dulles and the President of the importance of ACUSE which he proudly announced on October 13, 1955. Earlier in June, in the

wake of the Messina Conference and Monnet's replacement by René
Mayer at the head of the ECSC, the secretary of state had "expressed
regret that his friend Monnet was not longer in the position to help in
the field." [115]

Dulles soon resumed his association with Monnet, however,
even though his friend no longer occupied an official position. On
October 25, shortly after the Action Committee became a reality,
Dulles met with Monnet in Paris at his request, then again in December.
Monnet explained the efforts to establish a European pool for the
peaceful use of atomic energy, and informed Dulles of his committee's
intention to adopt a resolution in January 1956 on a European atomic
commission after the pattern of the coal and steel community. Monnet
asked for American backing of this initiative, notably in dealing with
the British, but also with the Germans. He was preoccupied that the
Germans might never sign or ratify the Euratom treaty if the United
States agreed to sign bilateral treaties with Germany. Would Dulles
please try to delay the bilaterals? Dulles assured him of the
cooperation of the United States.[116]

During the next few months top-level U.S. officials, mostly in
the state department, used diplomatic channels to convey to their
German counterparts that they could expect more cooperation from the
United States by dealing on a multilateral basis.[117] In late January
1956 Monnet sent Dulles a letter enclosing a copy of his committee's
resolution and underlying that it had every chance of being adopted by
each parliament because it already had the support of the political
leaders of all non-communist parties and of labor leaders. He also
suggested that there would "have to be an agreement between the
U.S.A. and the Community."

The following November, after the Suez crisis, Monnet
suggested a "broad scale and generous program of US support for
Euratom, both in the supply of materials and in technical cooperation,"
might help repair Atlantic solidarity.[118] Monnet's connection with
Dulles, and the indefatigable efforts of Max Kohnstamm, ACUSE vice-
president, played no small role in making the U S. agreement with
Euratom a reality. Dulles' sympathies for Monnet's proposal were
decisive in overcoming the strong reservations of the Atomic Energy
Commission, and its chairman Lewis Strauss. The secretary of state not
only attempted to convince Strauss to delay the bilateral discussions
with Germany, but also tried to impress on him that Euratom was not
socialistic, that it would not destroy free enterprise and that such a
large and responsible organization would provide adequate controls and

prevent the proliferation of "uncontrolled national atomic developments." [119]   In March 1957, three days before the Six signed the
Euratom and Common Market treaties, the secretary of state sent a
letter to Belgian Foreign Minister Spaak stating the department of
state and the Atomic Energy Commission saw "nothing which would
appear to preclude the subsequent negotiation of a fruitful cooperative
arrangement between the United States and Euratom." [120]

In August 1958, after much debate, Congress gave its approval
to an assistance program to Euratom. The official signing of the US-
Euratom agreement took place in Brussels on November 8, 1958. In the
spring, as the agreement seemed to run into some difficulties, Monnet
wrote Dulles emphasizing that Euratom was strictly limited to the
peaceful uses of atomic energy and that the US-Euratom joint program
for the development of atomic reactors would accordingly also be
"solely for peaceful purposes." In mid-July Monnet again wrote hoping
that Dulles would use his "influence and energy" to insure that the
agreement pass Congress soon to maintain the momentum, and thus
strengthen Euratom and the whole European integration movement.[121]

Dulles used both his influence and energy on the side of
Euratom. So too did many friends in the state department of Monnet
whose influence helped skew the administration's interest towards
Euratom rather than the common market. With European integration
on the move again after EDC, Monnet preferred Euratom over the more
ambitious proposal of creating a common market.

Whereas Euratom could "identify the Community with the
power of the future and capture public imagination," he felt the
common market would remain " a pretty nebulous project" [122] for the
Six, and especially for the French, with a slim chance of being ratified.
Priorities within the American administration paralleled this
tendency. Clear evidence of high-echelon American policy-making for
Euratom came not only in the lack of in-depth discussions of a European
common market on the United States, prior to the signing of the Rome
treaties, but also in repeated statements by Dulles, who insisted that
common market talks should not delay Euratom's approval.[123]

Monnet's association with Eisenhower and Dulles thus played
a key role in shaping American policy towards European integration
during the Eisenhower years. His personal diplomacy encouraged the
appointment of American Europeanists such as David Bruce to key
positions in Europe. His influence was decisive in obtaining American
backing for European endeavors such as the ECSC, the EDC and

Euratom, not only through public statements and back-channel diplomacy, but also through financial and technical contributions. It was similarly crucial in American support for supranational as opposed to British intergovernmental schemes. Monnet's initial inclination to give priority to functional or sectoral progress towards European integration as opposed to overall integration similarly found echoes in the state department, and particularly with Dulles. Although Monnet did not always agree with Dulles, Eisenhower, and other Europeanists on the best method of advancing European integration, they were united in their commitment to the goal of European unity, which they viewed as an essential element of peace and stability in the post-war world. Yet their relationship was not only that of an association of men with a common vision, but also a friendship.

In November 1956, Monnet wrote his friend Dulles that he planned to go to the United States "on a strictly private visit," to breathe "some other air than 'European'" and talk "to some of [his] old friends." Eisenhower and Dulles were high on his list, as evidenced by his frequent tokens of affection to both of them. After Jean Monnet retired as president of the High Authority of the ECSC, he asked his friend Samuel Waugh to deliver to Eisenhower a copy of his book *Les Etats Unis d'Europe ont commencé*. Waugh later wrote the President that Monnet had "expressed his deepest admiration and affection" for him in autographing the booklet.

Eisenhower thanked Monnet for his "expressions of friendship" which were "fully reciprocated." More delectable than books were the bottles of cognac Monnet regularly sent Eisenhower and Dulles for Christmas, and which both of them much appreciated. Monnet also occasionally remembered birthdays, but was particularly thoughtful in case of distress. When Eisenhower suffered a heart attack in September of 1955, Monnet telegraphed wishing him a speedy recovery.[124]

Yet of Eisenhower and Dulles, Dulles remained his closer friend. Jean Monnet frequently wrote and telegraphed him while he was fighting cancer at Walter Reed Hospital, sending him words of prayer, encouragement and support. In spring 1959, as Dulles was deathly ill, Monnet wrote him a long letter, in which he told him that his decision to transfer his responsibilities to others had been " a great shock" to him and "a subject of deep sorrow and worry." Monnet then looked back on Dulles achievements throughout his life, praising him for his wisdom:

It is very rare, if ever it happens, that one can in life accomplish an effort that is conclusive. In fact, conclusion is static and contrary to life which is made of constant adjustments and changes. The real accomplishment is in the contribution that one can bring to the development of affairs of the world, and in the change in the psychology of men -- and that you have done. You can look to your life and effort as having contributed to the development of the world at a vital moment of civilisation when hesitancy might have fatally turned the course of events towards compromise first and then to the defeat of liberty as we know it. When our children will look back and consider the period we are going through, I believe they will consider the history of the last 10 years as the "charnières" [hinges] in the course which the world will follow - and you as one of the main architects of it- and also the bravest.

After Dulles lost his battle against his terrible illness in May 1959, Monnet was the only foreigner among the honorary pallbearers. After the funeral, Janet Dulles gave Monnet private copies of the writings of her late husband as a final memento.[125]

Endnotes

[1] Jean Monnet, *Memoirs*, Garden City,NY, 1978,(hereafter JMM); Department of State Bulletin, Jul 30, 1951.

[2] Louis Galambos, ed., *The Papers of Dwight D. Eisenhower* Baltimore, MD; *Chief of Staff* 1987,no. 2023; *Columbia University*, 1984,nos. 1009 and 1051; *NATO and the Campaign of 1952*, 1989, no. 215; Diary, Jun 11, 1951.

[3] Galambos, *NATO and the Campaign of 1952*, no. 304, Aug 3, 1951.

[4] Note from J.S.W. for Jean Monnet, Pre-presidential papers, no. 75, McCloy, John (1), Eisenhower Library, Abeline,KS. (hereafter DDEL), and Jean Monnet's appointment books, Jun 21, 1951, Fondation Jean Monnet pour L'Europe, Lausanne (hereafter FJM)

[5] McCloy to Eisenhower, undated, pre-presidential papers, no. 75, DDEL .

[6] Ibid.

[7] Gruenther and Harriman were both present.

[8] JMM, p. 359.

[9] Galambos, *NATO and the Campaign of 1952*, no. 424. On Oct 10, the day after the creation of the special Executive-Bureau, a SHAPE picture showed a pensive Monnet with the two other wise men and Eisenhower.

[10] Galambos, *NATO and the Campaign of 1952*, no. 502.

[11] New York Times, Nov 27, 1951 and Galambos, *NATO and the Campaign of 1952*, no. 502.

[12] Gruenther to Monnet, Jan 2, 1952, Gruenther Papers, Box 13, "Jean Monnet", DDEL.

[13] Galambos, *NATO and the Campaign of 1952*, no. 542.

[14] JMM,p. 50.

[15] McCloy to Eisenhower, undated, DDEL pre-presidential papers, p. 1.

[16] Eisenhower to Monnet, Dec 28, 1951, Pre-presidential Papers, Box 78, Monn-(Misc), DDEL.

[17] Monnet to Eisenhower, Nov 8, 1952, AM 46/8/15, FJM.

[18] Eisenhower to Jean Monnet, Nov. 19, 1952, AM 46/8/16, FJM.

[19] JMM, p. 179.

[20] Monnet to Eisenhower, Dec 31, 1943, Pre-presidential Papers, Box 78, Monn-(Misc), DDEL.

[21] Henri Rieben, *Des guerres européennes à l'union de l'Europe*, Lausanne, 1987, p. 272.

[22] Ibid, p.286

[23] Pierre Mélandri,*Les Etats-Unis face à l'unification de l'Europe 1945-54*, Paris, 1980, p. 29.

[24] Ibid,, p. 27. Ronald Pruessen, *John Foster Dulles: The Road to Power*, New York, 1982, p. 334.

[25] Ibid,p. 309.

[26] John Foster Dulles, "Peace Without Platitudes", in Fortune, XXV, no 1, Jan 1942, p. 87.

[27] Pruessen, *op. cit.*, p. 309.

[28] Dulles to Frederick Stern, Nov 20, 1942, quoted in Pruessen, *op. cit.*, p. 312.

[29] Dulles to James Warburg, Sep 16, 1946, Dulles Papers,Princeton University Library, Princeton, NJ. (hereafter DP-PL,) quoted in Pruessen, *op. cit.*, p. 325.

[30] John Foster Dulles, "Address on Foreign Policy to the National Publishers Association," New York Herald Tribune, Jan 18, 1947. A copy is in John Foster Dulles Speeches and Press Releases, Box 20, DDEL

[31] Dulles to Arthur Vandenberg, Mar 22, 1947; undated Dulles memorandum, approximately Apr 7, 1947, item 12, MCFM, I Dulles Papers, DP-PL *FRUS, 1947*, II, p.323-328, Ronald Pruessen, *op. cit.*, pp. 345-346.

[32] "Discussion Meeting Report", Feb 2, 1948, DP-PL; See also Mélandri, *op. cit.*, p. 145.

[33] *FRUS, 1948*, II, pp. 98-99. On Monnet's possible influence on Robert Murphy and Lewis Douglas, see Mélandri, *op. cit.*, p. 155, who cites an interview with Robert Murphy in Jul 1974.

[34] Townsend Hoopes, *The Devil and John Foster Dulles*, Boston, 1973.

[35] Alfred Grosser, *The Western Alliance*, New York, 1980, p.104 On Dulles' friendship with Monnet, see Eleanor Dulles, interview by Douglas Brinkley, May 1987, and Eleanor Dulles, interview with the author in Apr 1990. On one occasion, Eleanor Dulles stated that "Monnet was the best friend Foster ever had;" in a later interview, she said he was a friend, but hesitated to call him the best friend her brother ever had.

[36] JMM, pp. 102-106

[37] JMM, pp. 102-106.

[38] Pruessen, *op. cit.*, p. 118-119.

[39] Jean Monnet to John Foster Dulles, May 14, 1959, FJM.

[40] JMM, p. 105.

[41] Hoopes, *op. cit.*, p. 18.

[42] Dulles to Monnet, Mar 30, 1950, Box 54, DP-PL.

[43] Monnet to Dulles, Apr 4, 1950, Box 54, DP-PL.

[44] Monnet to Dulles, Apr 19, 1950, Box 54, DP-PL.

[45] On another instance, Monnet wrote a letter of introduction for Walter Hallstein. On yet another, in 1957, he introduced Max Kohnstamm as " a very intimate friend" of his. Monnet to Dulles, Mar 9, 1952, Box 62,DP-PL; Monnet to Dulles, Jan 1957, Box 120, DP-PL

[46] John Foster Dulles, *War or Peace*, New York, 1950.

[47] Dulles to Jean Monnet, May 23, 1950, Box 54, DP-PL.

48 Mélandri, *op. cit.*, pp. 281-282.
49 David Bruce was appointed by Paul Hoffman as Marshall Plan Mission Chief at the beginning of the Marshall Plan. On David Bruce, Stanley Cleveland, William Tomlinson and the Schuman Plan see interview with Stanley Cleveland Jun 12, 1981, FJM. See also Mélandri, *op. cit.*, p 280.
50 Interview with Stanley Cleveland, *op. cit.*
51 Mélandri, *op. cit.*, p. 283.
52 Dulles to Monnet, May 23, 1950, DP-PL.
53 Ibid.
54 Dulles to Monnet, Jan 3, 1951, Box 54, DP-PL.
55 Dulles to Monnet, Dec 31, 1951, Box 62, DP-PL.
56 Dulles to Monnet, Jan 3, 1951, and Dulles to Monnet, Mar 21 1951, Box 54, DP-PL.
57 Ibid.
58 Monnet to Dulles, Apr 19, 1951,Box 54, DP-PL.
59 Dulles to Monnet, May 3, 1951, Box 54, DP-PL.
60 Monnet met Dulles on Jun 10 at six o'clock at the embassy residence and then again at eight at Houjarray that evening. The two men met again at the residence on Jun 12 at 11.15, Monnet's appointment books, FJM.
61 Dulles to Monnet, Mar 24, 1952, Box 62, DP-PL.
62 New York Times, Apr 19, 1952; and Mélandri, *op.cit.*, p. 366.
63 Monnet to Eisenhower, May 13,1952, Pre-presidential papers, Box 78, "Monn-(Misc), DDEL.
64 Dulles to Monnet, Apr 28, 1952, Box 62, DP-PL.
65 Monnet to Dulles, Nov 24, 1952, Box 62, DP-PL.
66 Dulles to Monnet, Nov 26, 1952, Box 62, DP-PL.
67 Monnet to Dulles, Apr 4, 1950, Box 54, DP-PL.
68 Monnet to Dulles, Jan 19, 1953, AMH 46/5/1,; Dulles to Monnet, Jan 23 1953, AMH 46/5/2, FJM.
69 Allocution de Jean Monnet, Feb 8, 1953, AMH 46/5/5, FJM.
70 Adenauer to McCloy, Dec 1, 1952, Ann Whitman File, Administration Series, Box 25, "McCloy, John", DDEL.
71 Gruenther to MacArthur II, Feb 9, 1953, Box 2, "MacArthur, Douglas II", NATO Series, DDEL.
72 Ibid.
73 Douglas Brinkley,"Jean Monnet and the American Connection, 1953-63," Paper presented at the European Community Studies Associations' Conference, Fairfax, Virginia, May 24, 1989.
74 Eleanor Schoeneabum, ed. *Political Profiles. The Eisenhower Years*, New York, 1977.
75 Gruenther to MacArthur, *op, cit.*, and MacArthur II to Gruenther, Feb 12, 1953, Gruenther, Alfred, Box 2, MacArthur II, Douglas, NATO Series, DDEL.
76 Dulles' Memorandum for the President, Feb 18, 1953, Dulles White House Memos, Box 1, "White House Correspondance:1953 "(5), DDEL.
77 *FRUS, 1952-1954,* Volume VI, pp. 276-277.
78 Dulles to Jean Monnet, Feb 19, 1953, AMF/46/6/1, FJM; see also JMM, p. 379.
79 Monnet's appointment books, FJM.
80 Mélandri, *op. cit.*, p. 155.
81 *FRUS 1952-1954,* VI, Part 1, p. xxii.

82 JMM, pp. 271, 352 and Robert Bowie, interview, Jun 15, 1981 FJM.

83 *Political Profiles, op. cit.*, p. 564, Smith to Eisenhower, Aug 17, 1954, Walter B. Smith, Box 5, "Appointment as Under Secretary"; Eisenhower to Bedell, Walter Bedell Smith, Box 5, "Appointment as Undersecretary; Smith to Donovan, Jan 12, 1953, Walter B. Smith, Box 4, "American Committee on United Europe (2), all in DDEL.

84 See for example, Reader's Digest, Apr 1953, pp. 44-47.

85 *FRUS 1952-1954*, VI, pp. 305-306, and John Foster Dulles, Memorandum for the President, Apr 28 1953, Eisenhower Papers, Official Files 260-2, Box 919,"European Coal and Steel Community", DDEL.

86 83d Congress., 1st session, U.S. Senate, Committee on Foreign Relations: *Hearings. European Coal and Steel Community*, Jun 4 and 5, 1953,p. 15-17.

87 Ibid.

88 AMH 47/8/1, Lettre de Monsieur Etzel, Washington, Jun 4, 1953, FJM.

89 All above quotations from: AMH/47/6, Monnet to Dulles, Jun 8, 1953, FJM.

90 *FRUS, 1952-54,* Volume VI, pp. 311-312; Department of State Bulletin, Jun 29, 1953, pp. 927-929; AMH/47/6/9, FJM.

91 Department of State Bulletin, Jul 27, 1953, pp. 107-108.

92 See the summary of conversations held in Paris, Dec 13-15, between Monnet, Dulles, Humphrey, Stassen and their advisers; *FRUS 1952-54,* VI, pp. 337-342.

93 Eisenhower to Adenauer, New York Times, Jan 7, 1953, p. 1.

94 George Ball to James Reston", Feb 17 1953;"James Reston to George Ball", Feb 20 1953; "George Ball to James Reston", Feb 22, 1953, in Adlai Stevenson Papers, Box 373. Quoted in Mélandri, *op. cit.*, p. 395.

95 Department of State Bulletin, Feb 23, 1953.

96 "Address before the National War College", Oct 26, 1953, DP-PL.

97 Monnet had met with Dulles the previous day, but he had also met with Adenauer who strongly recommended to be firm with the French, as too did his friend Bruce. Monnet met again with Dulles on the 15th. See Monnet's appointment books, FJM; See also: Mélandri, *op. cit.*, p. 428.

98 Mélandri, *op. cit.*, p. 427;*FRUS 1952-1954*, V, Part 1.

99 *FRUS 1952-1954,* VI, pp. 337-346.

100 Bruce to Monnet, Personal and Confidential, Dec 28, 1953, AMH/ 46/8, FJM.

101 *FRUS 1952-54,* VI, p. 355.

102 *FRUS 1952-54,* VI, Dulles to Stassen, Jan 9, 1954, p. 351; *FRUS 1952-1954,* Vol VI, Tomlinson to Bruce, Jan 26, 1954, pp. 356-358.

103 *FRUS 1952-54,* VI, pp. 360, 368; Monnet to Dulles, Mar 21, 1954, AMH/51/5, FJM.

104 Monnet's appointment books, FJM; *FRUS 1952-1954,* VI, pp. 377-385; Dulles to the President, Apr 12 1954, O.F. 260-A-2, DDE Central Files, DDEL; Department of State Bulletin, May 3, 1954; "Dwight Eisenhower 1890-1969", Samuel Waugh, Box 1, Mar 31, 1969, "Mr Waugh's experiences in D.C.", DDEL; JMM, p. 390.

105 Bruce to Dulles, Sept 16, 1954, AMH/60/2/4, FJM, Lausanne; *The Memoirs of Anthony Eden: Full Circle*, London, 1960, pp. 158-164.

106 Quoted in Pascal Fontaine, *Le Comité d'Action pour les Etats-Unis de Jean Monnet*, Lausanne, 1974; *FRUS 1952-54*, VI, The Secretary of State to the Office of the United States Representative to the ECSC, at Paris, Washington, Dec 13 1954, p. 418; The Secretary of State to the President of the High Authority of the ECSC (Monnet), Washington, Dec 14, 1954, p. 417.

107 *FRUS 1952-1954*, VI, Monnet to Dulles, Dec 1, 1954, Dulles to Monnet, Dec 13, 1954, Dulles to Monnet, Dec 14 1954, pp. 415-417; Dulles to Monnet, Oct 27, 1954, AMH 60/4/3, FJM.

108 *FRUS 1955-57*, IV, Memorandum prepared in the Office of European Regional Affairs, Washington, Dec 6, 1955, p. 358; *FRUS 1955-57*, Vol IV, Telegram from the Acting Secretary of State to the Embassy in Italy, May 30 1955, p. 290.

109 *FRUS 1952-54*, VI, Bonsal to the Department of State, Mar 20, 1952, pp. 28-29; *FRUS 1952-54*, VI, Dunn to the Department of States, Jun 22, 1953, pp. 89-92; *FRUS 1952-54*, VI, Dunn to Department of State, Jul 13, 1952, pp. 122-124.

110 *FRUS 1955-1957*, IV, Dulles to Macmillan, Dec 10, 1955, pp. 363-64.

111 *FRUS 1955-57*, Vol IV Memorandum of Conversation, Paris, Dec 17, 1955, and The Secretary of State to the President, Paris, Dec 17, 1955, pp. 367-369.

112 *Public Papers of the Presidents of the United States. Dwight D. Eisenhower*, Washington,1956, pp. 1038-1045; *FRUS 1955-57*, Circular Telegram from the Secretary of State to Certain Diplomatic Missions, Mar 6, 1957, pp. 534-536.

113 Fontaine, *op.cit.*, p.114.

114 *FRUS 1955-57*, IV, Martin to Timmons, Paris, Nov 10, 1955, p. 347 ; Secretary of State to the Department of State, Dec 17, 1955, p. 372.

115 Department of State, Cable Dulles to Bruce, Dec 13, 1954, *FRUS 1952-54*, VI,p.416.

116 *FRUS 1955-57*, Vol IV, Memorandum of Conversation, Paris, Oct 25, 1955, p. 337; *FRUS 1955-57*, Vol IV, Memorandum of Conversation, Paris, Dec 17, 1955, pp. 367-368.

117 For example, Report of a discussion between Brentano and Dulles on Dec 17, 1955, Ibid, p.372.

118 Monnet to Dulles, Jan 24, 1956, Dulles Papers, Box 106, PL; *FRUS 1955-57*, Vol IV, Dillon to the Department of State, Nov 19, 1956, p. 488.

119 *FRUS 1955-57*, Vol IV, Memorandum of Conversation, Department of State, May 14, 1956, p. 441.

120 *FRUS 1955-57*, IV, Letter from the Secretary of State to Foreign Minister Spaak, Washington D.C., Mar 22, 1957, p. 543.

121 Monnet to Dulles, Apr 26, 1958, Dulles folder, FJM; Monnet to Dulles, Jul 13, 1958, and Monnet to Dulles, Jan 30, 1957, DP-PL.

122 *FRUS 1955-57*, IV, Memorandum of Conversation, Department of State, Apr 20, 1955, Words from Mr. Albert Coppe, 2nd Vice President of the ECSC, p. 288; JMM, pp. 622-237.

123 For example:*FRUS 1955-57*, IV, Memorandum of Conversation, Department of State, May 14, 1956, p. 441.

124 Monnet to Dulles, Nov 26, 1956, Dulles Papers, PL.;Waugh to the President, Jun 20 1955, and Eisenhower to Monnet, Jul 1 1955, White House Central Files, PPF, I-L M, DDEL; Monnet to Eisenhower, Sept 27 1955, White House Central Files, PPF 1-ZZ, "Foreign rulers etc "M", DDEL..

125 Dulles to Monnet, Dec 28, 1956, Box 106; Monnet to Dulles, Feb 28, 1958, Monnet to Dulles, Nov 11, 1958, Monnet to Dulles, Dec 9, 1958, Box 132, Dulles to Monnet, Dec 12, 1958, Box 132, Monnet to Dulles, Dec 18, 1958, Box 132, Dulles to Monnet, Jan 8, 1959, Box 141, Monnet to Miss Bernau, Feb 14, 1959, Monnet to Dulles, Feb 16, 1959, Box 141, Dulles Papers, PL.; Monnet to Dulles, (translation), Mar 14, 1959, Dulles folder, FJM; Roscoe Drummond, *Duel at the Brink*, Garden City, NY, 1960, p. 55.

6
Catch the Night Plane for Paris:
George Ball and Jean Monnet

David L. DiLeo

Near the conclusion of her husband's memorial service, as the Battle Hymn of the Republic was being played, Silvia Monnet tenderly turned to George Ball, her treasured American friend, and asked, "Wasn't that wonderful?" "Yes," he acknowledged, "It was all wonderful -- all those years were wonderful." Notwithstanding what he described as the "blank looks of mystification" exhibited by a few of Jean Monnet's European admirers who had come to mourn the passing of their continent's "First Citizen," Ball thought the presentation of the American Civil War's fighting song was especially fitting for the occasion; after all, the conflict was waged to protect a community of commonwealths from political dismemberment, pernicious economic rivalry, and potentially, more war. Ball records that he and Jack McCloy, another of the Frenchmen's many influential American associates, delighted in the moment as five verses of the anthem aptly testified to Monnet's attachment to America, to individual Americans, and to the principle of federalism.[1]

Ball retells this story in the longest and most elegant segment of his memoirs in which his inspired friend is commemorated. The many extended passages devoted to Monnet are composed with great care and obvious affection, and disclose as much about the author as the subject. There were, in fact, four individuals in Ball's life whom he credits with the development of his interests and professional career. They were all exceptional men; all possessed extraordinary talents. He was motivated and inspired by a long affiliation with Adlai Stevenson whose unashamed embrace of liberal values, he once observed, "hit some deep Middle Western idealist root in [him]." [2] His easy rapport and close collaboration with Dean Acheson also proved to be mutually nourishing and, in terms of Ball's professional and political life, enormously consequential. His sometimes tempestuous relationship with Walter Lippmann, whom he credits with the sharpening of his strategic and political judgments for twenty years, was intellectually fertile and tremendously stimulating.

Despite the shaping influences of these three luminaries, Ball concedes that Monnet was the most influential of his mentors. Indeed, while he often speaks and writes admiringly of many distinguished acquaintances in both the United States and Europe, his spirited veneration of his French friend is unparalleled. Jean Monnet, it seems, is the only person for whom George Ball harbored unqualified admiration. Ball's concepts of the Atlantic Community, his career and, indeed, his personal life, were profoundly transformed by the long professional association and warm friendship they enjoyed. Working together in various capacities for 35 years, they moved governments on both sides of the Atlantic, sometimes in small steps, sometimes in great strides, toward a more vigorous support of the "European idea." As a consequence of his work with Monnet, Ball became an anointed "European-American," embraced his mentor's central thesis, and assimilated a good many of his acclaimed "pragmatic methods."

The effects of Monnet's vision and political technique on Ball's career are conspicuous and, at the same time, difficult to assess. Ball has himself, on occasion, depreciated Monnet's influence on his life.[3] At other times he has acknowledged a boundless debt.[4] It may even be that he loved Monnet but, as an American journalist who pondered the careers of both men once explained, "[he] may also have simply felt that he was [his] equal, and not his disciple." [5] Despite the under secretary's occasional declarations of intellectual and professional independence, there can be no doubt that Monnet's impact on his world view and intellectual processes was profound and transcending. The Frenchman's ebullient character, his great personal force, and the theory and substance of the projects on which they cooperated, made indelible imprints on Ball and, hence, the European-American relationship in the post-war era.

While Ball's great affinity for Monnet is commonly recognized in the foreign affairs literature of the past half-century, the extent of his "Frenchification" has, heretofore, never been systematically explained. As an attorney working for the French government and advising Monnet in what he once described as "a quite informal arrangement" [6] in the 1950s, he regularly dispensed advice to leaders of an industrial trade association called the French *Patronat*, edited a journal published to promote trans-Atlantic investment entitled *France Actuelle*, and wrote long papers for the advancement of Franco-American investment enterprises -- which, as was often noted by a few of his more xenophobic antagonists, were habitually advantageous to the French side of the commercial equation. Although Ball was uncomfortable with the perception, in many quarters during his government service and beyond, he was recognized primarily as Monnet's protégé, with all the attendant assets and liabilities of that identification.[7] In many ways then, Ball is a citizen of the old continent. For his services to European economic recovery after World War II and the advancement of the Atlantic partnership, he was made an Officer in the French Legion of Honor and was awarded the Belgian Grand Cross of the Order of the Crown.

During his tenure as under secretary of state from 1961 to 1966, Ball was very closely identified with French and European interests generally, and with Monnet specifically. Even his most acclaimed endeavor in government, his running disagreement with the escalation of the Vietnam involvement, was largely understood as a direct function of his general concern with Europe, and of his specific accord with Monnet. Ironically, critical analysis of his Vietnam dissent leads directly to an even deeper appreciation of his command of the intricacies of postwar Europe's economic and political problems. He argued against the war as a European would have, and as many Frenchmen did. Also ironically, deepening American involvement in Vietnam brought Ball only marginally closer to that crisis. As Secretary of State Dean Rusk turned more of his energies over to Indochina, he relied proportionally more on Ball to worry about Atlantic affairs. At the height of the Vietnam conflict, as Rusk became a sort of Southeast Asia desk-officer, Ball became the policy leader in the state department on European affairs. The Atlantic world was, in Rusk's mind, his under secretary's great strength, but his weakness as well. Rusk followed Ball's lead on Europe, but sharply differed with him on Indochina. Rusk respected the analytical power behind Ball's dissenting views on Vietnam, but discounted their sagacity: "George's long exposure to Europe," he once stated, "jaded his vision on Southeast Asia," and he has implied that Ball "lacked a comprehensive view of the world." [8]

So Ball came at Vietnam through Europe. Examination of his personal and professional life leaves little doubt that his dissent sprang primarily from an acquired Eurocentric world view and his seasoning with Monnet in postwar France, and only secondarily from what was an episodic investigation of Vietnam's political and military dynamics. Fundamentally, it was insight and a Europe-centered political ideology, shaped by experiences in private and public enterprises antedating his state department service, that informed his dissent. He was right on Vietnam. But, as Assistant Secretary of State for Far Eastern Affairs Roger Hilsman once griped, "he was right for the wrong reasons." [9] His more hawkish adversaries chided Ball for arguing against a commitment in Vietnam merely because it would divert political and material energies form the under secretary's principal concern, the building of Europe. Devotees of escalation routinely noted that his views did not spring from a particularly rich experience in Southeast Asian affairs, but rather a fixation with the Atlantic community.

An account of how Ball became a Europe-focused under secretary dissenting on Vietnam requires a brief digression into what he was "B.C." -- before collaboration with Monnet. The story begins in the American heartland. Ball often teasingly solemnizes his Middle-Western roots. In much the same way a veteran or an athlete might proudly brandish a battle scar, he periodically invokes his Middle-Western heritage for rhetorical or political effect, and revels in nostalgic talk of his austere social origins and the cultural and intellectual innocence of his early life. Hailing from Des Moines, Iowa, he followed his older brothers through the academic climes of Northwestern University where he received a Bachelor of Arts degree in English in 1930, and a Doctor of Law degree in 1933.

As a young attorney, he went directly to Washington from law school at the beginning of the New Deal to practice his new trade in the Farm Credit Administration. From 1934 to 1935 he worked in the office of the general counsel of the treasury department, and at the end of 1935, returned to the Middle-West to practice law until the onset of the Second World War.

After Pearl Harbor, he again entered government service in Washington as an associate general counsel of the Lend-Lease Administration. While Ball has no clear recollections of their first encounter, it was in this capacity that he first met Jean Monnet. A year later, he assumed the same position in the Foreign Economic Administration, of which the Lend-Lease Administration had become a part. In 1944 he was appointed a director of the U.S. Strategic Bombing Survey which President Roosevelt had commissioned to assess the economic, political, and physical effects of the strategic air offensive against Germany.

Returning to Washington toward the end of 1945, Ball was retained by the French Supply Council then charged with planning postwar recovery. In was in this capacity that his relationship with Monnet flourished. It was also then that he became a partner in the legal firm of Cleary, Gottlieb, Steen, and Hamilton, which was then in the process of establishing busy offices in New York, Washington, Paris, and

Brussels. From 1945 to 1961, as a member of the firm, and as a specialist in international law and commercial relations, he divided his time between Washington and Western Europe. During this period, and stemming from his public declarations on behalf of European economic integration, George Ball developed a constructive -- and decidedly peculiar -- friendship and professional association with Jean Monnet.

While Ball and Monnet collaborated only intermittently, they did so at an extraordinary rigorous pace, and under intense and unpredictable political pressures. In what was a most unusual lawyer-client relationship, they quickly earned each other's unconditional respect and affection. Ball's unquestioned professional ethics, his unwavering personal allegiance to Monnet, and his dexterous representation of French interests permitted him access to the highest level of discussion bearing upon the building of Europe. He became intimately acquainted with things French, including economics, politics, language, culture, intellectual processes, and habits of work. As he drew closer to the man whom he dubbed "the keeper of the conscience of Europe," Ball became habituated to one on Monnet's fundamental assumptions: If French recovery was going to be sustained, it must take place within the context of general European reconstruction, and this required no less than the "creation of Europe" as a cooperative industrial, commercial, and political entity.

From 1945 to 1954, Ball worked sporadically out of a small office in Monnet's Paris headquarters at 18 rue de Martignac, or conversed with him by means of the new trans-Atlantic telephone cable --- a device to which, he insisted, his client was maliciously addicted. It was during this period that Europe was being conceived. True, the mirage of a united Europe was as old as Charlemagne. But in 1945, as President de Gaulle's appointee to supervise France's industrial modernization, it was Monnet who began to envisage ways to give Europe palpable institutional form. In what has aptly been identified as a "creative conspiracy," [10] Monnet, Etienne Hirsch, Paul Reuter and others began to address the problems of French economic modernization and security within the context of general European recovery. Monnet's brilliance in conceiving arrangements by which problems related to control of industrial resources and German rearmament would be addressed simultaneously -- and seizing the political opportunities to affect change -- has become legendary.

Throughout this busy interval, and while he was not in Paris, Ball was a de facto political agent of the Fourth Republic, part of Monnet's much heralded American lobby -- or, as Monnet himself called the members, his "well informed friends." [11] His political contacts in Washington and his extraordinary abilities as an attorney were of great benefit to Monnet in his efforts to prudently frame France's requests for credit and technical assistance. Ball served French interests, and Monnet, in two capacities: as a lawyer, he drafted the specialized language required for commercial and legal documents that would inevitably be scrutinized by suspicious American legislators, finicky bureaucrats, skeptical economists, the Justice Department's anti-trust division, and apprehensive directors of industrial boards. As a friend, he helped Monnet think. There seems to be no doubt but that it was a reciprocal and mutually nourishing association. "While Monnet profited by what I called our 'collective spiral cognition'," Ball once remarked in evaluating the relationship, "I learned much from helping a wise man shape ideas like a sculptor with a knife." [12]

Monnet was equally appreciative of Ball's contribution to his efforts to shape ideas into proposals: "Many times I'd make a statement," Monnet once mused, and "[George] helped me to clarify the problem we had to deal with. He had an intellectual mechanism which I think functions quickly without any prejudice. Objective is a bad term -- he viewed problems simply," and "he has a great capacity for work." Monnet once declared that he felt complimented at the suggestion that he in some way provided a spark of inspiration to Ball, and described their friendship as "a creative relationship, an exchange, a collaboration and if he learned from me I certainly did learn from him, a great deal." [13]   It was in this later role, as intellectual conspirator, that the most distinguishing attributes of their relationship were nurtured. This is not to discount the value of Ball's evolving political influence in the United States. Certainly, he wielded considerable bureaucratic authority and was, as will be shown below, an enormously effective advocate of the "European agenda" as under secretary of state during the Kennedy-Johnson years. But their relationship was primarily cerebral, not political.

When he was in Monnet's sphere, Ball would acquiesce to his client's eccentric habits of thought and work. Monnet was a notoriously early riser. Each day, with his customary walking attire and stick, he would head off into the woods to think. When Ball was in France he would often stay with Monnet at his home in Houjarray and would invariably be summoned to join in the routine. Ball confesses that during their many long contemplative walks together, "trite civilities" always gave way to speculative conversation. How would the Truman administration react to a major European industrial merger arrangement? What would be the best way to convince American farmers to make short term concessions on agricultural products? How would the French stock market react to a substantive change in the American credit assistance policy? What would the attitude of the American president and Congress be to a European army?

Monnet was not the least bit averse to summoning Ball to a discussion group across the Atlantic in a manner that would, to the outsider, appear both arrogant and capricious. But Ball routinely submitted. Pleasantries were rare. Often ringing him up in the small hours of the morning, Monnet would succinctly beseech him in a terse instructive voice: "Catch the night plane for Paris." [14] Everything was subordinated to business. Late evenings, early mornings, deferred meals, declined social invitations, multiple redrafting of documents, telephone summons -- and unremitting deference to Monnet's legion of idiosyncrasies. Indeed, Ball was amazed "that [Monnet] seemed always able to find men willing to submit to his stimulating but exasperating methods of work." That he did so, Ball admits, "merely testified to his extraordinary charisma." [15]

Balefully recalling the rhythms of labor in Paris, Ball has noted that "[I]t was a rare paper of any importance that did not go through at least seventeen or eighteen drafts." (Insisting that documents were normally redone only six or seven times, Monnet himself once maintained that Ball exaggerated the extent of the revisions he asked for. Richard Mayne, however, recalls redrafting a document for Monnet 140 times).[16] Accentuating the severity of work for his French friend, he has more than once characterized himself as Monnet's "dialectical punching bag." His primary service was to transmute enigmatic thought into vibrant prose -- once described as struggle "to find the correct allusion or figure of speech to supply the vivid aphoristic summation [Monnet] habitually sought." [17]

Jean Monnet and George Ball toiled together in the depressed atmosphere of postwar France where defeat and disillusionment were pervasive. In those days, Ball was surrounded by those whose job it was to take the pulse of Europe. The signs were not good. Throughout the period, as he once perceptively diagnosed the malaise of the times, "even an itinerant American could sense a resurgence of introspection, a slackening of vitality, and the insidious exhumation of old, dark rivalries, fears, and complexes. No one was more worried than Jean Monnet by this accelerating trend. It was axiomatic to him -- as to all 'good Europeans' -- that lasting peace could be achieved only by bringing France and Germany together and exorcising the demons of the past." [18] Ball generously credits Monnet with a rarefied understanding of the perils as well as the opportunities of an era in which the seemingly irreconcilable aspirations of the Germans, for equality, and the French, for security, might be bridged.

In 1945, he advised Monnet on his Plan for Modernization and Investment. In 1946, he canvassed influential Americans and made substantive recommendations as the Committee (later the Organization) for European Economic Cooperation (OEEC) was taking shape. Throughout 1947, Ball apprised Monnet of developments respecting the proposed multi-billion dollar European Recovery Program. In 1948 he watched from the sidelines as Monnet become disenchanted with the OEEC.[19] In 1949, while he was not commiserating with his now-celebrated French client about the dark mood hanging over Europe, he counseled him on the administration of the materializing Marshall Plan. Between 1953 and 1954 he was seduced into supporting the ill-fated proposal for a European Defense Community. By the end of the 1950's he was retained by all the communities which Monnet helped create including Euratom and the European Economic Community.

An analysis of Ball's collaboration with Monnet on any one of these enterprises would provide a fascinating vista on the problems of postwar Europe, on Monnet's stature in the United States, and on their extraordinary collaboration. And while Ball is careful not to overstate his personal contribution to Monnet's successes (or failures) on any one of the projects, he is understandably proud to have worked closely with him on so many weighty projects. Perhaps the most auspicious, and fertile, example of their work together was the effort to achieve the consolidation of German and French coal and steel. It had all the trappings of a good drama, was exemplary of how complex and intellectually rigorous their work could be, and appropriately testifies to the distinctiveness of their personal and professional relationships. At the outset it was hoped that the fusion of French and German industries would provide a decisive building block to what Monnet was then proposing as a new European edifice. While this work would prove to have monumental effects on the continent (an enterprise the long range implications of which are even yet not fully realized), it was also, in style and substance, representative of the 35 year association they both valued and enjoyed.

While Ball's law practice kept him busy in the United States during the first half of 1950, he spoke often with Monnet by telephone, but only in what he has described as "cryptic terms," about the delicate issues surrounding the coal and steel concept -- word of which was not then in the public domain. In fact, Ball himself discovered in the newspaper that the French government had proposed a plan for pooling the two national industries on May 9. While he acknowledges that he was personally disappointed to have been "absent at the creation," he knew it would be only a matter of time before the inevitable summons would arrive. Ball remembers being relieved, but not surprised, when Monnet's call came: "Be here tomorrow." Hours later he was hip deep in what has been fittingly labeled "the parturition of Europe." [20]

In an episode that was repeated many times in his years with Monnet, Ball arrived in Europe midstream and was hastily brought up to speed on a lofty undertaking -- in this case the initial recommendations for the European Coal and Steel Community (ECSC). Immediately on his arrival in Paris, Monnet handed him a pile of papers and uttered characteristically terse instructions: "Big things are happening. Read this." Ball turned immediately to the successive drafts of French Foreign Minister Robert Schuman's May 9 proposal, entitled *"Notes de Reflexion,"* outlining the basic concept for the ECSC and predicting, among other things, French political anxieties about economic union with Germany at the height of the cold war. Ball thought the draft "a stirring manifesto for European unity" and immediately seized upon the grand and long range implications of the idea. The more cautious Schuman, like Monnet, realized that "Europe will not be made all at once, or according to a single general plan." The goal of the coal and steel concept, as Ball saw it, was to create de facto solidarity though a single concrete achievement -- a device that Schuman saw as "indispensable for the preservation of peace." [21]

At once Ball seized upon the logic and magnitude of what was being done. While he concedes that he was initially content to be "on the fringes" of such an ambitious undertaking, he instinctively sought a more active role.[22]   In due course, he maneuvered his way into the center of the storm of the so-called Schuman Plan. Consistent with a developing pattern in his work with Monnet, he made vital contributions as an intellectual springboard and draftsman. One of the documents he produced was unassumingly entitled "Note Regarding Proposed Articles." It is a exemplary effort by Ball to press Monnet's thoughts into compact and powerful sentences, a representative sample of Ball's elocution of Monnet's basic philosophy.

Striving to provide his client with the simplest formulations of a complex idea, Ball wrote that "The single market is an indispensable principle of the Schuman Plan." He succinctly captured the truly radical nature of the proposal: "The Schuman Plan involves a revolutionary change in the production and distribution of coal and steel. This implies

not only a change in the legislation which now controls the operation of
these industries, but a change in the habits of thought of the managers of
the individual enterprises [emphasis added]." Ball also directed himself
to the political ramifications of what was being proposed in arguing that
"in order to bring about this change it will be necessary to make effective
the institutions provided by the draft treaty. This necessarily means the
elimination of many of the existing national organizations of control.
Existing institutions are unsuitable for this [new concept] because they
have organized on a national basis." [23]

In proposing to act in the comparatively narrow sector of coal
and steel, Monnet and Schuman hoped and expected other nations to
eventually comprehend the inherent advantages. They calculated that
countries would ultimately be willing to delegate sovereign powers to
supranational institutions that could, in time, form the nucleus of a
European economic community. It was during this period that Ball
became a convert to the "logic of Europe" and an enthusiast of the
Schuman Plan. Indeed, "once coal and steel were pooled," he wrote, "it
would become imperative to pool other production as well." As an
added dividend to one of the more pressing problems of the mid-1950's,
he also came to the conclusion that pooling coal and steel "would render
moot the issue of German industrial domination." [24]

"But," as the brilliant French economist Robert Marjolin tells us in
his recollections of the period, "the idea uppermost in Jean Monnet's
mind at that time was a different one." [25] As early as 1950, Monnet
envisioned a Europe "endowed with efficient institutions resembling,
even very remotely, the United States constitution." While the time was
"not yet ripe" for a grandiose proposal for European economic or political
confederation, Monnet and Schuman set out, in Ball's words, "[to make] a
decisive breakthrough at a narrow point [and not] undertake an assault
on a wide front against entrenched concepts of sovereignty." [26]

In what was by then a characteristic pattern of work in Paris, an
inspired debate was unleashed among Monnet's cabal of technocrats,
economists, lawyers, and political onlookers. Because the implications of
the Schuman proposal were so profound -- and because the plan did no
less than call into question the viability of the nation-state as an
organizing institution -- apprehension and pessimism quickly surfaced.
Those in America and Europe with whom Ball had regular consultations
about the economic affairs of the old continent were not immediately
persuaded that Monnet was moving in the right direction. As a short
term practical concern, the propriety of the concept of pooling was called
into question. Indeed, even Secretary of State Dean Acheson, an

enthusiast for the plan, was dubious. At the outset he felt that "[t]he arrangement could become a giant cartel controlling the basic necessities of an industrial society." [27]

Additionally, long term concerns were raised about the ECSC's abridgment of French and German sovereignty. Seven years later, as the initial proposals for the European Economic Community were being conceived and debated, similar reservations were recalled by Marjolin, a Monnet confidant, secretary-general of the OEEC, and a man who became one of Ball's closest personal friends: "I thought that the nation-state was not on the way out and that one could not expect the emergence of a European state in the foreseeable future [emphasis added]." [28] Marjolin did not completely share Monnet's ultimate vision and did not hold the general view that supranational institutions could supplant national sovereignties in the near or even distant future.

Ball conceded the wisdom of Marjolin's views. It was possible that there was too much history weighted against the idea of nations voluntarily delegating national sovereignty to supranational organizations. Perhaps the Europeans had developed too many passions and prejudices. After all, Ball wrote, "Patriotism had been the coalescing force animating Germany's neighbors to resist her ravaging armies in two world wars, and Britain was not ready for Europe." He entertained seriously the notion that Marjolin might be right.

As a witness and participant in these intramural debates, Marjolin quickly came to appreciate Ball's acumen and force of character. He considered his new American friend "an extraordinarily clear sighted and courageous man." He was particularly interested in how Ball, as a representative of enlightened American thinking with respect to the concept of an economic community for Europe, assessed the fundamental problem of national sovereignties. For his part, Ball saw Monnet and Marjolin addressing the same European dilemmas, he once said, "from different angles of attack." Monnet, he suggested, "set goals that might be approached but never attained." On the other hand, Marjolin, because he was politically accountable as the OEEC's secretary general "was necessarily aware of the limits of the feasible and the need for compromise." [29]

Because of his personal devotion to both men, Ball initially forswore taking sides and, true to his calling as a lawyer, assisted each in the articulation of their views. But it was only a matter of time before the divergent attitudes held by Monnet and Marjolin raised fundamental questions in his own mind: "Was Monnet really right in believing that a change in institutions would cause men and women to conform their thoughts and actions to a new set of principles? Could allegiance to a united Europe some day play the same activating role that national sovereignty had played in the past? Or did it really matter whether [Monnet] was right or not? Would not the insistent pressure for the unattainable goal at least lead toward greater solidarity and common policies and actions that could never be achieved by more modest objectives?" [30]

By his recollection, Ball came out "roughly in the middle" of this argument. He was not, at least in 1950 as the coal and steel plan was being conceived, as optimistic as Monnet that traditional methods of doing business could easily be revamped, "even," as he wrote, "in the pressure chambers of new institutions." And respecting Monnet's ultimate vision of a consolidated Europe, he did not then have much faith in the viability of a "United States of Europe" on the American federal model. He did have two convictions however: The first was that it was imperative that something be accomplished in order to maintain the momentum for community; the second was that he sensed a willingness on the part of the European governments to act. Taking small steps toward a consensus was imperative. Monnet himself instinctively felt that "political unity could not be decreed," as he often pronounced to his confederates, "it had to be built." [31]

The history of 1950 records that Monnet skillfully and courageously led the charge of the idealists, and deftly neutralized the pessimists. The political miracle of the coal and steel community was made when the "original Six" (France, Germany, Italy and Benelux,) signed the treaty on April 18, 1951. Monnet had indeed set a goal "that might be approached but never attained" – and he attained it.

Not content merely to be a participant in the coal and steel proposal, Ball volunteered to become its chronicler. As the treaty that would ultimately create the community was being negotiated, Walter Lippmann approached him with an idea for a book, and even set about to secure a contract with Harper's. Ball immersed himself in the project and, as the manuscript progressed, funneled chapters to Lippmann who had agreed to edit the work and to write an introduction. When Monnet abruptly withdrew his initial endorsement of the project (believing, like the American Founding Fathers at the constitutional convention, that public disclosure of the debates ongoing within the group would only inform and energize the skeptics), the project withered and the manuscript was never published.[32] While its absence from the now considerable literature on the origins of the ECSC is lamentable from the scholar's perspective, the brief enterprise speaks volumes about Ball's enthusiasm for the proposal and his dedication to Monnet.

Notwithstanding the collapse of the book project, by the end of the 1950s Ball had developed solid convictions about European integration and America's role within the interdependent global economy. While initially torn between Monnet's idealism and Marjolin's realism, his papers and speeches from the period 1954 to 1961 suggest that he gravitated ever more closely toward Monnet's unique brand of pragmatic optimism about the future of European integration. With a head filled with neoclassical economic doctrines, with considerable political and bureaucratic experience, and with rich insights acquired from his work with Monnet, in 1958 Ball became a founding member of the "Committee for a National Trade Policy," the avowed objective of which was to defeat protectionist practices and policies.

It was partly through this organization that Ball's professional associations with America's most influential businessmen, financiers, and industrialists were augmented. While at the apex of his law career in January 1960, he was invited to address a joint session of the National Industrial Conference on the European Economic Community and European Free Trade Association in New York. His visionary message brought him to the attention for the first time of then Massachusetts senator John F. Kennedy. In what was a historically well-informed speech, Ball recounted the American economic experience of the 1780s and 1790s, during which time the country was transformed from what he termed a "Balkanized" economy to a vast internal market under a federal constitution. American economic success, he unambiguously declared, is to be understood not as a result of superior virtue, but primarily as a function of its political integration. While not abusing the historical analogy (and criticizing others for doing so), he maintained that Europe had recognized the veracity of this historical example be creating the European Economic Community (EEC) under the auspices of the Rome Treaty of 1957. What Ball regularly calls "the logic of Europe" was to extend, so far as possible, the integration of the yet politically undefined continent.

In his remarks at New York he lamented that the American posture at the inception of the EEC was merely benign neutrality. In time, as under secretary of state for economic affairs, and then under secretary, he would enthusiastically champion virtually all schemes to integrate Europe more completely. As an economic adjunct to that broad political goal, under secretary Ball would continually warn American producers that short-term trading disadvantages and sacrifices would be required of them in order to reap the long term commercial advantages of European economic and political consolidation.[33]

American politics once again began to consume Ball's interests and energies. In the summer of 1960, largely as a consequence of his seminal role in the Stevenson campaign entourages of 1952 and 1956, he became one of Kennedy's New Frontiersmen. With JFK's nomination in July, he was brought on board as a principal member of the foreign policy task force, and in fact ended up doing the lion's share of the labor. As he was temperamentally (perhaps compulsively) prone to do, Ball took the bull by the horns that summer and autumn. While the Democratic nominee was ambling about the country blowing wind into the sails of his campaign, a small group of former Adlai Stevenson men were writing a foreign policy agenda for the 1960s. The future under secretary of state organized committees, assigned them issues and regions, and generally orchestrated the work of the foreign policy brain trust.[34] Ball ably served as a rapporteur and made substantive contributions to the final report.

The most significant testimony to Ball's contribution to Kennedy's foreign policy initiatives are the integrationist and open door themes distinctively underscored throughout the document. His Euro-centrist conceptions of American foreign policy were conspicuous. The task force made particularly "urgent" proposals for a coordinated NATO nuclear force; it warned of "the dangerous trend on the part of the NATO Allies toward the development of independent national nuclear deterrents"; and it included a twenty page support paper developing a plan for "Partnership Between a United Europe and America within a Strong Atlantic Community" which, not surprisingly, directly paralleled the integrationist principles espoused by Jean Monnet's "Action Committee for a United States of Europe." [35] Ball's economic liberalism and advocacy of free trade were also abundantly evident in the task force report. In a section entitled "A Comprehensive Program for the Economic Progress of the Free World," the foreign policy committeemen lamented the "parochial attitude of the treasury department" under Eisenhower. In particular, Ball faulted the previous administration with failing to extend adequate credits and markets to developing nations (particularly in Latin America), called for the executive branch to be endowed with new and greater power to effect trade policy, and proposed a 50% across-the-board tariff reduction within five years. This last proposal would, two years hence, prove most fertile.[36]

With respect to the problem of decolonization, the task force report specifically recommended to Kennedy that a "high level approach to de Gaulle [be initiated immediately] to indicate the importance which the new Administration attaches to an early settlement of the Algerian conflict." Also predictably, given Ball's unique taxonomy of world problems, much smaller support papers on China, sub-Saharan Africa and Latin America were relegated to appendices. (In a particularly elucidating passage from a section entitled "The World in Revolution," and one directly bearing on Ball's unconventional views on Southeast Asia that would emerge within the year, the report declared that "it is important that we not try to impose our own political or economic ideas" on third world nations receiving American assistance.)[37]

In reflecting on the summer of 1960 as his career as a political appointee was about to be launched to new heights, Ball recorded that he felt "well prepared to deal with those areas under [his] jurisdiction -- principally trade, foreign assistance and monetary policy -- as a result of [his] work in the Lend-Lease and Foreign Economic Administration during the war, [his] representation of foreign clients fighting trade restrictions, [his] participation in the Committee for a National Trade Policy, [his] work with Monnet, and [his] role as chairman of a number of Kennedy task forces [emphasis added]." His close exposure to the pressure cooker of postwar France and the practical vision of Monnet in no small way helped prepare him to play a role in the American government of considerable importance.

In a somewhat circuitous manner, Ball was appointed under secretary of state for economic affairs and then was, within the year, elevated to under secretary. While he was generally recognized as informed, talented, and experienced, Ball was a bit of an outlander at Camelot. A consummate Europeanist, he felt "surrounded" by younger men in the administration who saw Africa, Asia, and Latin America as the first orders of business on America's new global agenda. "The young movers and shakers of the Kennedy Administration," he once mused, "thought of themselves as pragmatists, well equipped to resolve America's emergent international problems with flair and imagination," and generated a "surfeit of theories regarding the economic development of the Third World." They had, he once ruefully added, "fewer settled views on the structure of relations among the Western industrialized democracies," which he believed then, and continues to believe today, were the principal building blocks of a successful American foreign policy.[38]

The world had, in fact, changed a great deal, as Arthur Schlesinger, Jr. reminds us, between the time Ball first met Monnet in 1945 and when he came to office with the Kennedy team in 1961:

"Western Europe had been growing twice as fast as the United States for a decade; it had been drawing gold reserves from America; it had been out producing America in coal." The strategic equation of 1961 was also much different from 1945 or 1947. Few Europeans believed a Soviet invasion was imminent, and "the conditions which had given rise to the Marshall Plan and NATO were substantially gone." [39] What then, were the imperatives of a European policy?

By 1961, Ball had already accrued a long track record as a North Atlantic strategist, had been an outspoken and effective advocate of the European agenda as a private citizen, and was not the least bit reticent about his Western European seasoning. In his senate confirmation hearings, for example, Ball did little to dispel the perception of himself as primarily a North Atlantic man as he sought to be confirmed for a job with multi-regional responsibilities. He testified that he had "traveled and done business... as a private lawyer in almost all the countries of Western Europe," but conceded that his travels to other parts of the world "were not extensive." In speaking about Latin America, Ball admitted that he had "a great deal to learn," and within the context of specific remarks about Asia, he reported that he had "very little professional experience [emphases added]." [40] The congressional hearing clearly shows that Ball was dispassionate about the massive unilateral third world foreign aid programs (and their originators) that were anticipated by the new administration. He believed that they raised unrealizable expectations of industrial and social progress and, most importantly, diverted resources from the more important work to be accomplished in Europe.

Later, as a consequence of his exposure to Monnet's consummate practicality and what might be termed a "unromantic vision," Ball would become particularly disdainful of what he later called "the esoteric cult of academics" who "think they know a lot, but don't know anything." Once, in a particularly noteworthy fit of irritation, he reduced the entire lot of New Frontier developmental economists to "a few high priests, who talked a strange, sacerdotal language," and who were annoyingly predisposed to flamboyant neologisms with a "quaintly Madison Avenue ring" such as "take-off," "the big push," and "the great ascent." [41] Derogating the era's fashionable political and economic theories, then collectively known as "nation-building" as "a most presumptuous undertaking," Ball openly questioned whether it was ever realistic to expect that "American professors could make bricks without the straw of experience and with indifferent and infinitely various kinds of clay." [42]

His disdain for diversions from the project he had inherited from Jean Monnet -- the "building of Europe" -- only ripened with age. After his retirement from government for the fifth and final time, Ball continued to sardonically deflate Kennedy's academics and, in the process, an integral element in the New Frontier mentality by impugning what he called the "theological aspect" of foreign assistance: Brimming with an "overblown nomenclature," all manner of experts during the Kennedy years, including economists, sociologists, psychologists, city planners, political scientists, "and experts in chicken diseases," embarked for the distant corners of the globe to construct all manner of "new Jerusalem." With little meaningful impact on the developing nations, many Harvard and MIT economists Ball has concluded, "only succeeded in straining America's primary diplomatic relationships by their constant din of requests of more aid from European governments for America's daring projects in the emerging nations." [43]

Ball admits that he never fully harmonized with the intellectual style of the Kennedy clique, and once conceded that he "could not avoid feeling somewhat detached from the new team's exuberance and its confidence in the bright new plans and brilliant insights" that swarmed around the room during policy planning meetings.[44] "John Kennedy and George Ball," Schlesinger recently wrote, "never hit it off quite as they should have done." [45] But there was one subject on which they enjoyed unusual concordance, that being the idea for an Atlantic Partnership. "When Monnet carried the [Atlantic Community] gospel to Washington early in 1961," Schlesinger recalls, "he found that the ground had already been well tilled in the new administration." [46] Indeed, for six years as under secretary, Ball would tirelessly work to insure that the American government heard the case for European integration and for strengthened European-American relations. Even with the third world being recognized as the emergent diplomatic frontier in the new administration, Ball's European advocacy was a great weight in the second year of Kennedy's term. The Kennedy team, Ball retrospectively wrote, "was sympathetic to what was, to me, a familiar idea developed during my years with Jean Monnet: the long-term objective of building what we referred to as a European-American 'partnership.' " [47]

Monnet hoped for two things from the new American administration. He urgently sought more discernible American recognition of the EEC "in order to lend it the authority and international character of which de Gaulle was attempting to deprive it; [and] equal partnership between the United States and the European Community." [48]

The new American president was initially quite suspicious of the economic unification of Europe. The Common Market might trade unfavorably with the United States and the consolidation of the industrial democracies of Western Europe could only diminish American prestige. As American ambassador to the European Communities J. Robert Schaetzel insightfully noted, "there were both Americans and Europeans whose reservations about a united Europe sprang from a conviction that an integrated Europe would inevitably become a third force. The skeptics anticipated that, instead of cooperating with the United States in a true Atlantic Partnership, a united Europe would become increasingly independent, with opposition to the United States deemed essential to a separate European identity." [49] Shortly after his feet were solidly on the ground in the state department, Ball began to work personally on Kennedy's fears. While Ball was confident he could move Kennedy toward Europe, he instinctively felt that a direct encounter with his French friend might do much to allay apprehensions then swirling in Washington, and personally arranged for the President to meet Jean Monnet. After their initial encounter in 1961, the new President quickly became a convert to the "Atlantic Partnership" concept and at once gained "the greatest respect and affection for Jean Monnet."[50]

The first public disclosures of the administration's "Grand Design" -- as it would come to be called -- were made in the summer of 1962. Kennedy's "concrete Atlantic partnership" proposal, delivered in Philadelphia on July 4, generated considerable excitement. That month, inquiries about who was doing what with regard to Europe dominated press briefings: The new division in the state department created to manage consultations with European leaders was headed by Bob Schaetzel, formerly Ball's staff chief; Henry Owen was given specific responsibility to study the Atlantic Partnership problem; McGeorge Bundy would look after Europe in the White House. "But the mastermind behind the Atlantic partnership concept," as the administration conveyed the project to the press, "[was] Under Secretary of State George Ball, an old friend and associate of 'Mr. Europe,' France's Jean Monnet [emphasis added]." [51] To the end of the Kennedy administration, Ball served as a link between the European and the American view of the Atlantic Partnership. While his work was primarily political and diplomatic, he and Monnet continuously advanced the economic argument that the short term disadvantages of American exports being subjected to the EEC's common tariff would be more than compensated by the escalating volume of trade with a revitalized Europe.

There were conceptual clarifications to be made as well. What, after all, was this new Europe? "The phrase 'European political unity,' " Ball once wrote, "has always meant different things to different men. Like other abstract and spacious terms that cloud our political discourse... it often suggest[ed] a swampland of semantic confusion." Ball's conception of Europe and the Atlantic Partnership had been -- not surprisingly -- consistently analogous to Monnet's. Formal arrangements for "consultations" -- as the British preferred in the days of the OEEC, would simply not be satisfactory. Sharing Monnet's pronounced abhorrence for "intergovernmental debating societies" throughout the 1960s and 1970s, Ball boldly echoed Monnet's call for the creation of common Atlantic parliament believing that it would, "over the years, build up a body of European statesman by inducing politicians to seek careers for themselves in a larger political arena." [52]

When British reluctance and French *snobisme* halted progress toward the concept in the early 1960s, Ball withdrew from the front lines. Though he concedes that the Grand Design never became more than a "figure of speech," over the years he has stubbornly refused to concede that the proposal was without great merit. "If I look back with regret at events since the early 1960s," he muses in his memoirs, "it is not because I spent so much time and effort trying to advance the building of Europe, but because the effort failed. Although, God knows, American governments have made plenty of mistakes, our encouragement of a unified Europe was not one of them. We were persuing a worthy goal and -- at the time -- not a wildly unrealistic goal." [53]

Perhaps the most constructive work in pursuit of a closer relationship between the United States and Europe was the rethinking of American commercial policy and the passage of the Trade Expansion Act of 1962. As part of the New Frontier economics (clearly anticipated by the task force proposals of 1960), Kennedy renounced the old isolationism and economic nationalism of the past and sought to expand foreign markets for American goods. As part of the strategy he resuscitated an old commercial institution, the General Agreement on Tariffs and Trade (GATT), that had been created shortly after the end of World War II. The Trade Expansion Act would statutorily make explicit that which Kennedy implied, i.e. a desire to reduce significantly and comprehensively the trade obstacles to trade with Western Europe.

Monnet immediately saw possibilities: "An affair of big business, tariffs, big money," he told Ball that summer.[54] Indeed, editorials in the American press would soon be touting the legislation as "the crowning achievement of the Kennedy presidency in domestic legislation" and an enterprise "that ranks with the Marshall Plan in its constructive impact." House Majority Whip Hale Boggs of Louisiana called it "one of the significant events of this century." [55]   Boggs intuitively understood the significance of the constructive relationship that Monnet had developed with Ball in bringing about the legislation. Initially, Boggs was himself skeptical about the proposal and thought the immediate trading advantages for the EEC outweighed potential U.S. advantages. But when Boggs visited Europe in the summer of 1961` and met with Monnet he came away impressed with the trade message and with the Frenchman's ultimate vision. Like Kennedy before him, he was convinced that the increased volume of trade would offset short-term disadvantages to American exporters. Instead of an item by item approach, Boggs helped to sponsor legislation that called for sweeping across-the-board powers to reduce all tariffs and trade barriers. In the wake of the floor voles in the House and Senate, as the administration and congressional leaders were basking in the political success, Kennedy implored Boggs, "Tell me Hale, who is the Jean Monnet of this country?" Boggs replied: "We don't have a Jean Monnet, but there's one man in your administration who is closest in approach: George Ball." [56]   Boggs' salutary comment speaks volumes about Ball, as well as Monnet's continuing influence within the United States government in the 1960s and serves as a remainder of the extent to which all had internalized his objectives and methods.

The Europe-focused under secretary dutifully served as a bridge between the old Atlantic orientation of the Truman years and the new exuberance for the developing nations so enthusiastically exhibited by the New Frontiersmen. With so much emphasis and activity all around the globe, and the looming presence of an Asia-centric secretary of state, Ball's studied attention to European affairs was rendered even more distinguishing. While it can be said that Ball effectively used his rapport with Monnet and other Europeans to advance the American national interests, some were not so sure of his motives. His loyalty was impugned more than once. Was Ball Monnet's not-so-secret agent in the Kennedy Administration?   Indeed, while still in the American government, was Ball using Monnet as an agent for U.S. policy? At a time when the Washington-Paris relationship was strained, some were unnerved by Ball's zeal for representing the French or European side of a question. The under secretary loved Europe and, as Kennedy's national security advisor McGeorge Bundy recalls, reveled in being able to travel to the Old Continent as part of his official capacities. In his state department duties he continued the pattern he had established in private life by routinely making the exhausting Atlantic crossing. Rather than send a subordinate, Ball preferred to go himself. To this day, Bundy remains baffled that Ball actually sought, rather than avoided, travel as a part of his already exceedingly strenuous schedule as the number two foreign policy officer of the United States government.[57]

If there were obvious political assets to the under secretary's relationship with Monnet, there were obvious political liabilities as well. His extremely close association with European interests did not escape suspicious Ball-watchers. During the early 1950s, an era that sanctified "one-hundred-percent-Americanism," questions about Ball's patriotism surfaced. Though none of the allegations raised during that anxious age ever had the slightest foundation, they serve to illustrate the degree to which Ball had become a citizen of the world. An FBI background report assembled at the time of his confirmation hearing as under secretary for economic affairs, for example, described his law firm of Cleary, Gottlieb, Friendly, and Ball, as "acting agents" from 1951 to 1961 for the government of France, the European Coal and Steel Community, and the nation of Luxembourg. Federal investigators seemed particularly curious about his ties with Eastern European countries. The FBI conducted a separate investigation of Ball's passport record from 1945 to 1960, and found it unusual that Ball spent part of nearly every month during that time period in Paris.[58]

Perhaps too much the urbane "One Worlder" -- particularly for congressmen with primarily regional identifications and narrowly focused constituencies -- Ball was widely considered to be too cosmopolitan and too complex. Although he maintained excellent personal relations with key members of Congress, those not more than casually acquainted with him chided his vision of an Atlantic Partnership and of an interdependent world economy -- that is, before Kennedy made it fashionable in the summer of 1962. His close identification with European interests prompted occasional verbal jibes. In one appeared in 1962 before a congressional trade committee, for example, Ball was asked when he was going to take out American citizenship papers, and was sarcastically reminded by an American legislator that he was "no longer in the pay of the French Government." [59] As political scientist Alfred Grosser has noted, even at the pinnacle of his state department years, his allegiances were considered divided. "On Capitol Hill," Grosser tells us, "Ball's foreign ties were not forgotten." In another extraordinary encounter with the legislative branch as he was advancing a European perspective on trade, an impatient, senator caustically reminded him, "that he was in the pay, not of M. Monnet, but of the United States." [60] Ball simply, and sometimes impatiently, defended himself against these allegations by consistently asserting that the American national interest and the transcendent goal of European unification were not mutually exclusive.

Robert Schaetzel once compactly summarized the principles that dominated Monnet's thinking: The first was an aversion to nationalism; the second was a faith in the idea of community; and the third an emphasis on institutions. While it is of course impossible to calculate the extent of Monnet's direct influence on Ball in any category, it would not be idle speculation to suggest that Ball come to more fully appreciate the wisdom of these principles as a result of his work with the great Frenchman. He was married to the first principle. Perhaps the most enduring legacy of Monnet is that Ball developed his own free trade catechism, and later declared, as his banking career was getting off the ground in 1968, that he knew "of few things more hopeful for the future than the growing determination of American business to regard national boundaries as no longer fixing the horizons of their corporate activity." [61] Ball has effectively used each of the five government offices he has occupied to assert that the United States should liberalize its trading policies and seek a truly interdependent world economic structure of the type envisioned by Monnet.

Courageously, Ball long felt that the United States must give up the hope of competing with cheap labor markets in the secondary manufacturing sector, and more rigorously assert the American comparative advantage in the high technology industries. He simply believed that most nation states are inadequate as economic units, and that global politics and global economics are "out of phase" with each other. He applauded the multinationals for moving elements of production around the world with great facility, and for "planning and acting in terms that are well in advance of the political ideas by which the world is organized." With a particular eye on European interaction, Ball believed, like Monnet before him, that the significance of free trade principles and common markets "rests not only on their economic efficacy but also on the seed of political unity they carry with them." [62]

There can be no question that Ball became a convert to the idea of European political community as a function of his work with Monnet and that he zealously advanced the cause in his own career. It was Monnet's idealism and pragmatism that appealed to Ball. As an American nationalist, Ball inherently understood that it was "not just good will or piety but compelling considerations of national interest" that warranted American support of the initiatives to unite Europe. "We were firmly convinced," Ball wrote of the 1950s and 60s, "that a United Europe would be stronger and less dangerously unstable and no longer a seedbed of war." [63] Judging from the amount of ink he has expended on the subject -- and despite his reputation as a Vietnam dissenter -- it is clear that he took more satisfaction from his work to promote European integration that any other single endeavor. It was perhaps the only project in government big enough to capture his attention and tax his ingenuity. Like Monnet, and despite their occasional references to austere origins, there is a part of them both that was more patrician than populist. While they strive to promote the general good, they were both less democratic in their means than one might suppose. As a "structural elitist," one observer noted, Ball "simply dislikes small policies, or policies concerning small places, or even policies designed for small periods of time." [64]   Ball and Monnet were both grand strategists and easily perturbed with the more mundane details of administration.

And finally, Ball found a new faith in at least one institution. Although his latent contempt for the United Nations has always been well known (he once scornfully admitted that he was the only U.N. Ambassador to know in advance the "sterility" of the job) it should be noted that his harsh criticisms of the institution mellowed appreciably. "It is time to put aside our unilateral posturing," Ball instructed the American Society of International Law, "and begin once again to use the United Nations in the manner its framers originally intended." Sounding a good deal like Monnet, Ball told the group of lawyers that "an abrupt change in our national conduct would pose a considerable challenge but it would also open vast new possibilities." As a timely antidote to persistent unilateralism of the post quarter-century, Ball called for "a major reorientation in our thinking and a substantial reconsideration of our [global] strategy." Noting that the pernicious East-West struggle has had "for four decades effectively paralyzed the principal organ of the United Nations -- the Security Council," Ball forecast the dawn of a new era in east-west relations long before the concept became fashionable. In the manner in which France and Germany did so, Ball called upon the United States and the Soviet Union to create "an alliance of adversaries "to advance the cause of stability.[65]

Ball often confessed his genuine admiration for, and has acknowledged a great debt to, his French friend. Monnet's transcendent character and enigmatic talents fascinated Ball from their initial encounter. When they first met in 1945, Ball appreciated Monnet as "a figure about whom legends had already accumulated." [66] In his eyes, Monnet was always a little bit bigger than life. In the course of his long and varied career as a lawyer, banker, diplomat and author, Ball had countless occasions to observe prominent statesmen on both sides of the Atlantic. His letters, speeches, books, and editorials are a veritable archive of insight into the leadership of the Western World for the past forty-five years. At no time, and in no single other instance has he expressed more fervent adulation of another man.

Among Ball's more distinctive tributes is the way he has contrasted two prominent Frenchmen he has encountered. In befriending Monnet and embracing his central thesis and methods, he necessarily became an antagonist of Charles de Gaulle who distrusted Monnet's vision. While de Gaulle saw the various communities (ECSC, Euratom, EDC) as threats to French sovereignty and his own anachronistic dreams of hegemony, Monnet saw them as the only possible institutions in which the tangled problems of French security and economic recovery might be addressed. Monnet was able to set aside former animosities in the hope of creating a spirit of internationalism; de Gaulle fumed the fires of acrimony to generate French nationalism. While Monnet conceptualized Europe as a family of nations beset by common dangers, de Gaulle saw Europe as a stage set for himself -- and pursued his personal aspirations to recapture France's status as the preeminent European power.

Applauding Monnet for never indulging in "whimsical fantasy," Ball saw him as eminently realistic. In contrast, he has characterized de Gaulle as a "brilliant anachronism" and a statesman who "disrupted Europe by undertaking a *tour de force* beyond the reach of his extraordinary abilities." Ball sees de Gaulle as essentially a "superb actor," and like those in that craft, he left "only legends and transient playbills [but] nothing permanent that affects the lives or sensibilities of future generations." Monnet, in contrast, was "a superlative architect," and the master builder of structures that will outlive his generation. "I have no doubt," Ball unhesitatingly professes, "that of the two, Jean Monnet was the greater." [67]

Ball's personal correspondence with Monnet also permits a more objective appraisal of their peculiar relationship. Not at all reluctant to express his sincere affection for Ball, Monnet's letters leave little doubt about the sincerity of the warm feelings they regularly expressed. Their families shared an intimacy that neither man extended to many other.[68] In 1973, after an unusually long absence from each other, Monnet lamented the fact that they had "let so long a time pass without making a little effort to meet." He reminded Ball that they had been friends for a long time and in difficult periods, and credited his younger friend with contributing "a great deal to [his] thinking." In a most touching closing, Monnet said that he was confident that Ball shared similar affections for him.[69]

Quite apart from the enormous regard that Monnet had for Ball's powers of reasoning and persuasion, it is also obvious that there was something about him as a person that was greatly appealing to the older

Frenchman. Unlike other Americans such as Acheson, Dulles, and McCloy who were much closer to Monnet in age and experience, Ball's relationship with his French friend was based much more on a mutual appreciation of each other's processes of thought, character, and personality. A slight and fragile man, Monnet was enchanted with Ball's size and energy -- and often commented on his "striking command of both physical and intellectual resources." On those occasions when Monnet would reluctantly respond to inquiries about his private relationship with Ball, compliments flowed freely. He appreciated his friend's "wisdom," "boldness," "loyalty," and "great capacity to analyze." In Monnet's eyes, Ball was highly "cultured," and possessed an "intellectual force which always surprised Europeans." He took particular note of Ball's "steadiness of mind," his "capacity to adjust to conditions," and his "kindness." All these attributes, at least in Monnet's eyes, served to mitigate the stereotype of the "Ugly American." "With Ball," Monnet felt, "you could say the friendly American," and he perceived his American friend as a man who had "great experience" in the occidental way of life. "Civilization," Monnet was delighted to attest, "means something to him. Virtues came naturally to him. He's gay, very gay. He is clear, not tortured like Europeans. A man of good will who finds pleasure in helping others," and consistently demonstrates the "very broadest concern for the general interest." [70] Like German Chancellor Helmut Schmidt,[71] Monnet found in his friend the ability, rare among Americans, to comprehend European mentalities. "Often," Monnet once complained, "strong Americans are too simple; they don't see things in their complexity." But Ball "is a spirit who weighs things," a man of "real judgment," a person "remarkably well balanced," not a "divided personality," and "loyal [emphasis included]." [72]

When George Ball and Jean Monnet met on Thanksgiving Day in 1977, both men sensed that the visit might well be their last. On that occasion Ball found Monnet engaging and alert, but weak. "I'm not ill, George," Monnet announced in a reassuring tone, "just old." With an air of inspiration Monnet confidently pronounced, "It'll go on. What we've started will continue. It has momentum." [73] A few weeks later, Ball wrote Jean and Silvia Monnet to thank them for the splendid day: "Although I have not always been an apt pupil," Ball admitted, "Jean has been a magnificent teacher, and I think I have learned more from you Jean, than from anyone else." [74]

Even his adversaries concede that George Ball is endowed with an extraordinary intelligence and impressive abilities. It would be intellectually negligent to discuss him in this context without taking note of the consummate self-confidence and personal pride he takes in his

work. Surrounded by the "best and brightest" during the Kennedy-
Johnson years, Ball remained an independent thinker -- his own man.
Indeed, there have been very few in the business of statecraft in this
century to whom he did not feel at least equal. Monnet may not have
been "everything" in his life, as he once blithely remarked.[75] But clearly
he was a great deal, and their relationship was both personally enriching
and, to the great benefit of a Western World now poised on the threshold
of a new economic era, politically fertile. In a deeply reflective mood at
the end of the three day Hyde Park conference entitled "Monnet and the
Americans," Ball succinctly summed up his relationship with Monnet
and the rigors of work in his orbit: "I wouldn't have done it for anyone
else and I wouldn't have missed it for anything. Indeed, it was
wonderful. All those years were wonderful."

Endnotes

1 George W. Ball, *The Past Has Another Pattern: Memoirs* , New York, 1982 ,p.99.

2 William P. Bundy interview, Apr 6, 1985.

3 In describing Monnet's relationship with Ball, a Kennedy assistant wrote:
"Soon Ball became Under Secretary of State for Economic Affairs; on entering
his impressive new office in the State Department, he is said to have gaily
remarked, 'Monnet isn't everything.' But Monnet remained a great deal."
Arthur M. Schlesinger, Jr., *A Thousand Days: John F. Kennedy in the White House* ,
New York, 1967, p. 772. Ball also once remarked to the author: "Unlike your
friend [Ambassador J. Robert] Schaetzel, I never became a Monnet cultist." Ball
interview, Mar 2, 1990.

4 In thanking Jean and Silvia Monnet for a recent visit, Ball sensitively confessed:
"I was grateful, as always, for your sound advice and the wisdom that
informed your conversation. Although I have not always been an apt pupil,
Jean has been a magnificent teacher, and I think I have learned more from you,
Jean, than from anyone else." George W. Ball to Jean and Silvia Monnet, Dec
14, 1976, Papers of George W. Ball, (hereafter PGWB.) Also, Ball's wife of fifty
years, Ruth Murdoch Ball, unhesitatingly expresses the private conviction that
her husband respected and admired Monnet above anyone. Ruth Ball
interview, Apr 6, 1985.

5 Marilyn Berger interview, Sep 5, 1990.

6 Ball's retainer while working for Monnet, the communities created by Monnet,
or the French government, were clearly not among his most lucrative. He
recently described them a "monetarily incidental." Ball interview, Sep 28, 1990.

7 As a consequence of his nomination to become Under Secretary of State for
Economic Affairs, Ball was investigated by the FBI. The Bureau's background
report on Ball makes repeated references to the regularity of his travel to
Europe, and to his associations there. United States Department of Justice,
Federal Bureau of Investigation, *"Special Inquiry Into George Wildman Ball,
Results of Investigation,"* Freedom of Information Act Case no. 8600931. PGWB.

8 Dean Rusk interview, Mar 27, 1985.

9 Roger Hilsman interview, Apr 2, 1985.

10 Clifford P. Hackett *Cautious Revolution: The European Community Arrives,*
Westport, CT, 1990, p. 3.

11 Quoted in Richard Barnet, *The Alliance: America-Europe-Japan, Makers of the
Postwar World* , New York, 1983, p. 98.

12 Ball, *Past*, p.73.

13 Marilyn Berger interview, Sep 2, 1990.

14 Ball, *Past*, p.76.

15 Ball, *Past*, p. 73. There were more conventional aspects of the relationship as Ball was retained by all three of communities midwife by Monnet: The European Coal and Steel Community (ECSC), Euratom, and, later, the European Economic Community. While he had a formal relationship with these institutions, he continued to advise Monnet personally and informally on a range of matters, performing his familiar role as "amanuensis and intellectual punching bag whenever he came to the United States."

16 Richard Mayne, "Gray Eminence," The American Scholar, Aug 1984, p. 538. Also reprinted in D. Brinkley and C. Hackett, eds., *Jean Monnet: The Path to European Unity* , New York, 1991, p. 114.

17 Ball *Past* , p.73. Lessons from work with Monnet were not lost on Ball. When he became under secretary of state he too proved to be a notoriously exacting task master. Schooled on Monnet's habits, and endowed (or cursed) with his own idiosyncratic attention to detail, Ball demanded much of himself and required an exceedingly high standard of performance from subordinates. One of his assistants in the state department introduced him at a dinner in his honor by remarking that Ball "single-handedly worked a revolution in the use of the English language within the State Department," and that he served as a "one man remedial writing instructor." Thomas Ehrlich, remarks at Stanford University, Mar 31, 1971, PGWB.

18 Ball, *Past*, p.83.

19 Robert Marjolin said Monnet thought the OEEC was a wholly unsatisfactory arrangement: "At this juncture Monnet tried to push Europe forward, a Europe which could take its decisions by majority vote and which, in consequence, would go well beyond the Europe as represented by the OEEC where all decisions had to be unanimous. He made no attempt to hide his contempt for what he called 'intergovernmental cooperation'." Robert Marjolin, *Architect of European Unity; Memoirs 1911-1986*, London, 1989, p. 271.

20 Ball,*Past*, p. 84.

21 George W. Ball, *The Discipline of Power: Essentials of a Modern World Structure* , Boston,1968, p. 49.

22 Ball, *Past*, p.89.

23 "Note - G.W. Ball (Nov. 1950)," Foundation Jean Monnet Pour L'Europe, (hereafter FJM) Lausanne, Switzerland.

24 Ball, *Past*, p. 86-87.

25 Marjolin, *Memoirs* p. 270.

26 Ball, *Discipline*, p. 48.

27 Dean Acheson, *Sketches From Life*, p. 37. Acheson also writes in *Present at the Creation* that original apprehensions quickly subsided, p. 383.

28 Marjolin, *Memoirs* , p. 264.

29 Ball, *Past*, p. 81. Marjolin remained skeptical:

"The difference in standpoints which George Ball noticed between Jean Monnet and me was even more pronounced, as far as I am concerned, when it came to certain theories representing the views of a number of fervent 'Europeans', who were quite a strong force during the fifties and early sixties. For them, federal Europe was within reach, if the political will were there. Practically speaking, once the first step had been in this direction, events would necessarily follow on from one of the so-called theory of *engrenage* [chain reaction] or the 'spill-over effect'. It is set out in the fullest detail in what

maybe regarded as the political testament of Walter Hallstein, who, as a close
collaborator of Konrad Adenauer, then as President of the EEC Commission
from 1958 to 1967, played a large part in the construction of the Common
Market. The forces which the Europeans had let in deciding to create a
common market, so Hallstein's thinking went, must inevitably take Europe to
economic union, then to political union. If one started out with a customs
union and a common agricultural policy, one would inevitable be drawn much
further...."Marjolin, *Memoirs,* p. 265.

30 Ball, *Past,* pp. 81-82.

31 Quoted in Barnet, *The Alliance* , p. 124.

32 Ball, *Past,* p. 95. Ball had been pressed --- without success --- to revise and
publish the long lost manuscript.

33   George W. Ball, "The Period of Transition," in *Economic Unity in Europe:
Programs and Problems,* New York, 1960, pp.9-34.

34 *"Report to the Honorable John F. Kennedy from Adlai E. Stevenson, November,
1960,"* Personal Papers of J. Robert Schaetzel.

35 Ibid. pp. 5-7, & pp. 1-20.

36 Ibid., p.11.

37 Ibid., p.12, Part II p. 2, appendices.

38 Ball, *Past,* p. 164.

39 Schlesinger, *A Thousand Days,* p. 771.

40 *Hearings Before the Committee on Foreign Relations,* U.S. Senate,87th Congress,
First Session, Jan. 24, 1961, p. 10.

41 Ball, *Discipline,* p. 224.

42 Ball, *Past,* p. 183.

43 Ibid,.

44 Ibid, p. 164.

45   Quoted in David L. DiLeo, *George Ball, Vietnam, and the Rethinking of
Containment,* Chapel Hill, NC 1991, p. xii.

46 Schlesinger, *A Thousand Days,* p. 772.

47 Ball, *Past,* p. 208.

48   Merry and Serge Bromberger. *Jean Monnet and the United States of Europe,*
New York, 1969, p. 223.

49   J. Robert Schaetzel, *The Unhinged Alliance: America and the European
Community,* New York, 1975, p. 64.

50 Schlesinger, *A Thousand Days,* p. 782.

51 Washington Daily News, Jul 10, 1962.

52 Ball, *Discipline* , pp. 57-58.

53   Ball, *Past,* p. 222. In describing the evolution of the concept within the
Kennedy administration, political scientist Alfred Grosser notes: "The idea of a
'partnership' between the possible future of the Atlantic community had
already been publicly expressed in December [1961] by McGeorge Bundy, one
of the President's closest advisers. And in a speech entitled 'Toward an
Atlantic Partnership,' another adviser, George Ball, had pointed out in Feb 1962
how closely this idea corresponded to the aim of the builders of Europe,
among whom he had good reason to count himself. He stated: 'As long as
Europe remained fragmented, as long as it consisted merely of nations small
by modern standards, the potentials for true partnership were always limited.
It was in recognition of this fact that since the war we have consistently
encouraged the powerful drive toward European integration. We have wanted

a Europe united and strong that could serve as an equal partner in the achievement of our common endeavors as an equal partner committed to the some basic values and objectives as all Americans.' The Action Committee for the United States of Europe on Jun 26, eight days before Kennedy's Philadelphia speech: 'The Action Committee which comprises the vast majority of the political parties of our six countries as well as the free and Christian trade unions representing ten million workers is of the opinion that only through the economic and political unification of Europe, including the United Kingdom, and the establishment of a partnership of equals between Europe and the United States can the West be strengthened and the conditions created for peace between East and West.'" Alfred Grosser, *The Western Alliance: European-American Relations Since 1945* , New York, 1982, p. 201.

54 Bromberger, p. 222-223.

55 "Historic Victory for Freer Trade," Newsweek Oct. 1, 1962, p. 17-18.

56 Ibid.

57 McGeorge Bundy interview, Apr. 1, 1987.

58 Justice Department, FBI Special Inquiry, PGWB.

59 Grosser, *The Western Alliance*, pp. 103-104.

60 Ibid, p. 104. Also, Ball's censure was called for because of his "lack of manners." Congressional Record, Jan. 24, 1963, p. 981.

61 Ball, "The Promise of the Multinational Corporation," Fortune Jun 1, 1967,.

62 Ibid, p.9.

63 Ball, *Discipline*, p. 48.

64 Donald R. Katz, "The Grand Designer," New Republic, Jul 13, 1979, p. 23.

65 Ball, *Past*, p. 175 and his speech before the American Society of International Law, Apr 22 1988, in Washington.

66 Ball, *Past*, p. 69.

67 Ibid, pp. 97-8.

68 Douglas B. Ball testifies to this intimacy in recalling how Monnet accepted dinner invitations only if Ball's immediate family, and no other guests, were present. Monnet delighted in Douglas Ball's curiosity and keen knowledge of history. Douglas B. Ball interview, Apr 17, 1986.

69 Jean Monnet to George Ball, Dec 27, 1973, PGWB.

70 Washington Post correspondent Marilyn Berger interview with Monnet on Dec. 5, 1974, PGWB.

71 Helmut Schmidt, interview, Pomona College, Mar 15, 1986.

72 Jean Monnet, *Memoirs*, Garden City, NY, 1978,p. 465, and Monnet remarks from an interview with Marilyn Berger on Dec. 5, 1974, PGWB and confirmed in an interview witl. Berger, Sep 2, 1990.

73 Ball, *Past*, p. 95.

74 Ball to Jean and Silvia Monnet, Dec 14, 1976, PGWB.

75 Schlesinger, *A Thousand Days*, p.772.

7
The Transnational Partnership: Jean Monnet and Jack McCloy

Thomas Schwartz

Toward the end of his long and distinguished career, John J. McCloy, the "Chairman of the American Establishment," spoke often of his friendship with the French brandy salesman-turned-statesman, Jean Monnet. McCloy recalled their collaboration during the Second World War and its aftermath, and their shared conviction about the necessity of the partnership between the United States and the emerging European Community. McCloy also remembered that Monnet once compared him to a law partner of McCloy's, Donald Swatland, saying, "Jack, you're not as bright, but you also have a most admirable trait - you are very lucky, and I think I'll stay close to you because you're a lucky man." [1] Allowing for self-deprecating humor, there is in Monnet's remark a useful characterization of their friendship. Monnet genuinely liked and admired the energetic and optimistic McCloy, who had risen to the top echelons of American government despite the modest circumstances of his upbringing. Monnet relied upon some of his American friends for innovative ideas or technical skills, but the Frenchman respected McCloy's unerring sense of where power lay within the American government, and how to get things done. McCloy's accomplishments and reputation for quiet effectiveness further enhanced his value as a friend for Monnet.

This essay focuses on their relationship from 1940-1952, the twelve years which McCloy spent in public service. During World War II their relationship helped Monnet to penetrate American decision making at the highest levels of the Roosevelt Administration. After the war, the friendship gave Monnet a significant influence over the direction of American policies toward Europe, especially those promoting European unity and the integration of Germany into the West. The Monnet-McCloy relationship provides one of the most fascinating and important examples of the transnational partnerships that sustained American and European cooperation in the years after 1945.

When he received the Jean Monnet Award in October 1981, McCloy recalled that his association with the Frenchman went back to "the period immediately following World War I and the early days of the League of Nations." [2] Unfortunately neither man left any record of their first meeting or initial impressions, and there is some reason to doubt that they were acquainted as early as McCloy remembered. Most probably they met only after McCloy joined the Cravath law firm in December 1924. Donald Swatland, a man McCloy admired as "perhaps the ablest I have ever known," brought the two together. Swatland, who had finished at the top of McCloy's Harvard Law School class, lured McCloy to Cravath from the rival firm of Cadwalader, Wickersham, and Taft. Swatland met Monnet when serving as a lawyer for Monnet's investment banking firm of Blair and Company. Monnet and Swatland worked together on the reorganization of Transamerica and international loans, where, in Monnet's words, Swatland's "integrity and deep understanding guaranteed that all was well." [3]

In association with Swatland, McCloy began his involvement with Cravath's European clients, spending much time in Europe in 1927 and 1928, and heading Cravath's Paris office in 1930. This work brought him into frequent contact with Monnet.[4] McCloy later recalled socializing with Monnet when he was in Milan, and even remembered the gossip surrounding Monnet's relationship with his future wife, Silvia de Bondini, who was at the time married to an Italian businessman. "No one realized there was anything going on between Silvia and Jean until they went off together," McCloy later recalled. The American envied his French friend: "Silvia was one of the most beautiful women I'd ever seen before or since. I thought she was a star. But she was far beyond my reach." [5] Later in the 1930s, when McCloy pursued the Black Tom sabotage case, and Monnet worked in China, the two men's encounters were less frequent. But undoubtedly Monnet recognized in McCloy an able and talented lawyer, a profession whose importance the Frenchman had learned to appreciate. (As Monnet said in his *Memoirs*: "Nothing important is done in the United States without lawyers.") [6]

Monnet once said that in his experience, "friendship... is the result of joint action rather than the reason for it." [7] Monnet and McCloy's first "*action commune*" came when both arrived in Washington in the bleak autumn of 1940. After the fall of France in June 1940, Monnet became a member of the British Purchasing Commission, while McCloy became assistant secretary of war under the venerable Henry Stimson, who also developed a high regard for Monnet. From the Frenchman's tiny office on the eighth floor of

Washington's old Willard Hotel, Monnet became the "great, single-minded apostle of all-out production, preaching the doctrine that ten thousand tanks too many are far preferable to one tank too few." [8] Monnet argued that the United States and Britain were still approaching the task of production in a piecemeal fashion, and that this approach led to the under-utilization of America's enormous industrial capacity. Calling for an approach that put needs first before resources, Monnet insisted on an Anglo-American balance sheet of present and future production. In his characteristically unrelenting fashion, Monnet insisted on the urgency of the matter, telling his Washington friends that America must become a "great arsenal, the arsenal of democracy." [9] When Monnet used the phrase with McCloy, the war department official noted the expression and used it in speaking to his former law school professor, Supreme Court Justice Felix Frankfurter, who admonished McCloy not to use the expression again. Frankfurter passed the phrase along to one of the President's speechwriters, Robert Sherwood, and it soon appeared in a famous Roosevelt speech.[10]

The problems of mobilizing America's industrial power consumed the attentions of Monnet and McCloy throughout 1941. McCloy spoke with Monnet almost daily, either over the telephone or in McCloy's office, as the two men discussed and lamented the status of America's production effort. Robert Nathan, one of the young economists who worked with the two men, recalled that Monnet's persistent demands for more American production could irritate Americans, as the Frenchman dismissed their concerns that "highly excessive goals would almost certainly result in chaos in the armament industries." [11] McCloy, however, supported Monnet's calls for a greater American effort. After President Roosevelt's declaration of an "Unlimited National Emergency," McCloy and Monnet, along with the Nathan and fellow economist Stacy May, worked together to prepare war department orders for "a comprehensive Anglo-American balance-sheet" comparing American and British resources with estimates of German strength. The balance sheet showed that American production was lagging behind Britain and Canada, and that there were serious deficiencies in the number of heavy bombers and tanks. These conclusions led Roosevelt to give his approval on September 25, 1941 to the Victory Program for the army and navy. Monnet noted that this meant an "immense increase in American strength and, by implication, a decisive American impact on the future course of the war." [12]

McCloy's admiration for the role Monnet played in pre-Pearl Harbor Washington is captured best in a letter to Frankfurter in

November 1941. Lord Halifax, the new British Ambassador in
Washington, had asked Frankfurter to "put on paper the view taken
here of Jean Monnet and his services." Halifax's request was likely
prompted by the concerted efforts of treasury secretary Henry
Morgenthau to get Monnet fired. Along with his absolute loyalty to
Roosevelt, Morgenthau possessed an almost paranoid distaste for
international bankers. He distrusted Monnet's interwar connections to
the Republican law firm Sullivan and Cromwell --- John Foster Dulles's
firm --- and Monnet's supposed activities on behalf of German firms in
the United States.[13] Frankfurter, who considered Monnet "a teacher to
our Defense establishment," assembled a strong defense of Monnet to
present to Halifax. He spoke with numerous officials, including Harry
Hopkins, Henry Stimson, Robert Lovett, and McCloy, all of whom
praised Monnet's efforts. Frankfurter's letter to Halifax contains a long
quote from the letter he solicited from McCloy:

> On reflection I think [Monnet] has been responsible
> more than anyone connected with the British mission ... for the
> orientation of the men with whom he comes in contact in the
> War Department to the primary task which the United States
> must perform if it is to act effectively in the war. For one reason
> or another - perhaps because of diffidence, perhaps because so
> many are compelled to respond so continuously to the
> motivation of the last cable from London - the result is that
> Monnet is the only one from their shop who talks and presses to
> the point almost of irritation the broad picture of the United
> States obligation. He spares himself no indignity or rebuff but
> before long he has the Army officers repeating his arguments.
> He thinks on the basis of a wide experience and wide contacts
> with the men of influence in three different governments, all of
> whom struggled with the problems of supply in war, not only in
> this war but in the last, and the quality and plane of his
> thinking shows it. Monnet has the advantage of knowing both
> the British and Americans well, but he contributes his own
> method of thinking and working which neither the British nor
> the Americans seem to be able to duplicate for its effect. You
> know the regard in which he is held among those in high place. I
> see his influence on the hewers of wood and I repeat, in my
> judgment no one in the British mission, capable as so many of
> them are, is near the equal of Monnet, measured in terms of
> influence on the War Department's approach to British supply
> needs.

McCloy concluded his evaluation with a comment that
Frankfurter chose not to pass along to Halifax: "As for [Monnet's]
national loyalties, they are unimportant whatever they are. I know
you can depend on his loyalty to the main task." [14]

McCloy's letter is worth quoting at length because his
assessment of Monnet's influence and style changed little over the next
forty years. Not surprisingly, the self-made man in McCloy admired

some of the qualities he himself was known for, such as extraordinary tenacity and persistence in the face of overwhelming obstacles. McCloy also recognized in Monnet a man who combined vision with pragmatism in a manner that was rare in wartime Washington. Monnet's willingness to repeat the same arguments over and over, to be the "apostle of all-out production," and to suffer indignity and rebuff in this role, impressed McCloy. In contrast McCloy's own temperament was less obstinate than conciliatory, often seeking to find agreement between conflicting officials and bureaucracies. His numerous responsibilities as assistant secretary gave him much less time to devote to such matters as "the broad picture of the United States obligation." McCloy also admired the cosmopolitan character of Monnet's approach and experience, the "wide plane" of his thinking that contributed historical perspective and authority to his arguments. With a man of such qualities it was unimportant what his particular national loyalties were, though Morgenthau's suspicions had planted this doubt among some leaders in Washington and London.

After Pearl Harbor Monnet and McCloy continued to work together on America's Victory Program, a collaboration that was both business and social. McCloy and his wife Ellen dined regularly with the Monnets, often accompanied by the Frankfurters or the Stimsons, They celebrated New Year's Eve together in 1942. (Ellen McCloy and Silvia Monnet became particularly close, as both worked as volunteers in various wartime organizations.) McCloy even intervened in a personal matter for Monnet. When Monnet's Italian brother-in-law was arrested because of suspected involvement with fascist circles, the assistant secretary helped him obtain a furlough from prison.[15]

Although Monnet's official position remained with the British Purchasing Commission, both Stimson and McCloy regularly consulted him about the political situation in France. Disputes over America's policy toward France began shortly after that country's surrender in June 1940. Unlike the British, who adopted the Free French movement of General de Gaulle, the United States recognized the Vichy government of Marshall Petain, hoping to encourage its resistance to German demands. The state department's distrust of de Gaulle as a potential dictator, a sentiment shared by the President and fueled by such French exiles as Alexis Léger, made America's policy toward the Free French more hostile than many Americans thought wise.[16] The United States finally broke relations with Vichy after the Allies landed troops in North Africa in November 1942. However, the Roosevelt Administration was willing to make a deal in North Africa with a notorious Vichy official, Admiral Jean Darlan, to insure the safety of American troops. The "Darlan Deal" produced a public outcry against Washington's expediency, and forced the Administration to look for some alternative. Washington hoped that General Henri Giraud, a French military commander who had escaped from the Germans, might serve as that alternative to de Gaulle or Darlan.[17]

Monnet's position in this regard was delicate. He had refused to join forces with General de Gaulle's Free French Movement, preferring to work directly for the British. Yet as a French patriot he remained committed to the restoration of France as a vital part of any European settlement. To accomplish this Monnet believed that the French themselves would have to be united and obtain support from the United States and Britain. De Gaulle's unpopularity in official Washington made open sympathy for the general dangerous. Monnet worded his own sentiments in such a way that a memorandum he wrote to Hopkins after the Darlan affair could be used by Robert Sherwood as an expression of Roosevelt's own position at the Casablanca Conference in January 1943. In the memo, written the day Darlan was assassinated, Monnet argued that the United States and Great Britain must preserve the right of the French people to self-determination after liberation. Monnet drew a distinction between French support for de Gaulle as a symbol of continuing the fight against the Germans as opposed to support for de Gaulle as the head of a new French government. He also made it clear that although Darlan had served a useful function in ordering his subordinates not to resist the allied landings, the Allies could not allow him to claim any legitimacy. Monnet proposed forming a governing body composed of both Free French and former Vichy supporters that would be under allied supervision and limited to local administration. The main allied effort would go into creating a French national army that could support the liberation.[18]

During the Casablanca Conference, Roosevelt cabled Secretary of State Cordell Hull to suggest that Monnet be sent to Algiers to assist General Giraud in setting up his administration. Despite Morgenthau's continuing suspicions, in Roosevelt's view Monnet had "kept his skirts clear of political entanglements in recent years," and his views on the future of France impressed the President. Hull opposed the suggestion, claiming that Monnet was a secret supporter of General de Gaulle. But the idea met a favorable response in other circles in Washington, particularly those in Stimson and McCloy's War Department. A month later Harry Hopkins arranged for Monnet to be sent to Algiers to work on the handling of lend lease supplies for the equipping of the French Army. Before Monnet left, Frankfurter urged him not to throw in his lot completely with Giraud, but to maintain his independence from "the contending forces in the pull of French politics." [19] Frankfurter's words only served to reinforce Monnet's own intuition that the political situation remained fluid, and that the imperative of the moment was to unite the French and then seek some form of allied recognition.

Two weeks before Monnet arrived in North Africa McCloy himself had come to Algiers on behalf of the war department. McCloy was particularly concerned to see the formation of a strong French Army to assist the Allies in their liberation of Europe. Commenting that "Europe is not Anglo-Saxon by a longshot," he told General Eisenhower, "we gain vis-a-vis Europe by incorporating the French more closely into our effort." [20] Along with more specific matters related to the military situation, McCloy's mission was to "examine the civilian situation in North Africa as it affects the military problem." [21] Most importantly, McCloy was to establish contact with General Giraud, who, in the aftermath of Darlan's assassination, had emerged as the leading figure in the French Army in North Africa. But Giraud was primarily a military man, and he lacked political skill and imagination. His failure to purge his administration of Vichy collaborators or to insist on the repeal of Nazi-inspired anti-Jewish legislation led to strong criticism in Britain and the United States. McCloy recognized the political impossibility of rearming the French while the Vichy legacy remained. In his meetings with Giraud, McCloy pressed these "Nuremberg Laws" in North Africa, but found Giraud slow to respond. McCloy told the General and his advisors that the American people "needed... some definite and unequivocal step" to show that "Nazism and collaboration were a thing of the past." [22]

McCloy's mission to North Africa lasted only a month, as Stimson insisted that his assistant not be "tangled up with work which was not essentially his." [23] To continue these efforts, and to support a unified French resistance, McCloy relied on Monnet. The assistant secretary prepared the groundwork for Monnet, praising him to American and French officials and even arranging an apartment for him. He told General Eisenhower that he would get "real help in Monnet," and urged the General to "keep in touch with him from time to time to see how he is making out." [24] To Giraud's advisor, the controversial Marcel Peyrouton, McCloy described Monnet as "a man in whom he could have absolute confidence." [25] When Monnet arrived the two men met again with Giraud and pressed him to repeal the Vichy anti-Jewish decrees.[26] After McCloy left, Monnet eventually succeeded in convincing Giraud to deliver his speech of March 14, 1943, which repudiated the June 1940 armistice, reaffirmed the sovereignty of the

French people, and denounced the legality of the Vichy regime. However, the general's speech came so late that it appeared no more than a grudging concession to General de Gaulle's forces, who had arrived in Algiers to negotiate a unified French resistance.[27]

After McCloy returned to Washington, Monnet intensified his own efforts to unify the French resistance. In pursuit of this goal he continued to enjoy McCloy's political and personal support in Washington. At one point, when rumors of a putsch in Algiers reached Washington, McCloy arranged military protection for Monnet.[28] The French historian André Kaspi has described Monnet's complicated and secret efforts to secure an agreement between General Giraud and General de Gaulle.[29] Monnet's success with the creation of the French Committee of National Liberation (FCNL) earned him praise from his American friends like McCloy and Frankfurter, who attributed the formation of the committee to Monnet's "infinite patience and complete disinterestedness and extraordinary resourcefulness." [30] However, both General de Gaulle and those Americans who backed Giraud looked on Monnet's role in the FCNL with great suspicion. De Gaulle referred to Monnet as the "inspirer" who seemed to work as an American agent in bringing about the fusion of de Gaulle and Giraud's forces.[31]

On the other hand Robert Murphy, a key state department representative in Algiers, reported to Roosevelt that Monnet's secret expansion of the FCNL from seven to fourteen members, undertaken "without advising us... appears to give a preponderant influence to the de Gaulle group." De Gaulle's political movement also reminded Murphy of "the technique employed in the early twenties by the German National Socialist party." Murphy admitted that while Monnet "respects the United States and Britain and... will avoid giving offense to us," Monnet "is definitely out to gain every advantage for the French he possibly can." Because Monnet "knows our methods so well," Murphy feared that he would benefit from "every opportunity we offer him to seize advantage." He noted that Monnet "counts greatly on the support of Jack McCloy and Felix Frankfurter," and that he was loyal to neither Giraud nor de Gaulle but to "to France and to Monnet." [32]

Murphy's suspicions reflected the bitter disappointment of those American officials, including President Roosevelt, who supported Giraud against General de Gaulle. De Gaulle's eventual success in consolidating his support within the FCNL and ousting Giraud was a result which Monnet probably anticipated. When he returned to the United States as a representative of the FCNL in November 1943, Monnet pushed hard for official American recognition of the committee

as the government of France.[33]   In this new role as an official
representative of France, Monnet doubted whether "my friends in the
Administration would give me so much of their time." But Monnet soon
found himself once again working closely with the war department and
particularly McCloy. McCloy supported his friend when the state
department, holding to Hull's hostility toward all things associated
with General de Gaulle, treated Monnet in a "silly way." The assistant
secretary urged them to listen respectfully to Monnet as "an accredited
representative of France." [34]

Early in 1944 McCloy took up the cause of American recognition
of the FCNL. Although Monnet's influence was only one factor in
McCloy's thinking, there is little doubt that the friendship
strengthened McCloy's resolve. McCloy drafted a plan which called
for recognition of the FCNL, but coupling the recognition with a pledge
from the FCNL to relinquish its authority at the end of hostilities in
favor of a freely elected group.[35] The plan immediately faced the
opposition of Secretary of State Hull and President Roosevelt, and even
the doubts of his boss Secretary Stimson. As Stimson noted, "McCloy
wanted to enlist and recognize the Committee as the responsible
government all over France as soon as France was liberated and thought
that we could not differentiate the combat zones from the other parts of
France in this respect." [36]   Both Hull and Stimson disagreed with
McCloy, arguing that the committee was too fragile and might fall
apart after the Liberation. McCloy held to his plan even after a
"disastrous interview" with President Roosevelt, who continued to
distrust de Gaulle.[37] Indeed McCloy's continued support for de Gaulle's
recognition may have come close to getting him fired, so strongly had
the President come to detest the French general.[38] Roosevelt refused to
give the FCNL de facto recognition until July 11, 1944, more than a
month after the Normandy landings, and only grudgingly extended
official recognition in October of the same year.

McCloy supported the FCNL with the hope that it would help
the military effort. The assistant secretary disliked the fact that "not
enough of the French are involved in the war against Germany," and
that America's refusal to recognize the FCNL encouraged the French to
be "more political" rather than to engage in "military activity." [39]
Both McCloy and Monnet believed that Europe required the restoration
of a strong France to balance the greatly increased power of the Soviet
Union, though they could differ on what priority to give this objective.
Monnet's role in relief efforts in late 1944 found him repeatedly
pressing upon McCloy the need to expedite supplies to France.[40]

In one conversation, McCloy, with more than a hint of irritation, noted that Monnet "with his usual persistence" was pressing him "for treatment of the French on the same basis, so far as shipping is concerned, with the English, the United States, and Russia." McCloy had to tell Monnet that with a shipping shortage, priority had to go to supplies directly associated with shortening the war. McCloy was annoyed when Monnet brushed aside "as almost of no moment the enormous amount of material that is going into France on the military program from which the French economy will benefit." [41] But Monnet's warning that if the import program were not considered independently from military control, that further discussion would have to include General de Gaulle, led the Army to guarantee ships for France and Belgium for the first quarter of 1945.[42] Monnet's persistence won out again, and McCloy remained attentive to France's supply problems.[43]

With the end of the war both men moved on to new positions that limited their personal and official contact. Both regretted the change. On one of his last trips to Europe as assistant secretary in October 1945, McCloy spent an evening with the Monnets in their house near Rambouillet. Noting how "lovely" the Monnets' home was, McCloy commented wistfully that "it was fun to be with them [once again]." [44] McCloy briefly went back to the practice of law, only to be asked by President Truman in early 1947 to become president of the World Bank. Monnet led France's postwar economic recovery program, known as the Monnet Plan, and worked to modernize France's economy and infrastructure. McCloy's World Bank provided France with a $250 million loan in late 1947, but the bank's role was quickly superseded by the enormous quantities of assistance provided by the Marshall Plan. McCloy would not find himself plunged back into the problems of Europe until he became U.S. high commissioner to the new Federal Republic of Germany in July 1949.

It was during McCloy's tenure as high commissioner that Jean Monnet's ideas and initiatives were to have their most important influence on American policy toward European integration. Americans had been preaching the need for greater European unity since the end of the war, even conditioning Marshall Plan assistance on a coordinated European response and the creation of such bodies as the Organization of European Economic Cooperation. But with the intensification of the Cold War and the creation of the new West German state, American calls for greater European unity became even more insistent. The American strategy of containing the Soviet Union called for a revitalized Germany, but required that this Germany somehow be "integrated" (or contained) within Western Europe, so that it could not again pose a threat to the West.[45] Secretary of State Acheson pressed upon French Foreign Minister Robert Schuman the necessity of France taking the lead in the effort to integrate West Germany, but Schuman found himself trapped by the punitive policies toward Germany that had guided France in the early postwar years. In January 1950 when Schuman made a conciliatory visit to Bonn to meet with the new German Chancellor Konrad Adenauer, their negotiations were undermined by controversy over the Saar, a coal-rich province of Germany that had been detached and placed under French economic control. Franco-German antagonism, imbedded in these battles over coal and steel resources, seemed likely to frustrate the movement toward European unity.

Monnet had watched the Saar problem develop, convinced that "history was repeating itself" in the conflict between the two nations.[46] He had long been convinced of the need for some form of international control for the Ruhr region, telling a journalist in 1944 that "the great Rhine coal and iron fields" should be "run by a European authority for the benefit of all participating nations, including eventually a demilitarized Germany." [47] (Both he and McCloy opposed treasury secretary Morgenthau's Plan to deindustrialize Germany.) In early 1947 Monnet and McCloy discussed the latter's idea of a "Coal Authority" for the entire Ruhr region, an authority patterned after American inter-state authorities, and which could borrow money, operate and develop mines, and allocate production.[48] McCloy thought such a project would be popular with the "investing public" in the United States, but nothing came of it. Monnet himself, while heading the *Commissariat au Plan*, also recognized the need to deal with the Ruhr. As Irwin Wall has noted, the continuity between the Monnet and Schuman Plans was apparent "not only in Monnet's perception of the need to open up the French steel industry to foreign competition, but also in his early realization that the strength of French steel depended on German coke, and that French security depended upon continued access of France to the Ruhr and restriction of German sovereignty there." [49]

By late 1949 it became clear to Monnet that the Americans might support a proposal to achieve France's Ruhr objectives, if the proposal also promised greater European unity. In October 1949, in an interview with the London Times, McCloy expressed his hope that the Germans would join the International Authority for the Ruhr, an organization established by the Washington Agreements of April 1949, and that the authority could be expanded to cover all Western European heavy industry.[50] Early in April 1950 McCloy told the Pilgrims Club of Great Britain that there must be "prompt action" to

create a genuine European union.[51] Privately he urged Secretary of
State Acheson to tell the French that "we view the Federation of
Europe as a vital cornerstone upon which our whole fundamental policy
rests and that the barriers to effective progress along this line rest
primarily in the French attitude toward Germany." [52] But while
proclaiming the need for European union, McCloy was also made clear
to the French that, if necessary, America would proceed with
Germany's rehabilitation without her. During the Allied High
Commission's discussions of new laws to re-structure and regulate
Germany's heavy industry, McCloy said that the United States did not
support continued imposition of production quotas and other
prohibitions on Germany's industrial production. McCloy told
Washington that such controls did not make sense in the "present
divided world," and that Western countries must allow Germany the
realization of her "legitimate aspirations... [including] a rising
standard of living... a reasonable degree of economic stability, and a
respected voice in international affairs." [53]

       McCloy's twin messages --- support for a move toward European
union and the American determination to revive Germany --- became
two of the critical arguments that Monnet used within the French
government to convince Schuman to act. In his famous message to
Schuman, Monnet noted the German demand to increase their steel
quota, and commented, "We shall refuse, but the Americans will insist.
Finally we shall state our reservations, but we shall give in." [54]
Monnet knew that the futility of the French approach had been
underlined in a secret message from Acheson, who told Schuman that
the United States was prepared to allow "a freely elected German
government" to decide the question of ownership of its heavy
industry.[55] With a combination of pressure and support, Monnet led
Schuman to accept his "High Authority" proposal to control French and
German coal and steel industries. The Schuman Plan was born.

       Although the Americans had hoped for some type of French
initiative, Acheson was initially worried that the Schuman Plan was
simply a giant cartel, similar to the steel cartel of the 1920s. To
reassure Acheson, McCloy came to Paris to discuss the proposal with
Monnet. McCloy's subsequent enthusiasm for the proposal, and his
assurances that it would work to increase production within the two
countries, helped calm the secretary's fears. McCloy viewed the
proposed High Authority as similar to American creations like the
N.Y. Port Authority, the Tennessee Valley Authority, and the
Niagara Authority, and emphasized its political importance to the
skeptical Acheson. The extraordinary enthusiasm that the Schuman

Plan generated among American foreign policy officials, ranging from John Foster Dulles through Averell Harriman, brought the United States and France into close cooperation on matters involving Germany and the European integration. It was an unrivalled success for Monnet, encouraged greatly by his friendship with Jack McCloy.

When Monnet came to Bonn to present the plan to the Germans, McCloy used his authority as chairman of the Allied High Commission to block a British suggestion that a high commission official attend the negotiations. McCloy agreed with Monnet's argument that "given the scope of the commitments Germany will be undertaking in the Schuman Plan Treaty, it is vital that no one in the future should be able to claim that they were not freely accepted." [56] Less openly both men worried that giving the Allied High Commission a role would allow the British the opportunity to undermine Monnet's core idea: that the plan involve a real sacrifice of sovereignty by the nations involved.

Over the following months McCloy continually supported the Schuman Plan to the German government, leading industrialists, and trade union officials. Adenauer already suspected that although the "initiative [for the plan] is apparently purely French, Acheson... is the real instigator." [57] The American support strengthened the Chancellor's own sympathy for the plan, which he regarded as similar to his own ideas for a merger of German and French economic interests. To a more skeptical group of German industrialists from the Ruhr, McCloy proclaimed that the Schuman Plan had provided Europe with "renewed hope" for peace, and that its success could diminish the fear of Germany in other European countries. He added that "it is a political and economic fact of the first magnitude that France has proposed the idea and Germany has accepted it." McCloy also insisted that the German industrialists should accept and cooperate with allied plans to restructure the German coal and steel industry in the proposed Law 27. The high commissioner realized that outlines of the law had already provoked considerable opposition, but hoped that making it a pre-condition to entrance into the Schuman Plan would reduce German dissatisfaction.[58]

To encourage the close coordination of the Schuman Plan negotiations and the high commission's work on Law 27, McCloy, arranged the close cooperation between his own Office of Legal Counsel, headed by Harvard Law Professor Robert Bowie, with Ambassador David Bruce's staff in Paris, whose leading figure was the brilliant treasury official, William "Tommy" Tomlinson. Tomlinson and Bowie were very close to Monnet and his staff, which included Etienne Hirsch and Pierre Uri, and this arrangement allowed an extraordinarily close and careful coordination of American and French objectives. Monnet's men relied on Bowie to handle the Germans, especially the objections they anticipated from the Ruhr industrialists. For his part Bowie, along with George Ball, encouraged the French to make the Schuman Plan as unlike a cartel as possible, and most importantly, to include strong anti-trust provisions within the final treaty.

The close cooperation between the different American missions in Europe helped save the Schuman Plan from defeat, especially after the outbreak of the Korean War altered the European power equation. Monnet, as George Ball put it, saw the implication of the North Korean attack "almost faster than Washington." The Frenchman told Ball that the Americans "would never permit the Communists to succeed with such naked aggression.... Yet for America to intervene in Korea would not only jeopardize the Schuman Plan, it might well create panic in Europe and increase American insistence on a larger German role in the defense of the West." [59] The American demand for German rearmament endangered the delicate balance between France and Germany necessary for the Schuman Plan to succeed. Monnet also thought the Germans might try to encourage the Americans to undertake a war for the recovery of their "lost" eastern territories, a war which would bring destruction to all of Europe.[60]

The Frenchman also recognized the Americans might respond to a positive proposal from France that would allow German rearmament to take place "safely" within some type of European controls. He knew that in early August McCloy and Bowie had proposed a "European Army," which would incorporate German soldiers but avoid creating a new wehrmacht and a new German general staff. Monnet also knew that Pentagon objections had temporarily carried the day in Washington. In vain Monnet tried to warn Schuman that the Americans would take a firm line on German rearmament at the September foreign ministers meeting in New York.[61] But when the Americans proposed the re-creation of between ten to twelve German divisions as a pre-condition to sending American troops and a Supreme Commander to Europe, Schuman found himself in lonely opposition to the proposal.[62]

The public deadlock between the Americans and French over the rearmament issue threatened to undo the support which Monnet had won with the Schuman Plan. French opposition angered even McCloy, whose sympathy Monnet could not do without. The high commissioner feared that France's hostile attitude toward Germany might encourage Soviet aggression and increase support for neutrality in Germany.[63] Monnet also perceived a "stiffening of resistance" by the Germans on a number of issues.[64] Adenauer's appointment of an opponent of the Schuman Plan, Robert Lehr, as Interior Minister, also sent a disturbing signal. Monnet thought that "fresh winds were starting to blow Germany off course." [65] In his view the only solution was a French proposal on rearmament patterned after the Schuman Plan and designed, in effect, to save the Schuman Plan.[66]

The result of Monnet's efforts was the Pleven Plan. Prime Minister René Pleven's speech of October 24, 1950 announced French plans for a "European Army" of some 100,000 men, with German soldiers integrated "on the level of the smallest possible unit." However, the impracticality of integration at the battalion level led many to see the Pleven Plan as closer to a French Foreign Legion for Europe rather than a step toward a genuine European union. Pleven's insistence that the creation of such an army would have to await both the completion of the Schuman Plan and the negotiation of the "political institutions of a united Europe" seemed designed to delay German rearmament indefinitely.[67] As a result the proposal met a cool reaction from Washington, where Acheson privately termed the French ideas "hopeless." [68] When the French Defense Minister, Jules Moch, stubbornly insisted that the French proposal be accepted without changes, his behavior led Acheson to note that "Moch has dealt the cause of French leadership on Continental Europe, which we have encouraged, a severe blow." [69]

Monnet knew he would need to recoup American support in order for both the Schuman and Pleven Plans to have any chance for success. His immediate goal was to convince McCloy that the Pleven Plan was a genuine effort to solve the problem of German rearmament. McCloy had reacted skeptically to Pleven's speech, telling Acheson that "running through the whole document I see the possibility of delay and diminution of the vigor of the concept of prompt and decisive action." Yet he also welcomed an invitation from Monnet to visit Paris to discuss the proposal further, telling the secretary that "I believe we must make the best of the French proposal, if France's intentions are sincere, for I despair of an effective European defense without France." [70] Monnet was certain that if he could convince the high commissioner, whom he knew had the confidence of both Acheson and Adenauer, he could begin the process of bringing the Americans and Germans behind Pleven's proposal. McCloy would lend substance to their case, as "his independence and goodwill" inspired much respect. In the meeting attended by McCloy, Bowie, Schuman, Pleven, and Monnet, the French officials stressed the major issues to the high commissioner. First, they emphasized the "defensive" aspects of the Pleven Plan, an implicit contrast with the overly aggressive American ideas for German rearmament. The relatively small size of the army, and its control by Europeans, would avoid provoking the Russians to take any sort of preemptive action. It also avoided giving the Germans any opportunity to wage a war to regain their lost territories. Second, they insisted that only if the Americans gave their support to the French plan would the Germans agree to participate. The French leaders were convinced as with the Schuman Plan, that if the Germans perceived a choice between a French and American idea, there was no doubt which way they would choose.

Finally, the French promised that any discrimination would exist only in the transition, assuring McCloy that the "Foreign Legion" provisions would disappear when the organization became permanent. They also assured him that they would act as quickly as possible to finish the Schuman Plan negotiations, and set up the machinery for the army plan. Finally, they argued that German recruiting should only start under a European authority, and that the first German soldier should be in a European uniform.[71]

McCloy came away from the meeting convinced of the "sincerity" of the French and told Washington that France's "impelling fear was... that a new German national army and General Staff would immediately begin to plan in terms of war of revenge for the return of the eastern provinces." The French assured him they were "not seeking to follow a dilatory course in regard to this problem." When he returned to Germany, he told Adenauer that the French were prepared eventually to accept Germany's equality within the European Army. The American interest in the Plan softened the chancellor's reaction. Before he talked to McCloy, the chancellor told his advisors that the Pleven Plan was discriminatory toward the Germans. He also disliked the linkage with the Schuman Plan, which he viewed, quite correctly, as a form of French pressure on the Germans. Adenauer was also dismayed at the lack of any provision in the French proposal for American "leadership and participation" in working out the details of the European army. McCloy told Adenauer that while he himself could not endorse the plan in its present form---he still doubted its practicality---he did urge the chancellor to emphasize in general terms the importance of reaching an agreement with the French. McCloy's assurances led Adenauer to take a more favorable public position, calling the Pleven Plan an "important contribution to European integration, ever one of the main objectives of German policy," and agreeing to assist "consultations" on the plan.[72]

The crisis of late 1950---the Chinese intervention in the Korean War---led to a Franco-American agreement to begin talks on German rearmament without any preliminary accord on the manner, numbers, or provisions of that rearmament. However, at the level of the American embassies in Europe, the Schuman and Pleven Plans became part of a detailed plan to place European integration at the very center of America's plans to rearm Germany and end the occupation. Once again, the close cooperation between Monnet and McCloy, and the intimate working arrangements between their staffs, contributed to this process.[73] McCloy and Bowie now took over the final negotiations of Law 27, which Monnet had made a pre-condition for French approval of the coal and steel plan. The Americans hoped that Law 27 would equalize the competitive conditions between the French and German steel industries so that the French could enter into the Schuman Plan with greater assurance of their security.[74]

The major issue was the German control over the coking coal upon which the French steel industry was heavily dependent. Ruhr industrialists had persuaded the Adenauer government to demand that the *Verbundwirtschaft*, or the vertical integration of steel and coal, remain intact. The German steel companies wanted to maintain control of enough coal supplies to meet more than 100 percent of their prospective needs, as well as keeping in place the Ruhr's coal sales organization, the *Deutscher Kohlen-Verkauf* (DKV), to handle the distribution of the coal. The Americans were only willing to allow the companies to own 75 percent of their supplies, insisting that the rest be available on the open market to other producers, particularly the French. They also demanded that the DKV be abolished. When Adenauer protested, McCloy told Monnet he found the German proposals unacceptable and "animated by a spirit of domination." Monnet urged him to give the Germans an ultimatum: accept the American compromise as its own or the High Commission would impose a more draconian solution.[75]

McCloy remained firm in his position and Adenauer agreed on March 14, 1951 to submit the American proposals as his own proposal for Law 27. McCloy did help Adenauer by meeting individually with groups of German industrialists and trade unionists, explaining why the United States insisted on Law 27. In the meetings McCloy emphasized the "profound political significance of the Schuman Plan for Europe and the West," arguing that its approval would greatly affect American attitudes toward the Federal Republic. He further made clear that adoption of the plan would lead to a lifting of most controls on German economic development. The only compromise McCloy made was to accept the argument of German trade unionists that the DKV be phased out over a transitional period of some three years in order to avoid any dislocations from unemployment at more marginal mines. McCloy immediately cleared this compromise with Monnet, who was eager to secure German trade union support for the Schuman Plan.[76]

The signing of the Schuman Plan was one of McCloy's greatest achievements as high commissioner. Monnet admitted that the treaty "would never have been signed but for Mr. McCloy's support." [77] With Monnet's assistance, the high commissioner now used this success to push again for a realistic plan for German rearmament. Since January 1951, McCloy had been supervising talks on the Petersberg between the Germans and the deputy high commissioners which were designed to come up with a plan for rearmament. At the same time, and at a much slower pace, negotiators in Paris were considering the French proposal for a European army. These talks, and the whole European army concept, had come under withering criticism by the professional officers, both German and American. The state department also disliked the Paris embassy's enthusiasm for this approach, which Acheson termed Bruce's "cult of federation." In June 1951 the Petersberg negotiations came to an end, producing a plan which created a new German Army directly under the auspices of NATO. This approach appeared to many, including the state department, the Pentagon, and the Germans as the best way to proceed on rearmament. However, to the French it held all the dangers of an unrestricted German rearmament, and to Monnet and McCloy, this meant another deadlock and alliance crisis.[78]

One way to prevent the crisis was to convince the American military in Europe to support the French proposal. General Eisenhower, the new NATO Supreme Commander, was an old friend of McCloy's, and a man who understood the importance of alliance politics.[79] With the Petersberg negotiations over, McCloy sent the general a copy of the report along with a handwritten and personal note. He told Eisenhower that he was "anxious to achieve results," and "I would be glad to support [the European army] but only on that condition and only on the condition that the scheme was an effective one from a military point of view." As he had eight years earlier in Algiers, McCloy suggested that Eisenhower meet with Jean Monnet, a man who "thinks on broad terms and... can put the case for the European Army as well as any." The high commissioner told the general that he had already informed Monnet that he would have to convince those Americans concerned with the plan that it was not simply "a device to avoid and to delay a German contribution." Monnet would also have to convince the military people that the plan made sense from a military point of view, which meant dropping the idea of units smaller than divisions. McCloy reported to Eisenhower that he had told Monnet that "in the last analysis you [Eisenhower] were the one to decide the matter and that you were quite as well equipped to deal with the political nuances." McCloy knew that bringing Monnet together with Eisenhower was the best chance the European army concept would have to win American support.[80]

Monnet took the opportunity that his luncheon meeting with Eisenhower gave him. Repeating the arguments he had employed to sell the Schuman Plan, Monnet told the general that "Europe would become responsible and strong only if it were united." Without this unity, every nation would seek power for itself. This would be disastrous, especially in the case of Germany, which would try to seek power "in agreement with the East." A short-term Allied plan, which sought to "rush into raising a few German divisions on a national basis, at the cost of reviving enmity between peoples, would be catastrophic for the very security of Europe that such a step would be intended to ensure." A European army, which would "give France, Germany, and then their neighbors common resources to exploit and defend," would be a long-term solution which would help Europe to "recover the will to resist." Eisenhower was intrigued by this explanation, since it corresponded to his own beliefs about the necessity of restoring Europe's self-confidence and independence. He told Monnet that, "what you're proposing is that the French and the Germans should wear the same uniform. That's more a human problem than a military one." Sensing Eisenhower's increasing interest, Monnet added that, "What we have to do first of all is make people aware that they're facing the future together." General Gruenther, one of Eisenhower's chief aides, interrupted to attempt to bring the discussion down from abstract considerations to the size of the integrated divisions. But Eisenhower cut him off, dismissing his concerns as those of a "typical technician," who could "only see the part you're interested in --- you don't look at the problem as a whole." To Eisenhower the "real problem" with Europe was not "the strength of the divisions" but the "human" problem of how to "organize relations between people," and Eisenhower was "all for" taking the steps Monnet proposed.[81]

Monnet's persuasive abilities reinforced Eisenhower's own beliefs, and the general grew increasingly vocal in his call for European unity. On July 3 1951, Eisenhower delivered an address at the English Speaking Union in London, which was a clarion call for unity in Europe. He described how "with unity achieved, Europe could build adequate security and... continue the march of human betterment that has characterized western civilization." [82] The speech gave new momentum to the coalition in support of Monnet's Europe. With Eisenhower's support, the military objections to the European army crumbled. Eisenhower's intervention in the Paris negotiations changed the level of integration of the new European Army---from the battalion to the division---and renamed the project the European Defense Community, using as a model the Schuman Plan's "European Coal and Steel Community. By the end of summer of 1951, Washington swallowed its objections and proclaimed that the European Defense Community was America's choice as the method of German rearmament. For his part McCloy convinced the Germans that the EDC was the only way to proceed, even rejecting Adenauer's suggestion of a transitional arrangement which would rearm the Germans on a national basis. He told the chancellor that "efforts to find short-cuts outside the Treaty... will only divert energy from the main job, create doubts and suspicions, and delay the accomplishment of the final objectives." [83] The rejection of Adenauer's proposal demonstrates how thoroughly the Americans were committed to Monnet's approach to European union.

For Eisenhower, as for McCloy and Bruce, a united Europe, resembling in some form the United States, became the "skeleton key" to unlocking solutions to Europe's problems. It offered the promise of a solution to the Franco-German enmity as well as the containment of the Soviet "threat from the East." Greater unity would also end the need for extensive American involvement before isolationist sentiments returned, something which both Eisenhower and McCloy feared but expected. The European Defense Community seemed to solve so many problems---Soviet expansionism, German nationalism, European weakness, American isolationism---that one can understand, if not approve, the tenacious efforts of otherwise pragmatic leaders to promote such an idealistic and visionary proposal. It was also the case, as McCloy and Monnet might have noted, that the EDC was the only game in town, the only way to maintain the momentum of transnational political cooperation.   Repeated alliance crises threatened to undermine Western stability and encourage the Soviets. Despite EDC's many defects, it seemed the only way to "square the circle," and guarantee both French security and German equality.

With the ratification of the Schuman Plan treaty early in 1952, and the successful completion of both the EDC and contractual negotiations ending the occupation in May 1952, McCloy and Monnet seemed to have realized the fruits of their efforts. But their plans would not work out as expected. The French Assembly rejected the European Defense Community in August 1954, bringing on exactly the crisis that Monnet and McCloy had hoped to prevent. However, ironically enough, the long debate over the EDC probably made German rearmament within NATO more acceptable. The sweeping victory of Adenauer in September 1953 indicated that German nationalism and irredentism were not as strong as many had feared. The long debate gave the NATO organization time to develop its institutional legs. It now constituted a more realistic alternative for constraining a new German army than it had in 1951. And the French, having defeated their own proposal for a method of rearming the Germans, had less moral authority to stop British Foreign Secretary Eden's proposal that Germany join the Western European Union and, subsequently, NATO. Despite Monnet and McCloy's fears, time did not work against a practical and politically acceptable solution to German rearmament.

Jean Monnet and Jack McCloy remained friends long after each left public life. Both became influential private citizens, frequently called upon by political leaders for their advice and counsel. Both continued to rely on each other for advice, as Monnet sought to build his "Action Committee for a United States of Europe," and McCloy cultivated support for the alliance among Americans. Both enjoyed the singular honor of receiving the Presidential Medal of Freedom at the same time, enjoying the praise given them as architects of the new Europe and the Atlantic alliance. The two men remained friends till Monnet's death in March 1979. At Monnet's funeral, a solemn traditional Catholic ceremony, George Ball noted how he and McCloy smiled quietly when, in the midst of the largely European congregation, an American chorus began to sing the "Battle Hymn of the Republic," the "fighting song of the American Civil War---a song, as some of us knew, Jean had loved." [84] Ten years later the same song would echo at McCloy's memorial service.

The transnational partnership between the United States and Europe, symbolized in the friendship of Jean Monnet and Jack McCloy, was only partially successful in their lifetimes. Monnet did not live to see the movement toward a Europe without trade barriers in 1992 or the powerful effect Western European prosperity had on weakening the communist hold over Eastern Europe. McCloy died a few months before the collapse of the Berlin Wall brought a democratic and united Germany within the Western alliance. Both men would have welcomed these changes, and called for a renewal of the US-European relationship to address the continuing international problems of the environment, economic development, and human rights.

Jean Monnet and Jack McCloy were quite different men, but in their working relationship and personal characteristics they shared a number of important qualities: optimism about the human endeavor, a pragmatic approach to problems, a dislike for publicity, a faith in rationality, and a certainty that governments and individuals gained as much through cooperation as through competition. Both perceived that in a world of increasing economic interdependence, leaders needed to look beyond their immediate national interests and think in global terms. Both hoped that a united Europe would help preserve individual freedom, end the danger of war, and allow the progress of civilization. Both men deserve the encomium of "world citizens," men who sought peace and freedom for the world community.

Endnotes

[1] Interview with John C. McCloy, New York, Jun 28 1982.

[2] John J. McCloy, "Remarks on the Occasion of the Ceremony for the Presentation of the Jean Monnet Award," Oct 24 1981. This speech was made available to me by the Fondation Jean Monnet pour L'Europe, Lausanne, Switzerland (hereafter, FJM).

[3] Jean Monnet, *Memoirs*, trans. Richard Mayne, New York, 1978,(hereafter JMM) p.108.

[4] Robert T. Swaine, *The Cravath Firm and Its Predecessors 1819-1948*, Vol. II, New York, 1948, pp. 321 and 469.

[5] John J. McCloy, Oral History, Jul 15 1981, FJM.

[6] JMM p. 105. Monnet's comment was made in regard to John Foster Dulles, but it applies to McCloy as well.

[7] JMM p.76.

[8] Robert Sherwood, *Roosevelt and Hopkins*, New York, 1948, p. 288.

[9] JMM p. 160.

[10] Sherwood, *Roosevelt and Hopkins*, p. 226. There are several stories about the origins of the phrase "arsenal of democracy." McCloy always stressed his intermediary role in using the term.

[11] Robert Nathan, "An Unsung Hero of World War II," in *Jean Monnet: The Path to European Unity*, eds. Douglas Brinkley and Clifford Hackett.New York, 1991, p. 83.

[12] JMM pp. 169-172. Monnet's experience in encouraging America's production for war may have had an important effect on his later ideas about a United Europe. As McCloy later commented, Monnet became fascinated with "the continental sweep and depth of the American economy and its markets." According to McCloy, Monnet believed that a similar reduction of European tariffs and creation of a mass market could increase European living standards and overcome the class conflicts and national divisions that had so weakened the continent.

[13] Monnet's problems with Morgenthau are detailed in the perceptive article by Clifford Hackett on Jean Monnet and the Roosevelt Administration in this volume.

[14] McCloy to Frankfurter, Nov 1 1941, and Frankfurter to Halifax, Nov 14 1941, Papers of Felix Frankfurter, Library of Congress, Washington.

[15] McCloy diary, Jan 20 1942, Oct 25 1942, Papers of John J. McCloy, Amherst College, Amherst, Massachusetts.(hereafter JMP).

[16] Raoul Aglion, *Roosevelt and de Gaulle*. New York, 1988, p. 188.

[17] Julian G. Hurstfield, *America and the French Nation, 1939-1945* , Chapel Hill, 1986, pp. 162-183.

[18] George McJimsey, *Harry Hopkins*, Cambridge, 1987, p. 273, and Sherwood, *Roosevelt and Hopkins*, pp.680-681.

[19] Diary of Felix Frankfurter, Feb 7 1943, in Joseph P. Lash, *From the Diaries of Felix Frankfurter*, New York, 1974, p. 185.

[20] McCloy to Eisenhower, Mar 8 1943, Pre-Presidential Correspondence 16-52, Box 75, Papers of Dwight Eisenhower, Eisenhower Library, Abilene,KS. (hereafter DDEL).

[21] Diary of Henry Stimson, Jan 1943, p. 169, Papers of Henry Stimson, Yale University.

[22] McCloy diary, Feb 23 and 27 1942.

[23] Stimson diary, Jan 1943, p. 169.

[24] McCloy to Eisenhower, Mar 1 and 8 1943, PPC 16-52, Box 75, DDEL.

[25] McCloy diary, Feb 27 1943.

[26] Frankfurter diary, Mar 20 1943, in Lash, *Diaries of Felix Frankfurter*, p. 222.

[27] McCloy to Eisenhower, Mar 1 1943, PPC 16-52,DDEL.

[28] JMM p. 216.

[29] André Kaspi, *La mission de Jean Monnet `a Alger (mars-octobre 1943)*, Paris, 1971.

[30] Frankfurter diary, May 30 1943, in Lash, *Diaries of Felix Frankfurter*, p. 248.

[31] Charles de Gaulle, quoted in Alfred Grosser, *The Western Alliance*, trans. Michael Shaw, New York, 1982, p. 101.

[32] Murphy to Roosevelt, Jul 6 1943, President's Secretary's Files, Folder, France 1943, Box 42, Franklin D. Roosevelt Library, Hyde Park, NY (hereafter FDRL).

[33] JMM, pp. 215-220.

[34] McCloy diary, Nov 14 1943.

[35] McCloy diary, Jun 14 1944. This entry contains a record of McCloy's Jan 1944 plan.

[36] Stimson diary, Jan 14 1944.

[37] Stimson diary, Feb 29 1944.

[38] Robert Dallek, *Franklin D. Roosevelt and American Foreign Policy, 1932-1945*, New York, 1978, pp. 458-462.

[39] McCloy diary, Dec 15 1943.

[40] McCloy diary, Aug 27 1944, Jan 5, Feb 6, Apr 23, and May 15 1945.

[41] McCloy diary, Jan 11 1945.

[42] McJimsey, *Harry Hopkins*, p. 352.

[43] Even on his last official trip to France as assistant secretary, McCloy was solicitous of Monnet's concern for France's coal supplies. McCloy diary, Oct 3 1945.

[44] McCloy diary, Oct 3 1945.

[45] Much of the argument from this section of the paper comes from Thomas A. Schwartz, *America's Germany: John J. McCloy and the Federal Republic of Germany* , Cambridge, MA, 1991.

46 George Ball, *The Past Has Another Pattern: Memoirs*, New York, 1982, pp. 82-83.

47 John Davenport, "M. Jean Monnet of Cognac, " Fortune, Vol. 30, No. 2, (Aug 1944), p. 216.

48 McCloy to Douglas, Jun 10 1947, folder McCloy, Papers of William Clayton, Box 65, Truman Library, Independence (hereafter HSTL).

49 Irwin Wall, "Jean Monnet, the United States, and the French Economic Plan," in *Jean Monnet: The Path to European Unity*, eds. Brinkley and Hackett, p. 104.

50 The [London]Times, Oct 18 1949.

51 New York Times, Apr 5 1950. One French historian has used this speech as one of his main pieces of evidence in a chapter entitled, "The American Origins of the Schuman Plan." Pierre Melandri, *Les États-Unis Face a L'Unification de L'Europe, 1945-1954*, Paris, 1980, p. 272.

52 Memo, McCloy to Acheson, May 10 1950, D(50)1299, Box 13, RG 466, McCloy Papers, National Archives, Suitland MD (hereafter NARA).

53 *Foreign Relations of the United States (FRUS) 1950*, IV, pp. 633-634.

54 JMM p. 292.

55 Acheson to Paris Embassy, Apr 8 1950, D(50)1125, Box 12, RG 466, McCloy papers, NARA-Suitland.

56 *FRUS 1950*, III, pp. 706-708, and transcript, May 23 1950, AMG 2/3/8, FJM.

57 Bonn (Liaison) to Secretary of State, May 10 1950, 850.33/5-1050, RG 59, National Archives, Diplomatic Branch,Wash DC (hereafter NARA-DB).

58 Speech by John J. McCloy, Jun 16 1950, *Third Quarterly Report*, American High Commission (HICOG), pp. 85-90.

59 Ball, *Past Has Another Pattern*, p. 91.

60 Monnet to Pleven, Sep 3 1950, AMI 4/3/6, FJM.

61 JMM p. 341.

62 Schwartz, *America's Germany*, pp. 137-138.

63 McCloy to Acheson, Sep 20 1950, Memo of Conversation, Papers of Dean Acheson, Box 65, Truman Library (hereafter HSTL).

64 JMM, p. 344.

65 JMM p. 344.

66 As David Bruce recognized, "if Schuman could relay to his Cabinet a course of conduct inspired by us but giving the French government an opportunity to assert Continental leadership, we might possibly obtain a happy and even unexpected result." *FRUS 1950*, III, pp. 364-365.

67 Pleven's speech can be found in Margaret Carlyle, ed. *Documents on International Affairs*, London, 1953, pp. 339-344.

68 *FRUS 1950*, III, pp. 404-405.

69 Ibid, pp. 427-431.

70 McCloy to Byroade, Oct 26 1950, 762A.5/10-2650, NARA-DB.

71 JMM p. 348. Monnet's handwritten notes of the meeting, in English, are dated Oct 27 1950. AMI 5/2/2, FJM. McCloy's account of the meeting is in a cable to Byroade and Acheson, Oct 28 1950, 762A.5/10-2850, NARA-DB.

72 McCloy to Byroade, Oct 28 1950, 762A.5/10-2850, McCloy to Acheson, Nov 8, 1950, 762A.5/11-850, NARS-DA; Carlyle, *Documents on International Affairs, 1949-1950*, p. 344. At the same time McCloy also assisted Adenauer by calling Monnet and insisting that the Ruhr Authority would have to be abolished after the Schuman Plan came into effect, a concession the French would later be forced to grant. McCloy-Monnet telephone conversation, Nov 6 1950, AMI 5/7/2, FJM.

[73] *FRUS 1950*, IX, pp. 674-675, 791-792, and McCloy to Acheson, Nov 29 1950, 762.A.5/11-2950, NARA-DB.

[74] *FRUS 1951*, IV, p. 88.

[75] Notes on a conversation with McCloy, Feb 19 1951, AMG 12/3/6, FJM.

[76] Memorandum by Robert Bowie to McCloy, Mar 4 1951, D(51)289, McCloy papers, RG 466, Box 25, NARA-Suitland.

[77] Monnet made this statement to the British ambassador in Paris. Oliver Harvey to Morrison, May 4 1951, FO 1008/1, Public Record Office, London.

[78] The background to the EDC issue is discussed in Schwartz, *America's Germany*, pp. 210-234.

[79] Ibid. pp. 219-220.

[80] McCloy to Eisenhower, undated but either Jun 9 or 10 1951, PPC 16-52, Folder McCloy, Box 75, DDEL.

[81] JMM pp. 358-359.

[82] Speech by General Dwight Eisenhower before the English Speaking Union, Jul 3 1951, PPC 16-52, Box 163, DDEL.

[83] *FRUS 1951*, III, pp. 874-877.

[84] Ball, *Past Has Another Pattern*, p. 99.

8

Monnet and "The Insiders": Nathan, Tomlinson, Bowie, and Schaetzel

Sherrill Brown Wells

Jean Monnet worked with many Americans during his lifetime. Some became his good friends; many more came under his influence, especially in his work for European integration. But none was closer to him than four men who were decisionmakers inside the American bureaucracy: Robert Nathan, William Tomlinson, Robert Bowie, and J. Robert Schaetzel. These "insiders" were close to the senior policymakers, and they advised and influenced the men above them.

Part of Monnet's genius was that he could identify individuals at all levels of government who would be useful to him in carrying out his goals. He knew that many important decisions were made at the second level, by those who had the ear and confidence of the presidents, the secretaries and under secretaries of state, and the ambassadors. Because Monnet realized U.S. policy paralleled his own goals, he developed close relationships with these four men and worked with them as partners to strengthen and unite Europe.

All highly intelligent, well-educated, and articulate, these men moved at different times into Monnet's galaxy of friends on both sides of the Atlantic. They understood the importance of European integration for the nations of that continent as well as for the United States. Each with a different expertise, background and influence --- an economist and statistician, a lawyer and professor, and two civil servants --- these four individuals had relationships with Monnet which collectively covered a 35-year period, from 1940 to 1975. Each was at some point in a key position to influence U.S. policy.

Robert Roy Nathan

Economist Robert R. Nathan from Dayton, Ohio had an intense, rewarding, and productive relationship with Jean Monnet in the 1940s. Monnet learned a great deal from Nathan both before and during the war about mobilizing an economy and the critical role careful planning can play. Monnet applied what he had learned from Nathan when designing his own plan to revive the French economy soon after the war. Nathan, who earned his B.A. and M.A. from the University of Pennsylvania and his L.L.B. from Georgetown University, learned from Monnet about strategies and ways to get leaders to make important decisions and to execute programs.

After the fall of France in June 1940, Nathan left his position as a young economist in the Department of Commerce, where he was chief of the national income division, to become associate director of the bureau of research and statistics of the National Defense Advisory Commission. His new job was to collect information on military requirements and analyze the productive capacity of the economy, with emphasis on raw materials, processed components and machinery and equipment. His goal: to determine what bottlenecks would be encountered and what critical components would be needed if all-out defense mobilization became necessary. This analysis of requirements of essential materials under the concept of a full-employment economy led to significant early investments in new facilities, and increased stockpiles of strategic materials from abroad such as rubber, nickel, and steel alloys.

Monnet came to Washington in August 1940 as a member of the British Purchasing Commission and stayed until February 1943. Earlier in the fall of 1939, when war had become inevitable, France's prime minister Edouard Daladier had supported Monnet's idea for a French-British committee to purchase supplies and aircraft in the United States. Monnet was sent to London to explore the idea, and because Neville Chamberlain, the British prime minister, was receptive, an Anglo-French Coordinating Committee was created that fall with Monnet as its head. Simultaneously, an Anglo-French Purchasing Board was set up in New York (and later, in Washington) to coordinate the French and British purchasing missions. But once France fell, Monnet wrote to Britain's new prime minister, Winston Churchill, offering to serve the British government. The prime minister responded with alacrity.

As a member of this important mission in Washington, Monnet helped initiate and expand the American mobilization program. Robert Nathan was to play a central role in this mission. Using his knowledge of American decision-making machinery and his many friends among President Roosevelt's circle of advisers, Monnet gradually became indispensible, Nathan said, in helping coordinate British and U.S. efforts to match British needs against American capabilities.

Allied orders helped revive American production to some degree, but it was a challenge in 1940 and 1941 to mobilize American factories effectively to meet the growing needs of the allies, which after June 1941 included the Soviet Union. One problem was American isolationism. Another was the reluctance of American industrialists to take the risks of wartime investment. Monnet described his main contribution to the war effort at this time as tackling the enormous mobilization problems, stating them in simple terms and bringing them "into wide-ranging discussion." He wrote, "This time I had no difficulty in finding men who were ready to listen and to turn into practical decisions the plans we worked out together." [1]

With his ability to find persons who could be useful to him, Monnet learned about Nathan and his work, met him sometime in late 1940, and cultivated his friendship. "He was truly a great strategist and was always full of ideas," Nathan declared. "He loved to debate, argue, and disagree, and he stimulated you to take different approaches. He was always initiating and discussing ideas, but he also was anxious to know what you thought. He was a patient listener who tried to find practical solutions to problems. He was not an economist but a doer, and he believed in an orderly process." Whether on an early morning walk in Rock Creek Park or at an all-male dinner party at his home on Foxhall Road, Monnet stressed, Nathan recalled, the urgency of America's mobilization and the consequences for the allies as well as for Western democracy if it did not expand material output massively and quickly. "Monnet had one goal in Washington: to impress upon American decisionmakers that American production was needed to stop Hitler. He never suggested the United States send troops or advocated getting our nation involved. He just wanted Europe to be able to help defend itself with massive American production." [2]

In the first half of 1941, the two met often, for the Frenchman was trying to figure out how to obtain large and speedy increases in American production. Nathan explained that it was hard to get specific military requirements and that without this information, the

US Government could not get support to build and convert large industrial facilities. Through the Frenchman's manipulating and maneuvering, the "Victory Program" concept was gradually developed in mid-1941. A key step came Nathan said, when the request for specific U.S. military requirements was put to the military by the President in June 1941.[3] At the same time, British and Russian needs for American goods and supplies were determined.

Nathan's job in the summer of 1941 was estimating both the military requirements for America's defense and the inputs and production of a full employment economy. Once the data flowed in, Nathan began designing the program. Monnet watched him closely. By the summer's end, Nathan had figured out U.S. steel capacity and requirements for other metals such as aluminum and copper

Next Nathan had to schedule basic production. Monnet tried forcefully to persuade him to elevate the figures but Nathan refused to do anything that was not feasible. He argued with Monnet, tried to make him understand that their analyses would be useless if they were not feasible, and stressed that feasibility was essential for a successful mobilization. By mid-October, Nathan had designed a production schedule for the successive years 1942, 1943, and 1944. Roosevelt adopted it 10 days after the attack on Pearl Harbor.[4]

Nathan credits Monnet with being one of "the most important single contributors to the Allied victory in World War II. If it hadn't been for Monnet and his Victory Program effort," noted Nathan, "we would have lost months... of vital production."[5]

Once America entered the war, the challenge to U.S. officials was to calculate specific British, Soviet, and U.S. military requirements, and the pace at which items could be produced under maximum effort. Monnet supported the efforts of Nathan and another American economist, Stacy May. After Pearl Harbor, Nathan was made chairman of the Planning Committee of the War Production Board where he designed and submitted a feasiblity study for the mobilization and production effort. Monnet worked closely with him, debated schedules, and argued about the availability of raw materials, analyzed trends, and discussed statistics. Monnet wanted quick results, but he learned from Nathan that realistic planning and implementation were necessary to achieve results efficiently and speedily.

Monnet left Washington for Algiers in early 1943 to keep Harry Hopkins and the President informed on the split between Generals de Gaulle and Giraud and also, later, to handle supply and armament matters for the Comité Francais de Liberation Nationale (CFLN). In this period Monnet was not in touch with Nathan but he returned in October to lay the groundwork for American aid to France after the war. In the 1943-1945 period, he ran the French Supply Council and assembled an able Washington staff which became the core of his postwar team: the economist Robert Marjolin; the bright Felix Gaillard; and the chemical firm manager, Etienne Hirsch. He had learned much from the economists May and Nathan, and the success of the American war production programs convinced him that wartime mobilization techniques could readily be adapted to peacetime purposes. Monnet stressed to the CFLN the need to organize the ordering and distribution of foreign supplies once the allied invasion of France began. In August 1944, he proposed a six-month plan to cover imports for the liberation and subsequent "start-up" plan for raw material, machinery, food, and medical supplies. His proposals, which the CFLN endorsed, served as the basis for lend-lease negotiations with the American government.[6]

Monnet helped negotiate a French lend-lease agreement signed in February 1945 under which the U.S. Government gave military aid, raw materials, and food and provided capital equipment on the basis of a long-term, low-interest loan. Monnet was told in August that any further aid would be dependent upon the French formulating a precise program to restore its economy. Monnet was able to convince de Gaulle of the need to take advantage of American resources to reconstruct France in a pragmatic way, and this, he argued, required a modernization plan. De Gaulle assigned him the task, and after the French cabinet approved the idea in December 1945, Monnet and the able team of experts he assembled set out to develop such a plan. By tying aid to a modernization program and making the French accountable, the U.S. government spurred the French planning process.[7]

Monnet became head of the Planning Commission (Commissariat General du Plan) created in January 1946 by the French cabinet. Almost immediately, in early 1946, Monnet asked Nathan to serve as adviser and consultant to his planning group which eventually included Marjolin, Hirsch and economist Pierre Uri.

Monnet brought the first draft of the plan to Nathan in March 1946 when the Frenchman accompanied Léon Blum on a high level diplomatic mission to Washington. The mission was to settle French war debts, delineate trade policy, and negotiate credits for economic recovery. One of the principal tasks of the delegation was to convince the Americans that France was making a serious effort to rebuild. Monnet's draft plan achieved its goal. U.S. officials were convinced of the French determination to rebuild their economy and agreed to a loan.[8]

Nathan analyzed the draft plan and explained where the American experience of mobilizing its economy for war might be applicable to the French goal of renovation and reconstruction. In several lengthy papers given to Monnet in April 1946, Nathan commented on the quantitative analysis of the French economy prepared by the planners. He argued that France needed a fuller appreciation of the basic necessity of data and statistical analysis as a basis for economic and business planning. He recommended that a central group with top authority in the French government be established to collect, disseminate, and analyze essential data.[9]

In a second paper, Nathan assessed the national income estimates for France. He recommended that accurate and separate data be collected on each industrial activity, including textiles, food, electrical equipment, construction, and retail trade. He underlined that economic planning could only be based on accurate data and that France had to improve the quality and quantity of its collection and analysis of critical economic information.[10]

Nathan commented extensively on the general objectives of the draft plan. He stressed that while there was a need to develop a 5-year plan, the achievement of the objectives would depend to a considerable extent on the speed and significance of the measures taken in the succeeding 12 months. Immediate measures, he said, had to be taken in order to increase the production of coal, agricultural products, construction, and steel and to get inflation under control.[11]

At Monnet's request, Nathan came to Paris in August 1946 and spent most of the month in meetings with the planners analyzing the key elements of successive drafts of the plan. He underscored the need at the government level and that of the general public for substantial agreement on the general philosophy of the plan and its goals of modernization and increased productivity. "Having accepted the goals, then the field of discussion and argument is more limited and everything must fit into the pattern of accepted objectives," Nathan wrote. In order to achieve this public consensus, he stated, there should be a general campaign in the media to educate the government and the general public.[12]

Repeating the methods of the war experience, Nathan stressed the need for feasible goals and emphasized that a sound plan must be based on realistic estimates and objectives. He underscored the need for the scheduling of investments as well as production of consumer goods and services and that annual schedules must be based on both needs and feasibility.[13] Manpower was the most important limiting factor in the expansion of the French economy. Therefore, he argued that the French government must allocate labor to economic areas important to the country, increase the work week to 48 hours, and import labor.[14] He also stressed the importance of fiscal policies and vigorous efforts to reduce nonessential governmental expenditures as well as the need to balance the budget and to control inflation.[15]

Monnet and his colleagues incorporated many of Nathan's ideas in the plan. Accepting the American's judgment on the political questions of implementating the plan, they adopted his recommendation that the implementing group be a small apolitical staff of skilled planners attached to the head of the government. They followed his recommendation that the planning commission stay out of operations and that the ministries implementing the plan as well as representatives of labor, industry, and consumers be involved in the planning.

While Nathan saw Jean Monnet only infrequently after 1946, Nathan credits him with being an important influence in his life intellectually and personally. Nathan genuinely admired this man of vision who constantly learned from other people, who sought no political position for himself, and who was an amazing strategist with pragmatic solutions to difficult problems. Nathan credits Monnet with making an important contribution to the formulation of the American Victory Program because of his vision, his powers of manipulation and persuasion, his commitment to high goals, and his effective sense of strategy.[16] When reflecting on Monnet's whole life, Nathan remarked, "I was not surprised by the phenomenally successful role played by Monnet in the creation and implementation of the European Community because he often talked about the need to prevent another war. He expressed his distress that World War II followed so closely after World War I. Even though he was fully and deeply involved in the World War mobilization, he was looking ahead to the rehabilitation of the French economy and a peaceful and prosperous European

Community.   It reveals Monnet's vision, strategy and performance."
Nathan concluded: Monnet was truly an "unsung hero of World War II."

William Mahon Tomlinson

For William Tomlinson, knowing and working with Jean Monnet
became a central experience of his short life. Born in Moscow, Idaho on
February 8, 1918, he spent the year 1940-1941 studying economics at
Brown University following graduation from the University of Idaho.
After working for a brief time on Capitol Hill, he joined the
Department of the Treasury as the Second World War was drawing to a
close and was sent in 1945 to London as its official representative. In
1947, he was transferred to Paris where he served as the treasury
representative and the financial attache at the U.S. embassy. He first
met Monnet in this capacity when the French were beginning
negotiations with the American government for financial aid in which
both men were involved.

The 29-year old American soon developed a respect for Monnet
which gradually grew into a deep and trusting friendship. Friends
described a father-son relationship. (Monnet was almost 60). Their
families grew close.

Tomlinson gradually came to share Monnet's vision that many
of the world's troubles came from Europe's quarrels. Tomlinson also
embraced the view that the French-German animosity had to be
overcome after the wounds of two world wars and that the integration
of Europe was the way to achieve this. "Both had a fire burning in
them to change the world," remarked a colleague of Tomlinson, "and
this chemistry worked for both of them." [18]

Monnet introduced Tomlinson to most of the key officials in the
French economic and political centers of power. Tommy, as he was
called, became an informal member of Monnet's team of French economic
experts at the Commissariat du Plan on rue de Martignac. The team met
almost daily to thrash out ways to implement the Monnet plan for
France's reconstruction. This intellectual elite surrounding Monnet
included economists Uri and Marjolin and advisers Hirsch, Francois
Fontaine and Jacques Van Helmont. Tomlinson came to understand the
difficult economic and political problems facing France.

From listening to their discussions and watching how these men interacted, Tomlinson learned how Monnet operated, the details of the Plan and how it was to be implemented. As Van Helmont said, "Tomlinson was one of these people who worked closely with Monnet without regard to rank or nationality.... Tomlinson spent so much time with us around the table that he learned the division of labor between Monnet and his close associates. He worked with us so he knew how to get things done." [19] A state department colleague from that period remarked "Tomlinson shared a common trait with Monnet, one reason they got on so well together, which was that Tomlinson had a capacity for working with people for a singular objective regardless of who happened to be paying their salary or even what government they were working for." [20]

Tomlinson quickly developed a reputation, among both Americans and French, as a brilliant and penetrating mind, a tough and effective negotiator and for demanding the highest standards of performance from his colleagues and himself. To Arthur Hartman, who as a young economist worked with Tomlinson in Paris, he was "probably the most extraordinary man" he ever knew.[21] Stanley Cleveland,who worked for Tomlinson as a young foreign service officer, stated, "He was the only authentic genius I've ever known." [22]

Tomlinson had abilities for economic analysis that did not come from graduate school training. As Hartman said, Tomlinson did not use the techniques employed by other economists. "He had an instinctive way of analyzing an economic situation. He was very good with numbers, but didn't approach problems in the way a numbers man would. He came to the same conclusions as the other economists but in half the time." [23]

Tomlinson was handicapped by poor health but this did not interfere with his effectiveness as a link between Paris and Washington for most of the time he worked with Monnet. Childhood rheumatic fever left Tomlinson with an irreparable hole in his heart. In spite of doctors' warnings to take life easy because his life would be shorter than others, he was a workaholic, often spending seven days a week in his office. He demanded no less from those working for him. To his junior colleagues who survived this regimen of drafting exacting memos and compiling forceful and precise arguments, he was formidable, exciting, intense and demanding, but always fair. He never asked of them anything he did not ask of himself.[24]

Tomlinson's responsibilities increased when David Bruce became the first head of the Marshall Plan mission in Paris in 1948. Established by the Economic Cooperation Administration, which in turn was established by the Marshall Plan legislation, the aid mission became an important pressure point on French economic policy, partly because it controlled the release of counterpart funds.[25] Tomlinson and Bruce soon became trusted friends with the treasury official acting as the mission chief's senior economic advisor. Through Tomlinson, Bruce met and became friends with Jean Monnet whom he depicted with "an astoundingly quick and comprehensive mind." [26]

Bruce used Tomlinson to help run the aid mission, located in the annex of the American embassy. Bruce created a tripartite organization --- combining state department, treasury and ECA elements --- and, with treasury's approval, made Tomlinson its director. As treasury attache, Tomlinson had his own deputy as well as four foreign service officers and four ECA officials. Treasury secretary John Snyder and Paul Hoffman, ECA administrator, had agreed that Tomlinson would be allowed to concentrate on European, not just French, affairs.[27]

From 1948 to 1950, Bruce, Tomlinson, and Monnet worked closely together to achieve an important goal of each of their governments the stabilization of the French economy. Monnet and his planners provided stability and continuity through many government changes. As Etienne Hirsch remarked with a smile, "French governments came and went, and none lasted long enough to undo or change the direction of our economic policies. By the time the politicians decided to change one of our policies, their governments fell, and we, ignoring their directive, continued with our plan." [28]

As head of the planning commission, Monnet worked with the French cabinets in 1947 and 1948 to improve the French economy. He persuaded them to take some exceptional measures and adopt the stabilization program which helped reduce inflation from 45% to zero in 18 months and bring stability to France in 2 years.[29] He also collaborated with Bruce and Tomlinson on ways to utilize American influence to pressure the French political and economic leaders to bring about the needed economic stabilization.

Tomlinson's dual treasury and Marshall Plan mission roles facilitated his successful penetration of the second center of economic power in France, the ministry of finance. He learned how to work within the French bureaucracy at this ministry and gained unusual access and trust of officials in spite of his very limited ability to speak

French. He also worked with the interministerial committee for questions of European economic cooperation, a separate agency set up to deal directly with the ECA mission in Paris. He developed a good working relationship with Paul Schweitzer, the secretary general and head of this committee attached to the premier's office, and later with successors to Schweitzer like Marjolin.[30]

Tomlinson's unusual access to the major centers of economic power facilitated his work with Bruce and Monnet to attain French financial stability. The reduction of inflation was a goal of the U.S. government underlined by the terms of the bilateral agreement under the Marshall Plan signed in June 1948. Civil servants in the French bureaucracy were already working to combat inflationary policies and they agreed that these policies needed to be enforced. As a result of these pressures, the Bank of France did tighten credit considerably for the rest of 1948.[31]

The drastic reforms were desired by prominent Frenchmen like Pierre Mendes France, Guillaume Gindey, Francois Bloch-Lainé, President Vincent Auriol, and Hervé Alphand. Therefore when the *loi des maxima* was introduced on December 13, 1948 enacting a promising program of stabilization, the ECA mission and these prominent French officials and politicians were relieved.[32]

Tomlinson and Bruce, in collaboration with Monnet, worked hard in 1949 to secure counterpart funds to finance the plan. The effort had actually begun in late 1947 when Monnet started lobbying for the formation of an autonomous fund for his plan. By January 1948, he had persuaded the Schuman-Mayer government to authorize the new equipment funds, *Fonds de modernisation d'Equipement,* which would receive income from a special tax. This partial funding for the basic sectors was a considerable victory but insufficient for the needs of the plan.[33] It became clear the plan needed a continuous flow of capital that the fund could not supply, so he launched a fight to obtain the use of counterpart accounts for financing the basic sectors.

In May 1949, David Bruce. a Francophile who had acquired great influence among French politicians while head of the Marshall Plan mission, became the new Ambassador to France. Bruce appointed Tomlinson his deputy in charge of all economic matters at the embassy and financial and trade adviser to the ambassador. He still served as representative of the treasury but assigned all matters of that agency to his deputy, Donald McGrew, because he preferred to work on European issues.[34]

This powerful triumvirate --- Bruce, Monnet, Tomlinson --- achieved much of what they wanted for France. As a result of continual bargaining and negotiation during 1949-1950, these two American officials had obtained from Washington what they wanted: greater mission control over the funds, regularized quarterly releases of the funds as opposed to a project by project basis, and the ECA's commitment of most of the counterpart funds for the Monnet Plan. As a result of Monnet's persuasion backed by American pressure, the French cabinet consented to allocate these funds to the industries designated under the plan.[35]

The three had achieved an important victory for the plan and secured the financing of the basic sectors through 1952. This was a crucial and necessary step in the revitalization of the French economy. As Monnet later noted in his memoirs, "In 1948, without the help of Bruce and Tomlinson, I should never have succeeded in persuading the U.S. Administration to allow hundreds of billions of francs' worth of counterpart funds to be used by the French Government; and I should have found it hard to persuade the latter to allocate them to the Plan. As it was, in 1949, some 90% of the Modernization Fund's resources came from this unhoped-for-source, and 50% in 1950. Even more, the certainty that so prolonged an effort could be financed without fail gave a sense of confidence to the whole French economy. And the economy, at that time, was not just a matter of material well-being: it was the necessary basis for national independence and the preservation of democracy." [36] Uri paid tribute to Monnet and his American colleagues when he exclaimed, "They conducted a fantastic piece of diplomacy." [37]

By 1950, Monnet had, with American financial assistance, put the French economy on the road to recovery. He then turned to the challenge of improving his nation's relations with Germany. Monnet's basic plan to begin the reintegration of Germany into Europe was accepted by French foreign minister Robert Schuman, who announced it to the public on May 9, 1950. The Schuman Plan proposed to pool the heavy industries of France with its neighbors to form the European Coal and Steel Community (ECSC). The series of difficult negotiations concerning this six nation endeavor set in motion a process that brought Germany back into the European family. While the United States government enthusiastically supported the Schuman Plan, it did not participate in the treaty negotiations but it monitored them through close contacts with Monnet.

Tomlinson, who handled the economic and financial matters for David Bruce, headed a special working group on the Schuman proposal and served as the liaison between Monnet and U.S. policymakers on these negotiations. He also worked closely with Robert Bowie on the German issues. His staff of economists and specialists tracked the negotiations on a daily basis and acted as unofficial advisors to Monnet.[38]

As a result of the North Korean invasion of the South in June 1950, NATO was tranformed from a political to a military alliance. The focus in Franco-American relations shifted, therefore, from French economic recovery to military preparedness. Concern over Soviet intentions in Europe led to U.S. pressure to build up NATO forces, and to the American proposal in September 1950 to arm several German divisions revived French fears of German militarism. U.S. readiness to commit its own forces to Europe and to set up an integrated command structure of NATO did not fully assuage French fears of rearming Germany. In an attempt to defuse the issue, Monnet devised the so-called Pleven Plan in October 1950, a proposal for a European Defense Community (EDC) composed of small national fighting units. This plan was designed to preserve French military power by counter balancing the rearmament of Germany and to insure Germany did not form a national army. It also aimed to obtain French security within a unified Europe under the jurisdiction of supranational institutions.[39] The prospect of rearmament gave the Germans leverage which they used in the coal and steel negotiations to counter the Allied plan for decartelization of the German steel industry. The American high commissioner for Germany, John J. McCloy, mediated a settlement at French request, and the coal and steel treaty was signed on April 18, 1951.[40]

Tomlinson and Bruce worked closely with Monnet from the end of 1950 to early 1952 during Franco-American military aid talks to influence Washington to support the EDC proposal. The Americans finally agreed not to stand in the way of French efforts to create a European Defense Community including Germany on condition that it be organized within the framework of NATO. Washington approved the French plan to spend $2.4 billion (850 billion francs) from the United States on economic and military matters but offered only $200 million (70 billion francs) in military aid for the first half of 1951.[41]

Furthering Monnet's initiatives consumed Tomlinson in his last years in Paris, 1951-1954.[42] Bruce's term as ambassador to France ended in March 1952 when he returned to Washington to be under secretary of state. Once the European Coal and Steel Community (ECSC) began its operation in August 1952 with Monnet serving in Luxembourg as president of the High Authority, Tomlinson became the deputy U.S. representative to the Coal and Steel Community.

When Bruce was appointed the official representative to the coal and steel community by Eisenhower in February 1953, Tomlinson, Bruce, and Monnet worked together once again. During the years from 1952 to mid-1954, despite weakened health, Tomlinson dedicated himself to persuading the French government to submit the EDC Treaty to the French national assembly for ratification.[43] Since the Eisenhower administration strongly supported this plan as a way to rearm Germany, Tomlinson cabled Washington to use all the weapons it could muster --- including promises of more aid and later threats to withdraw it --- to pressure the French politicians. The state department followed Tomlinson's advice, but neither the carrot nor the stick worked.[44]

French Premier Pierre Mendès France decided not to submit the treaty before he had obtained additional provisions making it more favorable to France. One condition involved additional American aid for French forces in Indochina where disaster faced the colonial army. At the final round of foreign ministers' negotiations in Brussels, Mendes France demanded additional protocols. Tomlinson had traveled to Brussels with Hartman to follow the negotiations. At 1:00 a.m. August 22 after the fiery debates had concluded, Tomlinson got a call at his hotel from the French embassy and was told that the French Prime Minister wished to see him. Immediately upon arrival, he was ushered in to meet alone with Mendès France. For one hour and a half, the Prime Minister talked to him. He wished to explain personally to Tommy, one of France's most loyal friends, why he had taken the action on the protocols, why the treaty would be defeated, and asked him to explain it to his government.[45] Much to Hartman's surprise, Tomlinson came out of the meeting exhilarated instead of depressed. As they walked out of the hotel, Tomlinson exclaimed, "Who in their wildest dreams would have thought that a French prime minister would call in a young kid from Moscow, Idaho, and ask him to explain his actions to the United States Government?" [46]

Yet Tomlinson regarded the defeat of the EDC by the French Assembly August 30, 1954 as "a personal defeat that could have been avoided and believed that perhaps he and others could have done something more," one of his colleagues stated. Soon after the vote, Tomlinson had a stroke which left him partially paralyzed, and the following year, he died at 37 years of age. Soon after his death, Bruce and Monnet set up and became trustees of a fund to educate the Tomlinson children. In a tribute that is rarely paid to anyone non-French, Pierre Uri exclaimed, "Tommy loved France and was one of us." [47]

The relationship between Jean Monnet and his unofficial American partner centered around their work to implement step-by-step Monnet's vision of an integrated Europe. While perhaps not essential to Monnet's achievements, Tomlinson's efforts did facilitate the process of European integration and probably made it move more rapidly. Their partnership strengthened their individual effectiveness, for each found his role enhanced by the other.

Tomlinson was one of Monnet's closest American friends in this period and the one he worked with on almost a daily basis for the longest uninterrupted period of time, 1947 until 1955. A photo of Tomlinson and Monnet, each with an arm on the other's shoulder, remained on the Frenchman's desk in his study along with one of his wife for the rest of his life.[48] Similar in temperament and in their singular devotion to an ideal, each had the ability to penetrate the bureaucracies and power centers of the other's country, to identify persons who were influential and could make a difference, and to cultivate close friendships with the leaders who were making key decisions. Perhaps at no other time has Washington had such continuous and unqualified access to political and economic power centers in France, and this was largely due to the insight and ability of "Tommy" Tomlinson and his close relationship with Monnet.

Robert Richardson Bowie

Lawyer and educator, Robert Richardson Bowie, from Baltimore, Maryland had a close, long-lasting friendship with Jean Monnet. This policymaker, who received his B.A. from Princeton and his L.L.B. from Harvard, became a highly valued adviser to John J. McCloy and later to Secretary of State John Foster Dulles when not teaching at his alma mater. Bowie served as professor of law, the founding director of the Harvard Center for International Affairs, and Clarence Dillon professor of international affairs. His relationship with Monnet fell into two broad categories: collaborative during the Schuman plan negotiations and collegial and advisory during the Eisenhower administration and later years after Bowie's return to Harvard university.

Bowie first met Monnet early in the summer of 1950 when he was serving as general counsel to McCloy, the U.S. high commissioner in Germany. On leave from his professorship at Harvard, Bowie had been charged by McCloy with the responsibility of implementing Law 27, a ruling adopted by the Allied High Commission to deconcentrate the German coal and steel industry. The objective was to be fair to German industry but at the same time make sure that its units were comparable in size to the other European units. In addition, the aim was to ensure that German industry was not given unfair advantage over the other steel and coal plants in Europe in case of a shortage of coke or coal.[49]

McCloy, also a friend of Monnet, sent Bowie to Paris from Bonn to talk to this Frenchman in the early stages of the Schuman Plan negotiations. McCloy asked Bowie to see how to relate that plan, which involved the coal and steel industry, to Law 27.[50] Monnet and Bowie soon became friends. They worked very effectively together because U.S. policy goals for the reconstruction of Europe and its integration, which were being implemented by Bowie and McCloy, were shared by Monnet. And both Bowie and this Frenchman had a capacity to conceive practical solutions to difficult problems.

Monnet believed the goals of the allied commission were consistent with the goals of the Schuman Plan. He believed it important that the Germans be treated fairly. And he wanted both the Germans and the French to feel they had come into the plan on equal terms.

Bowie worked very closely with Monnet and Tomlinson in Paris on the German issues relating to the Schuman Plan. Travelling by train from Bonn to Paris almost weekly starting in the summer of 1950 and throughout the fall and winter, Bowie met with Tomlinson and Monnet either at Monnet's office at rue de Martignac or at the U.S. embassy to hammer out terms that were accceptable to both the French and the Germans. Bowie reported these discussions upon his return to Bonn to McCloy. He then began to negotiate with German officials and representatives of the coal and steel firms.[51]

Monnet respected Bowie's acute mind and careful judgment. He also utilized his legal training in drafting the Schuman plan treaty. At the Frenchman's request, Bowie drafted provisions of the treaty regarding restraint of trade and monopolies.[52] Monnet was familiar with American antitrust legislation because he had lived many years in the United States, and he insisted on strong provisions against cartels in the treaty. Bowie's drafts of proposed anticartel articles were rewritten in a European idiom by Maurice Lagrange of the *conseil d'etat* who had the responsibility for giving formal legal expression to the ideas of Monnet. As a result of Bowie's efforts, articles 65 and 66 of the final treaty embodied the most advanced American antitrust thinking.[53]

Law 27 on cartels provoked a major struggle between the French and the Germans and confronted Bowie, Monnet, and McCloy with a difficult problem. Since the Ruhr coal was marketed through a common sales agency, the French believed this would give the Germans too much bargaining power within the common market for coal which the treaty proposed. The French also feared that failure to break up the great steel concerns would reinforce German dominance of the pool. McCloy took the lead in the negotiations with the German political authorities and Ruhr industrialists as well as with the British and French authorities as occupying powers.

Monnet persuaded Adenauer to appoint a person who could appreciate the political significance of the task to represent Germany at the Schuman plan negotiations. Adenauer selected Walter Hallstein, a distinguished law professor, who had taught at Georgetown University in Washington and who thus understood the American federal system and American antitrust laws. As a result of Hallstein's influence and the persuasiveness of Bowie and McCloy, American deconcentration proposals and the Schuman plan treaty were shaped to reinforce one another. Adenauer was able to present the deconcentration provisions as his own government's proposals and they were accepted by the French.[54]

Bowie described his discussions with Monnet and Tomlinson as genuinely collaborative and illustrative of the method of operation that Monnet used to solve difficult problems. "The negotiations," Bowie said, "were conducted in a very intimate, frank, straightforward and cooperative arrangement. All issues were treated as problems for joint solutions, and they were debated and discussed in the Monnet approach with the negotiators on one side of the table and the problem on the other." Bowie recalled that this was a true collaboration with each influencing the other.[55]

Bowie, Tomlinson, and McCloy enabled the United States to further this bold French initiative constructively from the sidelines by working so closely with Monnet. By hammering out possible solutions to problems between the Germans and the French, American officials were

furthering the goal of the United States and Monnet of linking Germany
in cooperative relations with other major countries in Europe. The
United States had determined that the Schuman Plan was clearly in
its interest, and McCloy was convinced it was a constructive way to deal
with Germany. It represented a profound shift in policy toward
Germany --- from one of constraining Germany to one of trying to
integrate Germany and France and the other European countries into a
community. "It was a constructive initiative," noted Bowie, "which
linked Germany into cooperative relations with other major countries in
Europe." [56]

        Both Presidents Truman and Eisenhower viewed the Schuman
Plan and the European Community as very much in the U.S. interest
because it seemed likely to help end French-German animosity and
assist Europe recover its status. Anything that would benefit Germany
and Europe in a positive way was of vital and profound interest to the
U.S. These American leaders hoped this plan would help position
Europe as a valuable partner for the United States.[57]

        In 1953, Bowie took leave again from his teaching at the
Harvard Law School to head the policy planning staff and serve as
Dulles' adviser in the state department. He served from 1953 to 1957
and was assistant secretary of state from 1955-1957. During this period,
Bowie had official but limited contact with Monnet. Every time Bowie
went to Europe, he would call on Monnet who, in turn, would seek
Bowie's advice on European issues each time he came to Washington.

        After the failure of the EDC in 1954, Monnet and others groped
for a device to restart the move toward European union. The Messina
conference in 1955 settled on a common market for goods and on atomic
cooperation as the new means. Monnet found Bowie's support of the
European Atomic Energy Community (Euratom) invaluable since the
United States played a key world role in peaceful uses of atomic
energy. The Frenchman sought Bowie's advice on how to obtain U.S.
support and what kind of collaboration was possible. Bowie and Dulles
believed the initiative was worthwhile because it was beneficial both
to Europe and to the United States. Both men worked to gain support
for Euratom within the Washington scientific community and
bureaucracy, and Bowie was helpful in suggesting ways to handle Lewis
Strauss, chairman of the atomic energy commission (AEC), who had
serious reservations about the idea. Monnet always had direct access to
Dulles because these two men had been friends since they met in Paris
at the peace conferences at the end of the First World War. But Monnet
knew that Bowie's support for any endeavor was helpful because the

Frenchman was aware of Dulles' consistant reliance on the advice and opinions of this advisor.

In 1957, when Bowie returned to Harvard to teach and direct the Harvard Center for International Affairs, he and Monnet kept in touch and visited one another when they travelled across the ocean. Often Monnet would ask Bowie for comments on resolutions of his Action Committee for the United States of Europe which Monnet had founded in 1955 after resigning from the presidency of the High Authority of the coal and steel community.

As his committee moved to identify specific steps toward European integration, Monnet believed it very important to have support by the United States. Bowie believes Monnet never lost sight of the importance of the European-American partnership but was eager that it become more balanced.[58] Monnet cherished the idea of Europe and America as partners to all of his American friends until his death.[59]

In the 1960s and 1970s, Monnet continued to rely on Bowie for advice and counsel. In the early 1960's, Monnet decided that the multi-lateral force (MLF) issue should be endorsed by his action committee. The idea of a multi-lateral force --- nuclear weapons in the hands of units supplied by several NATO members --- originated with Bowie and was proposed in his August 1960 report, entitled "The North Atlantic Nations: Tasks for the 1960s." It was written at the request of Secretary of State Christian Herter in order to assist the state department in planning NATO's role for the 1960s.[60] Monnet invited Bowie to Europe to discuss the merits of this much debated idea. This professor discussed many ideas with Monnet during these decades including the implications of Britain's failure to join the EEC.

The Bowie-Monnet relationship was important in its longevity, its mutual flow of influence, and in its proximity to power. Monnet could usually speak for or influence the decisions of the French Government during the Schuman negotiations, while Bowie could speak for McCloy. Later Bowie effectively represented Dulles in articulating and carrying out U.S. foreign policy during the Eisenhower administration.

It is difficult to assess Bowie's influence on Monnet, but the fact that he continued to seek this American policymaker's advice from 1950 when he first met him to the end of his public life is evidence that it was highly valued. As Bowie stressed, Monnet always made up his own mind and was never unduly swayed by any person. But clearly this Harvard professor played a stimulating and useful role in Monnet's thinking process for about 25 years and an important role in achieving Monnet's goals in the Schuman plan.

In turn, Robert Bowie was personally and intellectually influenced by Monnet's ideas and his methods. Through collaboration as negotiators as well as advisers, Monnet sparked Bowie's interest in European integration and the EEC and made him aware of the potentialities of integration. Bowie describes Monnet as the "energizer" and "source of his interest in European integration." As a result, since 1950 Bowie did what he could in both his government and in the academy to foster the unification process.

Bowie also respected and was influenced by Monnet's integrity and his method of attacking problems. "It was heartening to know such a man with the qualities of dedication and deep commitment to a long-term goal, commitment to important principles, and determination to search for practical steps which moved men toward a solution," noted Bowie. "He genuinely sought advice, never treated anyone's thoughts as gospel, and then arrived at his own judgment." Above all, Bowie believes his own outlook was greatly enriched by working in such close proximity to a man who combined two rare qualities: long-range thinking and implementing larger goals through pragmatic steps.[61]

John Robert Schaetzel

For Californian John Robert Schaetzel, career state department officer who was ambassador to the European Communities from 1966 to 1973, Jean Monnet was the most important influence in his life. A graduate of Pomona College who became an administrator in the Bureau of the Budget and later at the Department of State, Schaetzel first met Monnet in 1956 when he was in charge of the peaceful uses of atomic energy in the department. This office was run by Gerard C. Smith who was the secretary of state's special assistant for atomic energy affairs from April 1954 to October 1957.

Because Monnet had a talent for ferreting out officials in the U.S. Government with expertise, he discovered Schaetzel. This young American official had acquired knowledge of the peaceful uses of atomic energy as a result of a year's research at the national war college in 1954-1955. Monnet believed Schaetzel could be useful in securing U.S. support for the Europeans' initiative in Euratom.

By 1955, Jean Monnet had concluded that Euratom was vital to European integration. The creation of a multinational program among the six ECSC members devoted to the peaceful uses of atomic energy would be the decisive step toward European unity especially after the failure of the EDC. Monnet, with other prominent Europeans, saw the advantages to Europe of drawing on the experience of the Americans who then had a monopoly on nuclear matters.

At the Messina conference in June 1955, the ECSC council of ministers formally agreed to discuss preliminary plans for a multilateral organization that would integrate European atomic energy development under the acronym of Euratom.[62] The new agency would develop an atomic energy industry similar to that of the coal and steel community but designed to promote the generation of electrical power for industrial uses. With European coal production on the decline and the best hydroelectric sites already exploited, nuclear energy seemed to offer Europeans an indigenous and unlimited source of electricity for industrial use. But this potential was limited by Europe's uranium resources unless supplemented by the United States.[63]

There were other practical attractions of Euratom to Monnet and to European leaders. In the mid-1950s, atomic energy was almost the exclusive domain not of private industry but of the U.S. government. As Schaetzel asserted, "It was attractive to the Europeans because it was the closest thing we had to a real state enterprise. The heavy government overlay made it doubly attractive." [64] In addition, Schaetzel stated "that from the standpoint of the nascent European Community, Euratom was a marvellous piece of business. Since there were no entrenched business or interest groups, you could do something without worrying about established interests in society. You didn't have to overcome the hurdles of heavily entrenched and established sectors. It was new to Europe and therefore there was no effective lobby to oppose it." [65]

Most importantly, Monnet viewed Euratom as an institution like the ECSC which would help break down nationalism and channel energies into cooperative ventures which would yield practical benefits to each participating nation and to the collective whole. Since no other path to integration seemed possible at that moment, he wrote, "The spearhead for the unification of Europe would have to be the peaceful atom." [66]

After the failure of the EDC in 1954, the Eisenhower Administration believed that continued progress toward a United

States of Europe must be achieved through European economic integration. Rejection by the French Assembly of the EDC and the subsequent admission of Germany into NATO only underlined the importance of promoting European cooperation by different means. Yet since progress toward economic and political union appeared to be faltering in 1955, it seemed to U.S. officials that progress toward integration might best be made in the field of atomic energy. As Eisenhower later wrote, "Euratom was one step; then would come the effort toward economic union." [67]

Eisenhower supported Euratom first of all because it built on his 1953 Atoms for Peace proposal which offered other nations fissionable materials to be controlled by an international atomic energy agency under United Nations auspices.[68] U.S. peaceful nuclear diplomacy was Europe-oriented and the Suez crisis in 1956 underscored Europe's need to develop atomic power rapidly as an alternative to Middle East oil and the Soviet influence in that area.[69]

The President also saw the plan strengthening ties between the United States and Europe which would benefit American firms seekings to sell reactors overseas. Moreover, he sought a near monopoly over the military atom while promoting peaceful atomic uses. Amid the negative publicity over the effects of nuclear fallout, Euratom also lent a "redeeming value" to what seemed an increasingly evil American engineering achievement.[70] But the plan had a final, and very useful purpose: it signaled that the United States was eager to cooperate with other nations and thus established a positive atmosphere, a kind of mystique, that was helpful to American efforts supporting Euratom. And, as Schaetzel noted, this positive attitude toward Euratom built on "a belief in the magical powers of atomic energy, a real conviction that there were large benefits to be derived from atomic energy. Even among the engineers and scientists, there was a belief that its cost would be so low that it would replace other means to generate electricity." [71]

Eisenhower, supported by Dulles, gave Euratom priority even while supporting other forms of international atomic cooperation like the international agency, bilateral agreements and the Organization of European Economic Cooperation (OEEC). Dulles was convinced that "only the Community of Six offers promise of opening the way to a genuine United States of Europe." He had serious concerns about resurgent German nationalism, the weakness of France and its tendency to neutralism and defeatism, and Franco-German relations which, while improving, needed constant encouragement. These problems, he believed, could be aided by a strong European atomic energy community which would have more immediate security or political significance than an economic community.[72]

If the atomic community succeeded, Dulles said, its members could proceed to other activities. "If they fail, the integration movement is apt to fall apart with little hope that it can be reconstituted, thus presenting a very bleak outlook for the future." [73]

The strong support of the Secretary of State muted the opposition of Lewis L. Strauss, head of the AEC, toward Euratom. Schaetzel, throughout 1955, in meetings with the AEC and state department officials, urged the United States to take timely action on Euratom.[74] Our government needed, he said, to make decisions about the pattern of atomic energy development before national interests and programs became entrenched.[75] Robert Bowie, then director of the state department's policy planning staff, noted that a joint agency could solve the security concerns of the AEC. A new agency starting afresh could "choose new staff and institute new procedures" with security standards acceptable to us.[76]

Monnet worked hard to facilitate both European and U.S. approval of Euratom.[77] He met in Washington in January 1957 with Dulles and other U.S. officials. He stressed to Dulles that giving bilateral atomic aid to Germany before it had signed on with Euratom would destroy the integration movement. After a long meeting with Admiral Strauss where he sought to ease the AEC leader's fears, he told Dulles that he "felt Strauss now understood better Euratom and how closely it was identified with the creation of Europe." Although Strauss had not committed himself, he had shown signs that "he would not press for the bilaterals [bilateral agreements with Germany] as long as there was early prospect of the Euratom treaty being signed." [78] Eventually, Dulles avoided a clash with Strauss by declaring that the Europeans themselves should decide the appropriateness of any bilateral accords required and their effect upon Euratom.[79]

In October 1956, an intergovernmental conference on the common market and Euratom established a committee of three "wise men" to define the broad technical goals of Euratom, to examine how it could best develop a nuclear energy program, and to stimulate further political interest in it. The members were Monnet's former deputy, Franz Etzel, vice president of the high authority of ECSC; Louis Armand, head of the French Railways; and Francesco Giordani, former head of the Italian atomic energy commission and prominent Italian scientist. Schaetzel, C. Burke Elbrick, and Gerard Smith with the support of Bowie, urged Dulles to invite this committee of wise men to visit the United States. The U.S. officials advised that "the presence of this group in the United States would permit a thorough exploration of prospects for Euratom and a systematic appraisal of the most mutually profitable U.S. collaboration with the Community." [80] Dulles agreed and invited the trio to Washington.

Schaetzel worked closely with Monnet to arrange the details of the visit of this high-level Euratom committee in early 1957. When they arrived at the end of January 1957, Dulles urged Strauss to be cooperative. He wrote him that it was a "unique opportunity to assist the Europeans in carrying out a concerted effort to solve a major European economic problem in a framework which will promote political solidarity in Europe." He argued that relationships strained by the Suez crisis (where the United States had opposed Britain and France, as well as Israel) might be strengthened and that new forms of U.S.-European collaboration might develop. [81]

Schaetzel escorted the three men around the country on a schedule arranged by the AEC. The Europeans met with the heads of nuclear installations and laboratories as well as leaders of industrial groups. Two days after meeting with Dulles on February 4, 1957, they met with Eisenhower. [82] "The President told them," recorded Andrew Goodpaster, "he thought Euratom was a great hope for the whole free world. He recalled that he has strongly supported a united Europe as a third great force in the world." Goodpaster noted the President "had urged Jean Monnet on, as he now urges this group on in the same direction." The President argued that "if they did not join together deterioration and ultimate disaster were inevitable. He had no hesitancy in declaring that the project would be to the benefit of the United States, of the Atlantic Community, and of all the world." [83]

The visit of the "wise men" advanced Euratom significantly as did the visit of Paul-Henri Spaak, the Belgian Foreign Minister, on February 8-9, 1957. Spaak's goal was to find out whether the newly drafted Euratom treaty provided an adequate basis for future cooperation between the U.S. and ECSC nations. Dulles wrote Spaak in March that the preliminary draft of the Euratom Treaty contained nothing "to preclude the subsequent negotiation of a fruitful cooperative arrangement between the United States and Euratom." [84]

On March 25, 1957, the ECSC nations signed treaties creating the economic community and the atomic energy community. The defeat suffered by Europeans in 1954 with the defeat of the defense community had been overcome, not frontally but by a "relaunching" of the idea of European unity in another direction.

Schaetzel believed Euratom could benefit both the United States and European unity and worked hard for its formation. While he, Monnet, French Prime Minister Guy Mollet, Spaak, American diplomat Livingston Merchant, Bowie, and some members of the atomic energy commission all influenced the positive attitude towards Euratom of the U.S. Government, it was the President's desire to promote the peaceful uses of atomic energy and European integration, ardently supported and implemented by Dulles, that determined U.S. policy. When obstacles arose within the government such as with Strauss, Bowie's support and access to Dulles were indispensable.

With presidential approval, a working party was established February 6, 1958 to negotiate the U.S.-Euratom cooperative agreement. The draft agreement was approved by Congress June 23, 1958.[85]

Schaetzel believed that the battles were won because of the convergence of two forces: the Eisenhower-Dulles commitment to European union and the romantic view of the Atoms for Peace program. There was genuine enthusiasm for this new technology which was seen at the time as having many peaceful applications, and a desire to transfer this peaceful knowledge to other countries. But there was also a keen awareness in the U.S. government, in Congress, and in scientific circles of the dangers of encouraging military nuclear programs, and all understood the need for proper safeguards.[86]

Schaetzel had an unparalleled opportunity to work closely with Monnet over a period of three months during 1959-1960 as a result of winning a Rockefeller public service award. Through travelling with Monnet in Europe, working with him on Avenue Foch, headquarters of the action committee, and meeting his colleagues, Schaetzel observed first hand the problems of European integration and how Monnet approached them.[87]

When John F. Kennedy became President in 1961, Schaetzel became special assistant to George W. Ball who served as under secretary of state for economic affairs throughout 1961 and under secretary of state from 1962 to 1966. Schaetzel was deputy assistant secretary of state for Atlantic affairs from 1962 to 1966 and was one of a small group of Europeanists in the department deeply committed to European unity. Under the strong leadership of Ball (and labelled "the theologians" by McGeorge Bundy for their fervid beliefs), this group sought ways to strengthen European unity and to persuade U.S. officials that European integration was in the interest of the United States.[88]

Kennedy gave Ball considerable freedom in the design and development of European policy and economic initiatives.[89] Ball was able to move effectively in Europe because the Kennedy administration, led by Kennedy himself and Dean Rusk, his Secretary of State, was increasingly preoccupied with southeast Asia. At Ball's urging, Kennedy emphasized U.S. support for the political and economic integration of Europe.[90] Ball, a longtime close friend and admirer of Jean Monnet with whom he worked in WWII and then in the late 1940s with the Monnet Plan, shared the Frenchman's view that Europe and America should forge a partnership. Ball and Schaetzel believed that Europeans should be encouraged to develop their own European identity and institutions, and Europe would share responsibility as America's "equal partner."

Both men worked closely with Monnet during the Kennedy and Johnson years. Schaetzel was valuable to Monnet in the 1960s, as he had been in the late 1950s, because he put the Frenchman in touch with the key people in the administration and Congress, briefed him on issues and conflicting currents of opinion, and told him what would work in Washington and what would not. Monnet would usually camp out in Schaetzel's office when he was in Washington, using his telephone and his secretary and would often drive out to Bethesda in Schaetzel's decrepit Hudson sedan for dinner with his family.[91]

Schaetzel saw that "Jean Monnet had frequently observed that one of the special American virtues is our willingness to accept change." [92] He spoke of economic interdependence and that it meant economic problems had to be solved by common action. In a 1962 speech, he pointed out that the challenge for the Common Market in the period immediately ahead was "to realize the extent of the common business to be done and to develop new processes for doing this business." [93]

Schaetzel served as ambassador to the European communities from 1966-1973 when he continued to see Monnet often. Their relationship was unusual in its intensity and closeness, its breadth and scope in time and issues, and its accomplishments. Monnet admired his skill in mobilizing bureaucratic support. He profited from Schaetzel's sharp mind and ability to debate issues from all perspectives and his determination to ensure that European union remained the centerpiece of American foreign policy.

For Bob Schaetzel, this Frenchman who profoundly influenced his life, was one of the few outstanding figures of the century. Schaetzel was influenced in three fundamental ways: by Monnet's ideas, his method, and his personal qualities. He believed Monnet displayed a kind of genius not only for identifying the problems of Europe brought about by two world wars but also for proposing methods and solutions to solve them. Most importantly, Monnet understood that old institutions no longer proved workable and that a reappraisal had to be done and new institutions put in place.

Second, Schaetzel was influenced by Monnet's strategic sense, his method of achieving his goals, his way of moving large bureaucracies, of solving practical problems, and of "extracting from people what was essential to the development of a scheme or approach to any problem he was dealing with."

Third, Schaetzel was moved by Monnet's personal qualities: his integrity, curiosity, his thoroughness and ability to pursue a single goal, and above all, an almost spiritual quality of being able to instill or revive faith in humans' ability to modify their assumptions, alter institutions, and change the course of events.[94]

*   *   *

For these four Americans, meeting and working with Jean Monnet was clearly one of the most important experiences of their lives. All had a close personal relationship with Monnet and were captivated by his personality and goals.

Some common threads emerge from Monnet's relationships with this diverse group of Americans. First, these working-level officials all strongly believed in and worked for the goals that motivated Monnet --- an integrated Europe and a strong European-American partnership. They shared his vision of a new Europe that would not be dominated by the classical nation-state system. They understood the needs of Europe after the war and fully comprehended that it was in the interests of the United States to have stability and peace on that continent. Monnet strengthened their determination to work for the shared goals.

Second, they were influenced by Monnet's methods and by being part of his process of solving international problems. They watched him turn crises into positive steps toward achieving goals and learned from his analysis of problems. They participated in his method of putting the problem on one side of the table while those trying to solve it sat on the other.

Third, Monnet imbued in these four men a conviction of the fundamental importance of effective international institutions. Monnet's coal and steel community served as a model institution for integrating antagonistic nations in a common endeavor.

Fourth, these case studies underscore how a few dedicated individuals within large bureaucracies, with the support of an influential American superior, could develop and carry out innovative policies. These individuals operated in bureaucracies that invited initiatives, but in each case, there were senior officials in authority who supported these innovations: With Robert Nathan, there were Donald Nelson and Harry Hopkins; McCloy and Dulles in the case of Bowie; Bruce in the case of Tomlinson, and Ball and Kennedy in the case of Schaetzel.

These relationships influenced the course of events in Europe and in U.S.-European relations. Each of the "insiders" facilitated an incremental and progressive step forward --- with each step being partially dependent on the previous step --- taken by the United States and France and other nations of Europe to help heal the wounds of the two world wars and bring integration nearer.

Each of these steps was influenced by, or partially or wholly dependent on, the United States, and these four men were instrumental in providing influence and mustering their country's support. Nathan helped Monnet understand the mechanics of effective planning required for successful mobilization of his nation's resources and economy. Tomlinson, along with David Bruce, was instrumental in securing aid for France that was so essential for France's postwar recovery and for helping to ensure continued U.S. support for the coal and steel community and the EDC.

Bowie was pivotal in the Schuman plan negotiations because he worked to balance French and German interests while helping to craft the treaty, at Monnet's insistence, to include the American deconcentration provisions. Bowie's support for Euratom reinforced Dulles' belief that the project served U.S. as well as European interests. Schaetzel was instrumental in mobilizing U.S. support in official and congressional circles for the creation of Euratom and sustaining that support for European integration, so essential to its success, against opponents in the late 1950s and in the 1960s.

The "insiders" played another important role. Their presence, along with other policymakers who were friends of Monnet's, guaranteed that any idea or proposal of the Frenchman which furthered European integration or the Atlantic partnership received a favorable hearing in Washington and within the administration.[95] With the exception of Tomlinson who died in the mid-1950s, the insiders, whether inside or outside the government, had the capacity to influence the decisionmaking process and lobby for the ideas or policies that they deemed important.

Monnet's close circle of friends in the United States believed that the European Community and its partnership with the United States served the mutual interests of each partner and sought to assist him in fostering it. Without the "insiders," Monnet would not have had as much support from the U.S. government for his great leaps forward and without them, European integration might not have progressed as smoothly or as fast as it did.

Endnotes

1 Jean Monnet, *Memoirs*, Garden City,N.Y., 1978, p.153 (hereafter JMM).

2 Interview with Robert Nathan Apr 17, 1989.

3 Ibid; interview with Robert Nathan by Leonard Tennyson, Dec 18, 1981. See also Nathan's article "An Unsung Hero of World War II" in *Jean Monnet: Path to European Unity*, edited by Douglas Brinkley and Clifford Hackett, New York, 1991, pp.67-85.

4 Interview with Robert Nathan, Apr 17, 1989.

5 Tennyson, *op. cit* JMM, p. 171.

6 Richard Kuisel, *Capitalism and the State in Modern France*, Cambridge,1981, pp. 219-221.

7 Edgar Beigel, "France Moves Toward National Planning," Political Science Quarterly, 62, Sept 1947, 388-9.

8 Sherrill Brown Wells, *French Industrial Policy: A History, 1945-1981*, Washington, 1991, pp.15-31.

9 Robert R. Nathan, "General Organization of Statistical Compilation and Analysis in the American Government," Apr 25, 1946, Papers of Jean Monnet, Fondation Jean Monnet pour l'Europe, Lausanne (hereafter FJM).

10 Ibid, Nathan, "Memorandum: Comments on National Income Estimates for France," Apr 25, 1946.

11 Ibid, Nathan, "Program of Action," Apr 30, 1946.

12 Ibid, Nathan, "Strategy of Presentation," Aug 13, 1946, and "Broad Philosophy and General Objectives of the Plan, Aug 16, 1946.

13 Ibid, Nathan, "Comments on Investment Tables," Aug 22, 1946.

14 Ibid, Robert R. Nathan, "Comment on the Preliminary Report of the Commission on Manpower Aug 12, 1946, and "Strategy of Presentation," Aug 13, 1946.

15 Ibid, Robert R. Nathan, "Major Policy Issues," Aug 11, 1946, and "Strategy of Presentation," Aug 13, 1946, and "Inflation and Fiscal Policy," Aug 17, 1946.

[16] Interviews with Robert Nathan Aug 15 and Sept 12, 1990.

[18] Interview with Donald McGrew May 29, 1992.

[19] Interview with Jacques Van Helmont by Clifford Hackett, Feb 11, 1990.

[20] Interview with Stanley Cleveland by Leonard Tennyson, Jul 12, 1981.

[21] Interview with Arthur Hartman Oct 15, 1990.

[22] Cleveland, *loc.cit.*

[23] Interview with Arthur Hartman Oct 15, 1990.

[24] Ibid, Interview with Donald McGrew May 29, 1991.

[25] Irwin M. Wall, *The United States and the Making of Postwar France*, Cambridge, 1991, pp.158-162.

[26] Interviews with Hartman and McGrew, *loc. cit.*; David Bruce diaries Mar 30 1950, Virginia Historical Society, Richmond, VA.

[27] Ibid; interview with Jacob Kaplan Mar 10, 1992.

[28] Interview with Etienne Hirsch Jun 24, 1984.

[29] Kuisel, *op . cit.*, pp.238-241; interview with Pierre Uri , May 29, 1984.

[30] Ibid, pp.158-9.

[31] Wall, *op . cit.*, p.165.

[32] Ibid,pp.170-2.

[33] Kuisel, *op. cit.*, pp.239-240. Counterpart funds were the francs accumulated by the French government by selling goods delivered and paid for by the American government through the Marshall Plan.

[34] Interview with McGrew , May 29, 1991.

[35] NARA, AID, RG 286, ECA, Office of the Administrator, Country Files, France, Box 70, Counterpart, Oct 14, 24, 17; Nov 10, 17, 21, 30; Dec 2, 13, 1949; ECA, European Programs, Mediterranean Branch, Country Subject Files, France, Feb 1, 1950; Foster to ECA Mission in France, Dec 6, 1949, *FRUS*, 1949, IV, 682-6; NARA, AID, RG 286, ECA, OCR, Central Secretariat, Country Subject Files, France, Box 2, Bingham to Katz, Apr 11, 1950; Wall, *op.cit.* pp.177-82; Kuisel, *op.cit.*, pp. 237-42.

[36] JMM p. 270.

[37] Interview with Pierre Uri May 29, 1984.

[38] John Gillingham, "Jean Monnet and the ECSC," in Brinkley and Hackett, *op.cit.*, pp.138-139; John Gillingham,*Coal, Steel , and the Rebirth of Europe, 1945-1955* Cambridge,UK,1990 , pp.235-6.

[39] Wall, *op.cit.*, pp.188-200; Hogan, *op.cit.*, p.276.

[40] Gillingham, *Coal, Steel*, pp 228-298; Hogan, *op.cit.* pp.376-9.

[41] Wall, *The United States and the Making of France*, pp.202-4; Acheson to Bruce, Nov 3, 1950 and Acheson to Bruce, Nov 29, 1950, *FRUS*, 1950, III, pp.426-31, 496-8.

[42] Bruce diaries, *passim* 1951-54.

[43] Ibid.

[44] Wall, *op .cit.* pp.268-70.

[45] Sprouse to Department of State, Telegram, Aug 22, 1954, *FRUS*, 1952-1954, I, pp.1064-7.

[46] Interview with Arthur Hartman , Oct 15, 1990.

[47] Interview with Pierre Uri , Oct 10, 1990.

[48] Interview with John W. Tuthill , Jun 22, 1992.

[49] Interview with Robert R. Bowie , Aug 15, 1990.

[50] See discussion of Schuman Plan in the previous section on William Tomlinson.

[51] Interview with Robert R. Bowie, Aug 15, 1990.

52 Ibid.
53 George W. Ball, *The Past Has Another Pattern* , New York, 1982, p.87.
54 Ibid, pp.88-89.
55 Interview with Robert R. Bowie, Aug 15, 1990.
56 Interview with Robert R. Bowie by Francois Duchene, May 17, 1987.
57 Interview with Robert R. Bowie , Sept 19, 1990.
58 Ibid.
59 Interview with John W. Tuthill Jun 22, 1992.
60 Robert R. Bowie, "The North Atlantic Nations: Tasks for the 1960s," Nuclear History Program, Occasional Paper 7, Center for International Security Studies at Maryland, School of Public Affairs, University of Maryland.
61 Interview with Robert R. Bowie, Sept 19, 1990; Robert R. Bowie, "Reflexions sur Jean Monnet"in *Temoinages a la Memoire de Jean Monnet* Lausanne, 1989 , pp.81-8.
62 Richard G.Hewett and Jack M. Holl, *Atoms for Peace and War*, Berkeley, 1989, p.308.
63 Ibid, pp. 320-321.
64 Interview with Robert Schaetzel Aug 30, 1991.
65 Ibid.
66 JMM, p.419; interview with Robert Schaetzel , Sept 12, 1990.
67 Dwight D. Eisenhower, *Waging the Peace, 1956-1961*, New York, 1965, p.125.
68 Hewett and Holl, *op. cit.* , pp.300-307.
69 Ibid pp.306-307.
70 Ibid.
71 Interview with Robert Schaetzel , Aug 30, 1991.
72 Ibid.
73 Memorandum of a Conversation, Jan 25, 1956, *FRUS, 1955-57*, IV, pp.390-399.
74 Ibid.
75 Ibid, Memorandum of Conversation by Schaetzel, Jul 15, 1955, pp.313-318.
76 Ibid,Memorandum of a Conversation, Jan. 25, 1956, p. 396.
77 Jonathan E.Helmreich, "The United States and the Formation of Euratom," Diplomatic History, Vol 15, No. 3, Summer 1991,pp. 404-5.
78 Memoranda of Conversation by Dulles, Jan 10 and 18, 1957, *FRUS*, 1955-57,IV, p.501.
79 Ibid, Letter from Dulles to Strauss, Jan 29, 1957, p.510.
80 Interview with Robert Schaetzel , September 12, 1990; memorandum from Elbrick and Smith to Dulles, December 3, 1956, *FRUS*, 1955-57 IV,pp.491-492.
81 Ibid, Letter from Dulles to Strauss, Feb 5, 1957, pp.515-16.
82 Ibid,Memorandum of Conversation of Dulles' Meeting with the Euratom"Wise Men," Feb 4, 1957, pp.512-15.
83 Ibid, Memorandum of Conversation with the President, Feb 6, 1957, pp.516-18.
84 Ibid,Letter from Dulles to Spaak, March 22, 1957, pp.543-544.
85 Hewett and Holl, *op. cit.*, pp.444-445.
86 Interview with Robert Schaetzel , Sept 12, 1990.
87 Ibid.
88 Ibid.

89 David L. DiLeo, *George Ball,Vietnam, and the Rethinking of Containment*, Chapel Hill,NC, 1991, pp.49-50.

90 Ibid pp.197-209.

91 Ibid.

92 Address by Schaetzel before the Summer Institute of the Mount Allison University, Sackville,NewBrunswick,Aug 18, 1962, Department of State Bulletin, Sept 3,1962, pp 350-355

93 Address by J. Robert Schaetzel before the World Affairs Council and the Boston Regional Conference on NATO Affairs, Boston, MA., Oct 6, 1962, Department of State Bulletin, Oct 29, 1962, pp.661-666.

94 Interviews with Schaetzel, Aug 15 and Sept 12, 1990.

95 Interview with George Vest, Sept 3, 1991

9

Monnet And The American Press

Don Cook and the Editor

INTRODUCTION BY THE EDITOR

Jean Monnet once speculated about how different his life would have been if it had ended when he was sixty. At that age he was engaged in planning France's post -war recovery. He was not well known in France and certainly not widely known elsewhere in Europe or even in the United States where he had spent the war years and part of his business career. He was also largely unknown to the press, except for those in France who followed the country's economic rebuilding in detail.

Yet just a few years later, Monnet was widely identified as Mr. Europe. He was acclaimed as the father of the Schuman Plan to create a European Coal and Steel Community (ECSC). He presided over the first High Authority, or executive body, of that community in Luxembourg. He was widely identified with the plan for a European Defense Community and, when that failed, with an alternative approach to a united Europe in the European Economic Community. It was only in the last third of Monnet's long life that the press, and through its work, the public, recognized the work of this child of France who spent so many years outside of his native country.

It is clear from Monnet's memoirs that he recognized the press before it recognized him. There he described the personal value he found in dealing with American journalists. The year was 1948 when Monnet turned sixty. He was in Washington to negotiate for wheat but also to take the temper of the land he had left only two years earlier. It was important, Monnet noted, to return often to the United States if you want to maintain an understanding of that country. Once there, he

said, one must meet with well-informed friends. Journalists, together
with bankers, industrialists and lawyers, were those people whose
information and judgment one could rely on in America, he noted.

Was America, and its press, different from other countries in
this regard? Monnet never makes an explicit comparison with other
countries and their journalists but he does not cite, in his memoirs, or
elsewhere, friendships with any journalists except Americans. There
he calls the American writers "practical men" whom he saw soon on
arrival in the country when he had a major decision to make. These
were men "who could not afford to make mistakes." [1]

The 1948 trip began Monnet's most active period of consultation
with American news people. He had met Walter Lippmann and James
Reston many years before but neither had mentioned Monnet's name in
print. His relations with these two were typical of the many other
American journalists who followed: private, inconspicuous meetings, an
exchange of information, total yet implicit respect for confidences on
both sides and a promise to meet again.

In the remaining 30 years of his life, Monnet would come to
know, trust and share information with many more American
journalists. Few notes were made of these meetings by either
participant and no major stories were based on them. Monnet did not
seem to provide the big news stories and certainly would not have
leaked privileged information even when he had it. But he gave a
perspective on events which reporters found valuable. This was a kind
of "noteless" journalism which is, as Don Cook points out below, very
far from the era of sound bites and confrontation on camera.

One of James Reston's first recollections of Monnet is from
London in the early years of World War II. Monnet had come from
France to head the Anglo French Coordinating Committee, a role which
continued the Allied supply cooperation he had pursued successfully in
the First World War. France survived only nine months before
collapsing in 1940 before the massive Nazi armies. When Britain stood
alone, Monnet became convinced that only America's industrial might
could stop the Germans from conquering all Europe. Reston recalls
Monnet's insistence that the American political system must be
mobilized to see the country's stake in the war. He soon followed that
insight with action.[2]

Monnet moved from London to Washington after the fall of
France. There he worked with the British Supply Council, encouraging

sharp increases in America's production of war materials on which Britain's survival depended. Soon the Soviet Union became similarly dependent on the American arsenal. Although Reston recalls meeting Monnet in this Washington period more frequently than he did before or after, Monnet's work kept him out of public attention. Only after he was sent to Algiers by the Roosevelt administration to help make peace among warring French generals did his role change. He returned to Washington from eight months in North Africa in November 1943 as a representative of the new provisional French government. A few months later, just as the Allied forces were invading western France, Monnet was prominently interviewed by John Davenport, a well-known writer, in Fortune magazine.

The article, reflecting Monnet's new prominence, described his past activities as a businessman and international civil servant but emphasized his views of what post-war Europe would encounter. He spoke freely of the problem of Germany and of France's central role in Europe. Today the article seems significant because it was the first time Monnet had ever been interviewed as a public personality. His lifetime --- he was now 56 --- had been spent largely outside France and often either in Britain or America or with important connections to the Anglo-Saxon world. Yet neither the French nor the English language press seemed to know him until he was close to age 60.

This year --- 1944 --- marked Monnet's debut as an advocate of a united Europe. He moved cautiously from a role behind the New Deal wartime leaders toward prominence with the North Africa episode; now, representing the government that would initially govern a liberated France, he spoke more freely about the dangers of nationalism and the need for a federation of some kind to restrain Germany and to replace the system which had twice brought war to Europe in a single generation. A few months earlier Monnet's views were also the subject of a long report in the New York Times on a speech he gave in New York's Metropolitan Opera House. He spoke at a victory rally and presented a vision of Europe rebuilding after an allied victory.[3]

But these wartime press encounters did not reflect a developed approach to the American journalist nor was he born with an ease of dealing with American journalists. His reflections about the 1948 trip and the importance of the informed American newspaperman were made, after all, as he wrote his memoirs in the early 1970's when Monnet was over 80.

Even after his prominence as the man behind the Schuman Plan in 1950, he needed guidance in approaching the Americans. He had a conversation in 1952 with Secretary of State Dean Acheson in Paris. The coal and steel community was just getting underway and Acheson advised Monnet to get some important American correspondents interested in the importance of the opening of the first common markets in coal and steel, of the first European taxes and the first meeting of the community's assembly. Monnet agreed but asked for advice on how exactly such a publicity effort should be started.[4]

Not many years later, Monnet was considered a master at managing these campaigns to gain and hold attention for the growing integration of Europe. What happened in these years after Monnet started working on European issues --- he was already 62 when the Schuman plan was announced --- which developed his skills in using the press and especially the American journalists to tell his story? We must look at some of the details of what Monnet was learning in these years and how he applied this learning to the new problems of making Europe work.

When Monnet returned to France at the end of 1945, it was to take the challenge offered by General de Gaulle to guide the rebuilding of the French economy. Monnet's role was important in France and directly related to the success of American aid for rebuilding Europe which eventually produced the Marshall Plan. He was also involved in the creation of the Organization for European Economic Cooperation (OEEC) which the Americans insisted upon as a unified interlocutor for American aid missions to western Europe. But these tasks drew little press attention in the United States and Monnet's brief prominence in the late wartime American press was followed by an anonymity which would be broken only in 1950 when a coal and steel community was proposed by Robert Schuman, the French foreign minister, at Monnet's suggestion.

Monnet was usually as interested in receiving as in imparting information when he met the press. Theodore White, another of his earliest journalist friends, recalled that he learned just by listening to the questions Monnet would ask him after White returned from a trip.[5] In fact, Monnet embraced a variation of Thomas Carlyle's theory that history is made by great men; the Frenchman believed that history is managed, moved and manipulated by leaders. For Monnet, this group certainly includes journalists.

In some cases, the encounters had nothing to do with journalism commonly defined. In 1950 Monnet wrote Walter Lippmann for advice: should Monnet come to Washington to explain the Schuman Plan? No, Lippmann answered, the plan seems well protected at the top levels of government. Stay in Europe and keep up the work there. Later, Lippmann, though sympathetic to Charles de Gaulle's historic vision, supported Monnet's position during the difficult de Gaulle years and advocated, in a letter to Barbara Ward Jackson in 1962, that Monnet's vision of a united Europe continue to be pressed by the American government.

But Monnet was not hesitant in correcting his journalist-friends when he found it necessary. In 1964 he complained gently to Lippmann about a column which implicitly criticised the European Community for having too small a vision of Europe, and specifically, for one that did not include a united Germany, eastern Europe and the Soviet Union. Monnet said that the European Community had to start with the realities of Europe in 1950 but that its vision did not end with the original six members.[6]

The American press who were close to Monnet are hard to classify. Some, like columnist Joseph Alsop and even Lippmann, kept in close touch with Monnet but were either skeptical of his vision of a united Europe or at least not committed to it in print. Others, like Don Cook of the NY Herald Tribune and Robert Estabrook and Chalmers Roberts of the Washington Post, saw themselves as working reporters who went to Monnet for insights and perspectives but seldom for headlined stories. Another group were friends, like Phil and Katherine Graham (whom he met in Washington in 1940 soon after arriving there from London), Lippmann and Reston, who happened to be in journalism.

Some were close to Monnet for decades while others came in and out of his life for brief periods. Monnet probably met Lippmann at the Versailles Peace Conference in 1919; he met Reston in 1939 in London just after Reston left the Associated Press for the New York Times. Monnet stayed close to both for the remainder of his life. He also kept in fairly close contact with Kay Graham after her husband's death in 1963. She helped Monnet see people on his trips to Washington in the 1960s. [7]

Circumstance affected some relationships. He met David Schoenbrun and Theodore White in Paris in the early postwar years when Monnet was principally known for the Monnet plan for France's postwar recovery. He was close to them for a few years but later their respective activities caused them to drift apart. Harold Callender of the New York Times was very close to Monnet during the early 1950s until his premature death.

Monnet was open to meeting new journalists; he read their work carefully, compared their judgments with his own and valued well-constructed opinions. He asked, for example, to meet Francois Duchene, a young British journalist, whose articles on European integration in the Manchester Guardian impressed the Frenchman. Duchene subsequently worked twice for Monnet, principally in dealing with the British and American press.[8]

The respect Monnet found among journalists is also elusive. Reston attributes much of Monnet's influence to never seeking credit for himself. Monnet was explicit on this point in his memoirs, citing an old friend, Dwight Morrow, who distinguished between people who wanted to be someone and those who wanted to do something. Despite a comfortably sized ego, Monnet never wanted to be "someone" whom the press credited with actions and decisions. Instead he pushed forward the politicians whose survival, he said, depended on public recognition. [9]

Theodore White attributes the special strength of Monnet to his skills as a manager of ideas:

> This majestic little man, tart of tongue, brusque of manner, never elected by any vote to any public office, has remained the most mysterious major public figure of modern times because of the peculiar nature of his art. His art is the brokerage of ideas.... Monnet's skill lies in recognizing a valid idea, knowing the men to whom it can be sold, sensing the time they need it, and then locating the technicians to make the ideas work. [10]

Reston emphasized Monnet's personal convictions:

> It was from him... that I came to believe that you can defend a nation in this modern world only by defending its civilization. He had more maxims than McGuffey's Reader. 'It is only when we climb that we see the new horizons.' he would say. Or, 'When you see a difficulty, never think that people are solving it. See to it yourself.' He talked to people to nourish their hopes, lift their imagination, and inspire them not only to think but to act. He hated shoddiness, triviality, vulgarity and brutality. He... was always confident that, as cooperation had led to progress in the village, and moved then from the village to

> the region, later from the region to the nation, so the nations
> would move in ever wider circles of cooperation." [11]

Not all journalists responded to Monnet. Some defined their jobs more narrowly, looking for the major stories or the striking leads which Monnet did not offer. Others were not matched to Monnet's style. Don Cook, in the essay below, says he found intellectual stimulation with Monnet but notes that Cyrus Sulzberger of the New York Times found only platitudes. Other reporters may have missed the inside information which some officials gave but which was not found with Monnet, especially after 1955 when he left roles in the government and the ECSC High Authority and concentrated on his high-level pressure group, the Action Committee for the United States of Europe. But if he could not always provide headlines, the man who could get useful perspectives from talking with hotel doormen and railroad porters was never heard to complain about finding journalists who had some useful bit of knowledge he could extract.

Here an American journalist takes over to give a personal account of Monnet's influence on the generation of newsmen who follow the uniting of Europe for the first thirty postwar years. Don Cook was the correspondent of the New York Herald Tribune and the Los Angeles Times who watched and wrote about these changes in postwar Europe both for the daily press and in several books, including *Floodtide in Europe* (1956) and *Ten Men and History* (1981).

JEAN MONNET AND THE AMERICAN PRESS

by Don Cook

When I was preparing to return home after more than forty years as a correspondent in Europe, and was asked to do a personal backward glance piece about covering the crowded panorama of postwar European history, I wrote without hesitation that "of all the men I have known or covered, Jean Monnet, that great Frenchman, stands out in a particular way."

I went on to explain that while I could not recall that I ever wrote a headline story out of many conversations with Monnet across a quarter of a century, "to spend an hour with Monnet was intellectual stimulation and conversational delight, and I always came away with a clearer sense of what was important and what was not, with a sense of how history was moving, of the future shaping of events."

Soon after my return from Europe to take up what turned out to be fairly active retirement in my native Philadelphia, my old cohort James Reston also wound down after fifty years of reporting and writing his column for the New York Times. In a backward-glance interview, he unhesitatingly cited Jean Monnet as the greatest man he had known in his professional life.

"Monnet proved that if you don't demand credit for things you can push them through," Scotty told an colleague. "In this town everyone wants credit for everything. Monnet also saw one of the central things in my lifetime --- that it's only partly true that progress is made by competition. It's also made by cooperation, and with government and labor and management and academics working together on things you can make more progress." [12]

I was not surprised to find myself in agreement with Scotty, or vice-versa, for it happened often over the years, both at a distance and at close encounter. What was unique was the fact that two American journalists in the twilight of careers --- one who had worked almost entirely in Europe and the other almost entirely in Washington --- each warmly remembered Jean Monnet as the outstanding personality of their reportorial experience.

Was there a unique affinity between Jean Monnet and the American press? As far as Scotty and I were concerned, there certainly was, but that of course was only a very small part of a broad international picture, for Monnet's friends and contacts were legion. Moreover, the subject of Monnet and the American press is very illusive to document, rather abstract to define and difficult to qualify or quantify. Richard Mayne, who served as Monnet's press contact and personal assistant for several years, says that "Monnet always had a very soft spot for the U.S. press", but there is virtually no record at all, no documentation of his press contacts. Monnet was not a publicity seeker or a headline seeker --- he was a conversationalist. Each of his journalist interlocutors took away and conserved his own impressions, each found his own particular attraction and usefulness in talking with Monnet, and each made his own judgments and interpretations. But few kept any notes or records --- unlike the "paper trail" of notes of conversations made by officials or memorandums and correspondence that went back and forth with government leaders, politicians, bankers, economists and industrialists. So the record of "Monnet and the American press" is pretty skimpy except in the memory of those who were fortunate enought to have enjoyed his company. [13]

For his part, he made his own estimate of the usefulness of press contacts soon after he arrived in Washington during World War II. In his *Memoirs* he wrote:

> It was in Washington that I grew accustomed to working on a basis of total trust with outstanding newspapermen, such as Walter Lippmann and James Reston, who could be brought in on the most serious discussions, where their experience was useful, without ever being tempted to give away secrets. The secret elements in these talks, in any case, were less important than the public debate, which helped move men's minds toward our objective --- throwing the weight of American power into the struggle.[14]

This implicit trust in American newspapermen remained unbroken for Monnet through his life. Of course trust can only be maintained if it is not betrayed, and here, I think, the normal working habits of reporters in the pre-television era of journalism simply created a very different atmosphere of mutual trust. Generally speaking, in all my years in Europe, when you saw a government official or a politician or any useful source for a personal talk it was automatically assumed that the conversation was "off the record" --- that is, the material could be used by the reporter without attribution to its source, and no official was ever named or quoted directly. Moreover, most correspondents in this kind of contact avoided taking notes, for note-taking could inhibit an easy conversational flow. Sometimes I would go to a typewriter after a particularly important or interesting session and dash off a hasty summary of what had been said, but I never kept any of those summaries after their immediate usefulness was over. For European officials, there was no such thing as "on the record" except at open news conferences. You did not need to establish rules of "trust" before you started to talk. You then shared discreetly with your readers what you learned without identifying sources, and your byline was supposed to be sufficient to vouch for the accuracy of your reporting, your judgments of a situation, and the fact that you were not producing copy out of thin air or making it all up. It was really only in American embassies overseas that an officials would inevitably greet a journalist by saying "Now we are talking off the record, aren't we?"

In today's world dominated by television journalism, everything tends to center around on-the-record sound-bites, as if there is no point in talking to a man to find out what he thinks unless he's going to be on camera. Television has created an adversarial quality of journalism and reporting that I think would have been quite out of place in any meeting with Jean Monnet. As far as I am concerned, it would have been a crass intrusion ever to have plunked down a tape recorder on Monnet's coffee table.

Can you see a Sam Donaldson shoving a microphone at Monnet and growling: "Now Mister Monnet, if you are going to put all the German and French coal and steel industries together under one management, surely that's going to be the biggest cartel in all history, no matter what you try to call it, isn't it?"

The trust that Monnet felt in his dealings with journalists was to a large degree engendered by the discipline and working standards of journalism of that era. Indeed, for the American press it was the golden age of written journalism --- particularly for foreign correspondents. The written word was the conduit of informing Americans of what was going on in Europe, as America finally turned away from its old isolationism and marched into its new superpower role in the world. Postwar Europe was swarming with vigorous and experienced American journalists, most of them ex-war correspondents. All of us were learning to master an entirely new field of reporting about such arcane matters as balance of payments, trade deficits, inflation rates, recovery programs, international credit and currency values, counterpart funds, productivity curves and all the other complexities of the story of European recovery.

In the prewar years of the world depression in the 1930s, and the rise of fascism, we had all grown up at a distance from Europe asking outselves "Why can't all those little countries get together?" Now we were in Europe watching it happen, helping to make it happen. Sooner or later any American correspondent seeking seriously to inform and be informed about Europe would seek out Jean Monnet.

I am quite certain that it was perfectly possible for French journalists or English journalists or German journalists to establish themselves on a basis of trust with Monnet, and some certainly did. His door was open and he liked to talk to journalists --- as both Richard Mayne and Francois Duchene attest. But the American press was different for Monnet primarily, I think, because of the nature of its reporting and the professional outlook and approach and background of its reporters. Moreover, America was the powerhouse of postwar European recovery, and it became, then, the powerhouse behind European unity as well. Clearly it was important to Monnet to keep plugged in with the American press both to educate and to be informed, simply by talking and listening.

American reporting out of Europe, the American perspective, the American point-of-view always tended to be more of an overview of problems, almost more European in approach than that of the Europeans themselves. This I am sure Monnet sensed in talking with American reporters, and this is one of the things that drew him to the American press and vice-versa.

It is neither a surprise nor a criticism of European journalism to note simply that the press in Europe will always basically report any international diplomatic, economic or political development on its doorstep primarily from a national perspective. The English will see it their way in terms of British politics, the French their way and the Germans another way. They will be more concerned about how they are doing vis-a-vis each other in any European argument than they are likely to be about how Europe might be doing. Fair enough --- why not? That's journalism. But American reporters on the European scene, covering this European kaleidoscope, were constantly facing the problem of piecing together a French view, a British view, a Dutch view, a German view, weighing up differences and trying to make sense of it all for distant Americans.

This does not mean that European journalism is parochial or superficial --- far from it. Newspapers like the Financial Times, The Times or The Guardian in London, Le Monde in Paris, Die Welt or Die Zeit in German are thorough, distinguished and first-rate in their news coverage. They are staffed by intelligent and knowledgeable reporters who are excellent at their craft. But the American approach, the American interest was broadened by the simple fact that the Marshall Plan placed the United States at the heart of Europe's economic recovery from 1947 to 1952, and the birth of the NATO Treaty placed the United States on the front-line of European security from 1949.

These two American commitments, pan-European in nature, in fact laid the political, economic and security groundwork for Monnet's great innovation of the European Coal and Steel Community. It would have been impossible for Monnet to have launched the idea of pooling French and German heavy industry, or the French ever to have accepted it, without already having in place those vital European foundations of American-backed recovery and security. So it was in this context that American reporters would seek out Jean Monnet to understand the framework of Europe, which was the focus of just about any and every Monnet conversation at the end of his days.

Among the American correspondents, Scotty Reston knew Monnet longer than any of us. Later, of course, the American journalists Monnet saw most regularly were those based in Paris: Cyrus L. Sulzberger and Harold Callender of The New York Times; David Schoenbrun of CBS; Ben Bradlee in his days with Newsweek Magazine in Paris; Alfred Friendly when he was European correspondent for the Washington Post; Crosby Noyes of the Washington Star; Robert Kleiman with U.S. News and World Report and later, briefly, with CBS; Theodore H. White when he was in Paris doing daily and magazine writing; Joseph Alsop who saw Monnet regularly on reporting trips from Washington and then lived in Paris for more than a year in the 1950s; and Joseph Kraft on his reporting trips to Europe in the 1960s. Monnet saw Philip and Kay Graham regularly on their visits to Paris and on his visits to Washington.

I was in the New York Herald Tribune bureau from 1945 to 1949, and then in Bonn from 1949 to 1952, and although Monnet's name and activities were well known to me I did not actually meet him and take up regular contact with him until I was assigned to the paper's Paris bureau early in 1952. This was the period of the founding of the coal and steel community by Monnet in Luxembourg and of the ill-fated European army plan. I was covering both of these stories on a roving European assignment out of Paris which took me regularly to Luxembourg to see Monnet and his press man at that time, Francois Duchene.

From those days, Duchene recalls:

> Any press acquaintance who called was sure of a pretty good welcome. It all happened spontaneously. That was the hallmark of Monnet's press relations. They were natural and informal human relationships, all the more effective for that. With rare exceptions --- which I cannot even recall precisely --- he liked and trusted journalists. He thought they stood somehow as proxies for the citizens as against, for example, industrialists, who in his view, most definitely did not. Monnet would not invariably say all the truth. He could believe his own propaganda and sometimes sounded more optimistic than he felt. It was part of his basic mechanism to turn every development good or bad to positive account for his own turns. But I never heard him deliberately mislead a pressman.[15]

Of course for Monnet any meeting with a journalist was always a two-way affair --- more so, I believe, than with any other public figure, political figure or government official I ever dealt with. He was quite insatiable in his desire to know, along with his readiness to inform.

Theodore H. White, who has now faded away like so many other friends of that era, wrote of his Monnet experience:

> I learned much from Monnet's questionings. After each major trip I made out of Paris, I would visit him, and he would suck me dry of observations. He had an irritating habit of abruptly presenting an important question; you would open your mouth to answer; he would snap, "Don't explain. Just answer yes or no. We both know your reasoning either way. I just what to see how you add things up."
> He loved maps, and was his most eloquent talking in front of a map. He was both warm-hearted and cold-blooded. I remember talking about several problems of European unity and the need of a particular decision. "Right," said Monnet. "*Exacte* ! But, *dites-moi* on whose table should I pound to get the decision?" Monnet was convinced that ideas marched into politics only by reaching key people; his job was to find those people and use them, to pass the proper tables to get the effects he wanted.[16]

Of course Monnet used the press --- just as he used everybody to move a whole era of European history on the never-ending goal of European unity. What made this perfectly acceptable to those who were being "used" --- whether they were journalists or academics or politicians or government officials --- was the selflessness of Jean Monnet and the political purity of his ideals and proposals. He was not an ambitious man of power. He was not a scheming politician. He was not seeking publicity or headlines. He was not trying to sell something. He was simply lighting a light at the end of a long, long tunnel of European history, taking Europe collectively by the hand, through every visitor who came to see him, point to the light and starting Europe on the path.

Francois Duchene elaborates on this Monnet relationship.

> He did not see good journalists just as conduits for his own point of view. He regarded them as vital sources of intelligence and soundingboards for ideas. He always saw journalists before approaching the politicos to sell his wares. I think there was a special affinity for Americans, but there were specific reasons for it. They were better respected in their society than the Europeans, and support of that society was one of Monnet's key assets. They were thus better informed and more influential, more valuable to him at both ends of the relationship. Also he liked a set-up where he could influence matters by what he was best at --- personal relations.

The American style favored this. It was not distorted
by the omnipresent notion of the State. The French reporter was
listened to by the establishment with less respect --- he was an
inferior, since he had patently not triumphed in the exams to
become a mandarin. There was also a greater risk that a French
reporter might slant what he heard. And then most Americans
liked what Monnet had to say. Frenchmen were divided and the
Brits cool and at first distant. In general Monnet's relations
with Britain, as a society --- not with individuals --- were more
ambivalent than with America.

Richard Mayne also observed that "in American company,
Monnet changed character, laughing more, being more one of the boys ---
it wasn't false, but it was switching into a different mode, a slight
high."

With the British, Monnet's friends tended to be influential men
of the City, the treasury, foreign office officials, and a few key
politicians such as Edward Heath or Roy Jenkins. English journalists
did not seek him out on any very regular or sustained basis, probably
because they found, in the 1950s and 1960s, that England's long exclusion
from Europe, and General de Gaulle's veto on their first efforts to join
the Common Market, left them without much to discuss with Monnet.
Nor did he see all that much of French journalists. Occasionally André
Fontaine, René Dabernat, Henri Pierre, Adolphe Max would seek him
out, but he almost never saw France's leading political writer,
Raymond Aron.

Monnet's relatons with Hubert Beuve-Mery, the olympian
editor of Le Monde, were rather curious. It was always Monnet who
went to the Le Monde offices, not the other way, although occasionally
Beuve-Mery went to luncheon at Monnet's country home. Editorially Le
Monde was ambivalent about Monnet's European policies and ideas, to
say the least, but when the paper got into deep financial troubles in the
1960s, Monnet played a vital and totally discreet role in raising funds to
insure its continued independence, simply because he regarded it to be
vital to the journalistic, political and intellectual health of the
country that Le Monde not be taken over by a private owner.

Monnet, for his part, did not simply wait for the press to come
to him. He was not a man to call press conferences --- that was not his
style or an arena which he enjoyed. But when they wanted to try out an
idea he would phone and invite journalist friends to drop by and see
him, and on his travels to the United States he always sought out
newspapermen he had come to know and value. In his *Memoirs* he
wrote:

To understand America, its people and its leaders, one has to go back regularly and form some idea of the changes that ceaselessly carry it forward. That was the real reason for my visits, which always began with calls on well-informed friends. In places like London, New York and Washington, where big decisions are made, my first talks have always been with men who cannot afford to make mistakes --- bankers, industrialists, lawyers and newspapermen. What others say may be colored by imagination, ambition or doctrine. I certainly respect their influence; but I base my judgment on the wisdom of practical men.... I learned a very great deal from talks with friends in the press world. I gave them news of Europe, it is true; but in return they shared with me the world panorama they enjoyed from such vantage points as the New York Times, the Washington Post, or CBS.[17]

Francois Fontaine, who collaborated with Monnet on his *Memoirs*, adds this elaboration on his relations with journalists:

He was familiar with journalists the way one is in the United States, at all levels --- it is better to invite them yourself into your company than to have to put up with their indiscretion. He respected their job and had no prejudice against their methods. 'Their work is difficult and indispensable,' he said "so one should be very clear right from the start. There should be confidence on both sides.' He hardly ever needed to regret that he had spoken too frankly with one of them. The newsman who is explicitly given secret information knows what he risks if he betrays it. Jean Monnet had every kind of security at his disposal. Newspaper owners used to come for an intimate chat with him once or twice a year. Nobody was present during their general exchange of views, which led to no particular piece of news. Press conferences were ordeals for him and so were held as rarely as possible. Formal interviews were dramas where ever word was carefully traded; they were only reluctantly granted. Wide ranging conversations, by contrast, happened almost every day without any difficulty.[18]

Not only were Monnet press conferences very rare; he was not much of a public speaker. I never head him deliver a speech, but Francois Duchene says that "he was inaudible most of the time and when you did hear him, he stumbled over his text so much one doubled up with embarassment --- it was a wonder anyone ever understood a word." Nevertheless, he always talked with great precision in expounding and elaborating his ideas. He knew exactly what he wanted to say, even if he sounded like his own record --- for he was the most persistent of men.

Moreover, Monnet's use of the English language was a joy of precision and choice of words. He had learned English when he was a very young man as part of "on the job" training in the City of London.

Since he was totally bilingual, and since French is a language of fewer words with a variety of meanings, Monnet would automatically search out English words to use in unexpected but apt expression that would delight and surprise an American or English listener.

Monnet's persistence in bringing every conversation back to the subject Europe, no matter what the starting point, was unquenchable. Scotty Reston recalls a family lunch at Monnet's country home at Houjarray when the talk wandered briefly to the subject of grandchildren. After a couple of exchanges at the table, Monnet interjected to bring everybody back to the subject of Europe. His wife said, "Oh Jean, we were just starting to talk about grandchildren. Why do you always have to talk about Europe." Monnet replied with a twinkle: "Silvia, dear, it for our grandchildren that we are building Europe." [19]

I mentioned earlier that Monnet and the American press was an elusive subject and difficult to document because few notes were kept or records made of his meetings with journalists. A case in point was Walter Lippmann. The two men saw each other regularly in Washington and in Paris and I am sure that they enjoyed their conversations. Yet in the publication of collected Lippmann columns in my possession there is not a single mention of Monnet. Moreover, in Ronald Steel's massive 650 page biography of Lippmann there are only two references to Monnet, neither of any substance. He was simply listed as one of the people Lippmann saw while in Paris, with the notation of one mention that "everyone in Paris from de Gaulle to Mendes-France to Jean Monnet told him that the EDC would never clear the French Parliament."

My own impression is that Lippmann was not particularly attracted or stimulated by Monnet's ideas. I saw Lippmann myself pretty regularly across forty years on his visits to Europe or when I was back in Washington, and he was clearly much more intrigued, intellectually, by General de Gaulle than he was by Monnet. Perhaps it was a throw back to post-World War I for Lippmann --- Woodrow Wilson and Versailles and all that. But it seemed to be competition among men and nations that fed Lippmann's mind and writings rather than the process of coming together.

One American journalist who was a pretty indefatigible diarist was Cyrus Sulzberger. Cy did not always take notes but he did always dictate prompt memorandums to his secretary when he came back from lunch or meetings. In his diaries of about a thousand pages from 1954 to

1963 there are four accounts of meetings with Monnet, at which the discussions dealt in general with problems of the moment but also much about General de Gaulle and where he was heading. One of Sulzberger's entries on Monnet --- the last in the volume --- was dated July 3, 1963, something of a low point for Monnet after de Gaulle's veto of British entry into the common market. It reads:

> Jean Monnet, as usual, was exceedingly nice when I saw him this afternoon, but also, neither facinating nor thought-provoking. He is widely acknowledged as an inspiring man but to me he seems intent on talking in platitudes. He has much common sense but little originality. [20]

I was also seeing Monnet fairly regularly in those years and whatever the slowdown in Europe, he always looked to the future which he knew for certain would come --- even if it was not a certainty that a journalist could always readily accept or endorse. But his Action Committee for the United States of Europe was of course the place where he was constantly seeding and watering and preparing the somewhat stony soil. I would telephone to suggest a talk at his convenience. Sometimes there would be a luncheon invitation but usually I would be asked to come to his apartment-office at the foot of the Avenue Foch around 4 or 5 in the afternoon.

Monnet would settle in a worn, comfortable little arm-chair, his back to a french window opening out onto the trees, a late afternoon sun often filling the room. I would be motioned to a sofa at his right and his faithful assistant of many years, Jacques Van Helmont, usually took another armchair. The conversation would open slowly.

I would bring up this or that current problem with the British or de Gaulle or the Americans, and Monnet would respond briefly at first, tapping the tips of his fingers, sometimes closing his eyes, and Van Helmont would interject a remark to keep things moving. But I had learned from past talks that this was not any indifference on Monnet's part but simply the care with which he collected his thoughts for any visitor. Then the observations, the comments, the ideas would begin to flow, often with unexpected statements of sudden diamond-hard clarity.

On one occasion, I recall, we were discussing some current impediment de Gaulle had thrown up in his almost pathological disdain for "integration" and I said something about "negotiating" with the general. Monnet stopped me abruptly. "My friend, you do not negotiate with General de Gaulle," he said. "He does not negotiate once his mind is made up. What you must do is to arrange conditions, set up hard facts, realities that he must take into account in making decisions. Then he can be very realistic and flexible. But he does not negotiate."

This was, of course, a simple truth about de Gaulle that any number of political leaders and heads of government and diplomats had to learn the hard way. When Monnet said that to me, it became a sudden illumination about dealing with de Gaulle, a pivotal point of reporting, writing and interpreting de Gaulle for me from then on. As Scotty Reston said of Monnet, "He taught me the importance of people" --- of how to deal with people to achieve something, how to get things done, how to use people, the need to understand people.

Monnet and de Gaulle were the two greatest Frenchmen of the twentieth century --- one a man of influence, the other a man of power. Monnet simply did not like de Gaulle, who was not a very likeable man. But they understood each other and I believe respected each other for the men they were.

It was de Gaulle after all who unhesitatingly adopted Monnet's proposal in 1945 to establish the all-embracing and powerful *Commissariat du Plan* and put Monnet in charge practically to run the French economy while governments came and went in the Fourth Republic. De Gaulle killed off the British efforts to substitute the European Free Trade Area for the European common market in 1958, and then insured that France carried the common market treaty into force--- even if the direction he then took once inside the common market was scarcely one of Monnet idealism.

After de Gaulle was gone, and the British had finally joined the common market (and had become rather gaullist in their own behavior once inside) I found myself on one of my visits to Monnet caught up peripherally and unexpectedly in his way of conducting his European business. At the time the British were demanding a far larger allocation of common market regional development funds for depressed areas, as a means of compensating and balancing the excessive costs that the British were having to pay into the common agricultural program. But the common market was supposed to operate on a balanced budget --- and this meant that others would have to take a smaller share of the available development funds in order to compensate the British. The British budgetary contribution was a continuing annual argument for years until it was finally resolved at a European summit meeting in 1984.

As we talked, I remarked to Monnet: "I don't see why the common market doesn't just go out and borrow the money, sell bonds to finance regional development and turn the proceeds over to the British. After all they don't have to operate a balanced budget in Brussels, and the common market ought to be a pretty good credit risk for any investor."

And then I added off-handedly: "Anyway, debt was one of the things that unified the American states in the early days of the federal government."

Monnet's interest was instantly piqued --- not by the idea of borrowing money to help the British but by my remark about debt having been a unifying force for the American states. What was this, he said, what was I referring to? I said I could not recall the details but I did know that Alexander Hamilton had insisted in the early days that the federal government should take over all of the public debts of the individual thirteen states and that this had become one of the basic unifying forces of the federal system of the United States.

"Is it in the Federalist Papers?" Monnet asked, getting up to go to the phone on his table-desk. He spoke to a secretary and a minute or two later she plunked down a hefty volume of the French translation of the Federalist Papers on the coffee table. "Find it," Monnet ordered. I leafed through authors and dates and quickly realized that since all of these had been written before the Constitution came into force it would not be there. Well, Monnet said, where could I get more detail about this for him? I said that perhaps I had an American history at home.

Next morning I dropped off a history volume at Avenue Foch. The story is a true vignette of the federal process at work. Early in 1790, Hamilton introduced in the First Congress, which met in New York, legislation for the federal government to take over all state debts. He believed firmly and rightly that without federal control of the monetary system, of which borrowing was of course a key element, there could be no strong central federal government. But in one of the first constitutional arguments over states' rights, he was opposed by the influential Virginians, Thomas Jefferson and James Madison, and the bill was defeated. At that time Virginia was the most populous state in the Union, thanks to some 150,000 black slaves.

Hamilton, however, persisted. He embarked on a shrewd political deal with the Virginians to get his way. Virginia had been fighting hard to have the federal capital located permanently on the banks of the Potomac. Hamilton proposed to Jefferson that he would deliver the New York votes in Congress to move the capital south if Jefferson would deliver the Virginia votes to take over the state debts. Jefferson and Madison agreed and the deal was done. Debt was successfully used to strengthen the federal government, and the capitol is in Washington.

A week or so after my talk with Monnet I was in Brussels and went to see Sir Michael Palliser, then British permanent representative to the common market, and later permanent undersecretary at the foreign office. I asked how things stood on the budget fight. Deadlocked still. So I tried again --- why didn't the common market just borrow the money the way the coal and steel community had always borrowed money to pay for rationalizing steel mills and modernizing coal mines, instead of worrying about paying for development programs out of a balanced budget.

Palliser smiled and said: "Jean Monnet has been on the phone all over Europe trying to sell that one. But as far as we are concerned it won't work because the common market would simply borrow the money on the London market. What we want is foreign currency coming into Britain from the outside, money across the foreign exchanges." All I could do was smile, too, at this response.

Nevertheless, when Britain's Roy Jenkins, a "Monnet man", became president of the common market commission in Brussels in 1977, one of his first actions (as a former British Chancellor of the Exchequer) was to press for authority from governments to borrow money to finance community development projects, instead of having to do it out of the community budget. It took Jenkins nearly eighteen months to get clearance to raise an initial $600 million but this then became routine practice.

Of course one of Monnet's salient characteristics was his determined optimism, his unshakeable belief that the European idea would prevail, his infinite resourcefulness in pursuit of his European goal no matter how dark or dismal the immediate political outlook. Richard Mayne recalls an occasion when a bookcase collapsed in his office, and Monnet looking in to find him ankle-deep in file-boxes and papers and books and starting to clean up. Monnet grinned and said: "Nothing ever gets done except in disorder."

One of my earliest contacts with him was in Luxembourg soon after the High Authority of the coal and steel community had been established and was getting down to business. It was a rare occasion when I asked Monnet if he would go "on the record" because I was writing an article for the New York Herald Tribune's Sunday magazine on the launching of Europe. Already there was a bureaucratic and political deadlock over the initial problems of harmonization of national tariffs and freight rates for moving steel and coal across borders. I started to cross-examine Monnet closely about the problem and how it was going to be resolved. He responded patiently at first, like a teacher explaining algebra to a new pupil, but he got a look of polite irritation, and finally he said:

> Look, my friend --- this is a process in which we are involved, not a tariff negotiation. We are building a market for all of Europe. We are at the beginning of a process, and this problem you are talking about will be solved because there is no other way, because the process that we are beginning is so much greater that this problem.[21]

As I wrapped up my last common market news story, I thought back to that early talk with Monnet. Once again the Monnet "process" had triumphed over the problem.

General de Gaulle's abrupt resignation from office in April, 1969 rolled away a heavy stone that sat like a deadweight on the Monnet process for more than a decade. But there is a rather fascinating footnote as to how he himself outmanuevered General de Gaulle to ensure that the opening would indeed happen. De Gaulle's immediate successor as interim president when he resigned from office was Alain Poher, the senate president, who then ran for election in his own right and forced de Gaulle's former prime minister, Georges Pompidou, into a surprising and unexpected second round of voting to win the office. Poher campaigned on a strong European appeal, to end France's isolation from Europe and open the Common Market to other members.

After the election, Monnet told me, with amused satisfaction, how Poher had become senate president and the man in line to succeed de Gaulle: The Senate, he said, was about the only institution of the French state that the Gaullists had never taken over completely. Because of a special system of electing senators, the Gaullists had never been able to capture a majority of its seats and it remained a pretty independent-minded body and often a political thorn for General de Gaulle. For years he chaffed at what he regarded as a mistake of his own in the constitution for the fifth republic and he finally determined to abolish it as part of the April 1969 referendum.

But some months before the referendum, Gaston Monnerville, long-time senate president, died. He and de Gaulle hated each other with public loathing. A new senate president would now have to be elected. Moreover, in the fifth republic, he would automatically become president of the republic if that office fell vacant. But since General de Gaulle had made up his mind to abolish the senate, he ignored completely its choice of a new president to succeed Monnerville. So, Monnet began to make a few telephone calls.

Alain Poher was an old fourth republic politician from the MRP Christian Democratic Party of Robert Schuman and Georges Bidault who had been elected to the senate in the early days of the fifth republic and was a true French European. He was a decent, honorable work-horse political figure who had helped push the coal and steel community treaty through the National Assembly.

As Monnet related, he first contacted Poher to see if he was prepared to make a bid for the senate presidency which of course he was. Monnet then got in touch with independent-minded senators and his old friends in the Socialist Party to put together a coalition to back Poher, who was personally well liked. With de Gaulle's back turned, and the Gaullists with neither a candidate of their own or any instructions from the Elysee Palace, a Monnet European politician became senate president and the man to succeed de Gaulle.

When Poher moved into the Elysee Palace after de Gaulle's resignation, he proved to be much more effective and appealing as a presidential candidate with the voters than anyone could have imagined or expected. By campaigning openly on the European issue, he forced Georges Pompidou to take a much more open and positive stance on the question as well --- much to the disgust of the "ultras" of the Gaullist camp, who regarded Pompidou as betraying their leader. Thus, the French door on enlargement of the European Community was pushed open by Poher in the first weeks after de Gaulle's resignation.

Jean Monnet had played out a last "check" move on the political chess board of Europe against General de Gaulle. The man of influence prevailed over the man of power.

I do not know what the contributions of the American press to the workings of the Monnet "process" might have been but I do not pretend that it was very great. I do know what a great contribution Monnet made to those of us who availed themselves of the open door and the ready privilege of knowing him and enjoying his company.

And today, half a century later, the Monnet "process" is still bigger than the problems. The process goes on.

POSTSCRIPT BY THE EDITOR

Monnet's relation to the American newsmen had a mysterious aspect, as White noted, and some obscurity, as Cook admits, yet his approach was usually quite direct. He never revealed all of his thoughts to anyone but he dealt with people, including journalists, quite openly. He would use anyone for his purposes but those purposes were always pure. Monnet never wanted anything for himself but he wanted everything for the enterprise, whatever that happened to be at the moment. Part of the mystery seemed to be a man operating so effectively in the world of politics who sought nothing for himself.

Monnet never concealed his eagerness to exploit the news gatherers who followed him especially closely in the 1950s. James Reston recalls Monnet as a diligent questioner; White, as Cook reports, as a sometimes abrupt one. Monnet undoubtedly believed he, not the journalist, was the principal beneficiary of their contacts. A senior U.S. official recalled Monnet in Washington during the Kennedy years. Just before returning to Europe, he insisted on telephoning Joseph Alsop. The official remonstrated: "Jean, why bother with Alsop. He doesn't care about the things you are doing." "I know," Monnet replied, "but we can never tell when we might need him." [22]

Alsop recalled meeting Monnet one day at lunch with Arthur Purvis, Monnet's new boss in Washington at the British Supply Council. The same evening, Alsop invited Monnet to a dinner attended also by Felix Frankfurter. The French exile went on to gain and keep a closer friendship with Frankfurter and the circle which the supreme court justice gathered about him than with Alsop himself. But in the 1950s Alsop visited Paris often and then lived there one year in mid-decade. He often saw Monnet and occasionally reported on European integration but without great enthusiasm or insight.

David Bruce, a friend and admirer of Monnet, worked closely with him while American ambassador to France, especially during the 1952-54 fight for the European Defense Community. Bruce once described Alsop as exhibiting "inpenetrable gloom" in the midst of this fight. The occasion for Bruce's comment was the all-out commitment by Secretary of State Dulles for the defense treaty which eventually failed in the French National Assembly, despite the best efforts of Bruce, Dulles and Monnet. This pessimism, while well-founded in this case, was an acknowledged characteristic of columnist Alsop. It must have been a barrier between him and Monnet since the Frenchman tended to avoid people who emphasized the obstacles to action instead of seeing them as stepping stones toward solutions.

Phil Graham was a friend of Monnet even before he worked for the Washington Post where he finally became publisher. They met through Felix Frankfurter in 1940-41, the year Graham was Frankfurter's law clerk. It was the same time that Alsop met Monnet but, as with Frankfurter, Graham and Monnet developed an affinity which never flourished with Alsop. When Graham took over the paper from his father-in-law, Eugene Meyer, the relations with Monnet deepened since by that time Graham had become a convinced European integrationist. When Graham and Meyer went to Europe, they always arranged to meet Monnet. They also directed Washington Post writers like Robert Estabrook and Chalmers Roberts to Monnet who, with David Bruce, were judged by the publishers to be the best informed people in Europe. These new journalistic sources were carefully serviced by Monnet both in Paris and when he came to Washington.[23]

Katherine Graham, who became publisher of the Washington Post in 1963 after her husband's death, recalls that she never really had a personal relationship with Monnet until Phil Graham was gone. After that time, Kay Graham became more important in Washington and, for Monnet, she became both a source of information in her own right for him and someone who could help him keep in touch with the right people on his increasingly rare visits to Washington. She became someone Monnet used in his benign but direct way with people.

Did Monnet rely on Kay Graham in the mid and late 1960s because he had fewer friends in the Johnson administration and was losing influence in Europe himself? Mrs. Graham thinks this possible. "The relationship [I had with him] was still personal. I did not have the experience or the accumulated knowledge to guide him. I was new at my responsibilities. But I did try to help him [by bringing him together with people]."

Thus, Monnet seemed to treat the American press as he did all other human resources he found along his way. He used people with a directness that often overwhelmed them. He trusted journalists so he probed their insights and assessed their sources. They trusted him because he had no reason to deceive them.

His optimism about building Europe was on constant display. But he did not hid the difficulties; instead he used them to move on. The American press was especially important in this movement because Europe could not be built without American understanding. And the press in America was essential to that understanding. It was too simple to write down.

Endnotes

1   Monnet's reflections on his life at age 60 are from Francois Fontaine's essay, "Forward with Jean Monnet," in D. Brinkley and C. Hackett, eds, *Jean Monnet: The Path to European Unity*, New York, 1991,p.65. His view of journalists as practical and reliable is from Jean Monnet, *Memoirs*, New York, 1978, p.271 (hereafter, JMM).

2   James Reston's recollections are from his memoirs, *Deadline*, New York, 1991, especially pp. 168-9, supplemented by a telephone interview with him in December, 1991 by the editor.

3   Fortune, Aug 1944; NY Times, Mar 12 1944

4   Memorandum of conversation between Monnet and Dean Acheson in Paris, Dec 15 1952. Dean Acheson papers, Truman Library, Independence, MO.

5   Theodore H White, *In Search of History* New York, 1978, p.334.

6   John Morton Blum, Jr, ed., *Public Philosopher, Selected Letters of Walter Lippmann*, New York,1985, pp. 551-2, 607.

7   Robert Estabrook recalled his experiences and those of other Washington Post writers with Monnet to the editor in a telephone conversation.
The relation of Monnet and the Grahams are from an interview with Katherine Graham by the editor in March, 1990.

8   JMM, p.456.

9   JMM, p. 272.

10   Theodore H White, *Fire in the Ashes* ,New York, 1953, pp. 260-1.

11   Reston, *Deadline*, p.171.

12   NY Times. Nov 5 1989.

13   This and subsequent quotations are from the author's correspondence with Mayne in 1990.

14   JMM, p.155

15   This and subsequent quotations are from the author's 1990 correspondence with Duchene.

16   White, *In Search of History*, p.333.

17   JMM, p.271

18   Fontaine, *op. cit.* p.9.

19   Reston,*Deadline,* p.170

20   Cyrus L Sulzberger, *The Last of the Giants*, New York, 1970, p.990.

21   NY Herald Tribune, Feb 8 1953.

22   Interview with J Robert Schaetzel, 1990. Schaetzel worked closely with Monnet in the 1960s and provided him a base in the state department during Washington visits.

---

23 Interviews with Estabrook and Roberts by the editor in fall, 1991. The meeting
with Alsop is described in Joseph W. Alsop, *"I've Seen the Best of It"*, *Memoirs*
New York, 1992, p.144. David Bruce's comment on Alsop is from his diary of
Dec 28 1953, located in the Virginia Historical Society, Richmond, VA.

Selected Bibliography

These books are chosen for their relevance to the principal American figures with whom Monnet worked and whose relationships are described in this book.

Autobiographies and Memoirs

Acheson, Dean. *Present at the Creation.* New York, 1969.

Alsop, Joseph. *"I've Seen the Best of It."* Memoirs. New York, 1992.

Ball, George W. *The Past Has Another Pattern.* Memoirs. New York, 1982.

Kennan, George C. Memoirs (1925-1950). Boston, 1967.

Macmillan, Harold. *War Diaries* January 1943-May 1945. London, 1984.

Monnet, Jean. *Memoirs.* New York, 1978.

Murphy, Robert. *Diplomat Among Warriors.* New York, 1964.

Stimson, Henry L. and McGeorge Bundy. *On Active Service in Peace and War.* New York, 1948.

Reston, James. *Deadline. A Memoir.* New York, 1991.

White, Theodore. *In Search of History.* New York, 1978.

Biographical Works

Ambrose, Stephen E. *Eisenhower: Solder, General of the Army, President-Elect.* New York, 1983.

------------------ *Eisenhower: President and Elder Statesman,* 1952-59. New York, 1984.

Bird, Kai. *The Chairman: John J. McCloy: The Making of the American Establishment.* New York, 1992.

Blum, John Morton. *From the Morgenthau Diaries.* Boston, 1954.

Brinkley, Douglas. *After the Creation:Dean Acheson and American Foreign Policy* 1953-1971. New Haven, CT, 1991.

-----------------and Clifford Hackett.(Eds.) *Jean Monnet: The Path to European Unity.* New York, 1991.

Brownell, Will and Richard N. Billings, *So Close to Greatness: A Biography of William C. Bullitt.* New York, 1987.

Bullitt, Orville. *For the President: Personal and Secret, Correspondence Between Franklin D. Roosevelt and William C. Bullitt,* Boston, 1972.

Burns, James MacGregor. *Roosevelt: The Soldier of Freedom.* New York, 1970.

Caro, Robert A. *The Years of Lyndon Johnson: The Path to Power.* New York,1982.

Cook, Don. *Ten Men and History*. New York, 1981.

Dallek, Robert. *Lone Star Rising: Lyndon Johnson and His Times*. New York, 1991.

DiLio, David. *George Ball, Vietnam, and the Politics of Containment*. Chapel Hill, NC, 1991.

Donovan, Robert J. *The Presidency of Harry S. Truman*. 2 vol. New York, 1977,1982.

Duchene, Francois. *Jean Monnet: The First Statesman of Interdependence*. New York, 1994.

Hoopes, Townsend. *The Devil and John Foster Dulles*. Boston, 1973.

Isaacson, Walter and Evan Thomas. *The Wise Men. (Acheson, Bohlen, Harriman, Kennan, Lovett, McCloy)* New York, 1986.

Jenkins, Roy. *Truman*. New York, 1986.

Kearns, Doris. *Lyndon B. Johnson and the American Dream*. New York, 1976.

Lash, Joseph P. *Roosevelt and Churchill 1939-1941*. New York, 1976.

McCullough, David. *Truman*. New York, 1992.

McClellan, David S. *Dean Acheson. The State Department Years*. New York, 1976.

Newhouse, John. *DeGaulle and the Anglo Saxons*. New York, 1980.

Pogue, Forrest C. *George C. Marshall*, 4 vols, New York, 1963-87.

Rosenman, Samuel. *Working with Roosevelt*. New York, 1952.

Preussen, Ronald. *John Foster Dulles: the Road to Power*. New York, 1982.

Sherwood, Robert. Roosevelt and Hopkins, New York, 1948.

Smith, Gaddis. *Dean Acheson 1949-1953*. New York, 1972.

Schlesinger, Arthur. M., Jr. *A Thousand Days. John F Kennedy in the White House*. Boston, 1965

Schwartz, Thomas. *America's Germany: John J. McCloy and the Federal Republic of Germany*. Cambridge, 1991.

Sorenson, Theodore C. *Kennedy*. New York, 1965.

Steel, Ronald. *Walter Lippmann and the American Century*. Boston, 1980.

Truman, Margaret. *Harry S. Truman*. New York, 1973.

Winand, Pascaline.*Eisenhower, Kennedy and the United States of Europe*. New York, 1993.

Histories and Commentaries

Barnet, Richard. *The Alliance: American-Europe-Japan: Makers of the Postwar World*. New York, 1983.

Diebold, William. *The Schuman Plan. A Study in Economic Cooperation, 1950 -1959*. New York, 1959.

Churchill, Winston. *The Second World War*. 6 vols. Boston, 1964.

Kennan, George C. *American Diplomacy, 1900-1950.* New York, 1950.

Macmillan, Harold. *The Blast of War 1939-1945.* New York, 1968.

Milward, Alan. *The Reconstruction of Western Europe 1945-51.* London, 1984.

Schaetzel, J. Robert. *The Unhinged Alliance: America and the European Community.* New York, 1975.

Spierenburg, Dirk and Raymond Poidevin. *The History of the High Authority of the European Coal and Steel Community.* London, 1994.

Unwin, Derek. *The Community of Europe: A History of European Integration Since 1945.* London, 1991.

Van der Beugel, *From Marshall Aid to Atlantic Partnership.* Amsterdam, 1966.

White, Theodore. *Fire in the Ashes. Europe in Mid Century.* New York, 1953.

Zurcher, Arnold. *The Struggle to Unite Europe, 1940-1958.* New York, 1958.

INDEX

N.B. Index references to Jean Monnet (JM) are found under subject or person entries e.g. family, Morgenthau, etc., not under his name.

Euratom continued
  and JM 133
  wise men 219-20
Euro[pean] army 84,105,117,
  147,184,186-8
Europe, united 1,59,60,72,73,
  83,86,88,91,92,94,96,97,103,
  109,112,116-118,152,190, 192
European Coal and Steel
  Community (ECSC)
  7,21,72,80,83,87,116,118-23,
  149,152,161,208,210,217,
  229,235,239
  assembly 123-6
  loan from US for, 121,123,
  124-6
European Community 7,73,90,
  92,129,203
  US support for, 125
European Council 23
European Economic
  Community (EEC) 7, 23,
  72,79,88,90,94,95,96,
  120,129,132,133,246
European Defense Community
  See also Pleven Plan 72,84-5,
  104,106,107,116,120,124,
  190,209-10,217-218,229
  opposed 117,123,125,127
European Free Trade Area
  (EFTA) 130,131,153
European Political Community
  120,162,153
European Recovery Program
  See Marshall Plan
European Union 19,182

family (JM) 8,10,11,
  15,30,31,33,62
Farm Credit Administration
  144
father (JM) 8,30,58
feasibility studies 42
Federal Council of Churches
  109
Federalist Papers 247
finances (JM) 33,43-4

Financial Times 239
Finletter, Tom 91
fireside chats (FDR) 15
Fontaine, Francois 24,204
force de frappe 90
foreign ministers meetings
  (1950) 18,184
Ford Foundation 86
Foreign Economic
  Administration (FEA) 144
Foreign Operations
  Administration (FOA)
  125,127
Forrestal, James 75
Fortune magazine 16,109
Foxhall Road 43,199
Four Freedoms 39
France 9,16,18,26,27,49
  in WWII 31,37,38,51,
  52,75,77-8,177
  postwar
  59,61,63,81,83,95,106,
  114,145,202,205
  modernization (Monnet)
  plan 7,16,17,81,113,201,
  204-206,246
France Actuelle 142
Franco, Francisco 29
Franco-British Union of 1940 7
Frankfurter, Felix 3,14,27-8,
  36,39,42,45,47,58,60,64,
  74,122,252
F.D.Roosevelt Library
  Association 5
Franks, Oliver 79
Free French 26,38,51,52,175
Freedom medal (JM) 92
Free world 82
French Committee of Nat'l
  Liberation (FCNL) 4,15,
  55,59,61,63,77,178
French Foreign Legion 185,186
French-German relations
  147,214
French-German treaties 84,95
French Supply Council 144
Friendly, Alfred 240
Fulbright, Senator 123

The pages for *Monnet and the Americans* were set in 10 point Palatino by Andrew P. Hackett for N.M.N.F.Y.S. Productions. The book was offset printed on fifty pound Harrison Trade Opaque Cream White Antique paper by RR Donnelley Information Services in Scranton, Pennsylvania.